The Complete Idiot's Bird Care Reference Card

Buying a Bird

1. Choose a species that fits your personality.
2. Buy your bird from a person or pet shop you trust.
3. Take a good look at your potential pet. She should show all the signs of good health and no signs of sickness.
4. Buy a responsive bird who seems to like you.
5. Inexpensive birds often make wonderful pets. The price of a bird is determined by the rarity of the species, not by how good a pet the bird will be.

Choosing a Cage

1. Buy your bird the biggest cage you have room for and can afford.
2. Rectangles and squares are the best shapes for birdcages.
3. Buy a cage created for a bird's comfort and safety. Your bird's exercise requirements, wingspan and tail length should determine the size and shape.
4. Avoid cages with guillotine doors, if possible.
5. Never buy a bamboo or wooden cage for a hookbill, not even one as small as a budgie (parakeet).
6. Make sure the wire is strong enough to withstand your big bird's beak.

Creating a Happy, Healthy Home

1. Place the cage in a draft-free area where the family congregates—but not in the kitchen, unless you have no other choice.
2. Provide dishes, perches and toys suitable for the size of your bird.
3. Keep your bird high off the floor if you have other pets.
4. Design the interior of your bird's cage so your pet can spread her wings and move from perch to perch easily. Perches should be placed at different heights and should be located where droppings won't land in the food and water dishes.
5. Many houseplants are poisonous to birds. If you aren't sure about yours, ask at the plant nursery.
6. Bird-proof your home so your pet won't poison herself.
7. Beware of nonstick cookware. When overheated, it emits fumes deadly to birds.
8. Fresh air is good for your bird on a nice day, but keep your pet out of direct sunlight.
9. Change your bird's cage papers and wash her dishes daily.
10. Make sure your bird has safe, stimulating toys to play with.

tear here

alpha books

What Birds Should Eat

1. Birds need variety in their diet, including fresh veggies and fruit. Wash produce well.
2. Different species have different nutritional needs. For example, canaries and finches need a little grit to help with digestion; while lories, toucans and mynah birds eat only soft food. Chapter 10 tells you what your species needs.
3. A diet of only seeds is inadequate for a bird.
4. Formulated foods, commonly called pellets, contain all the nutrition birds are known to need, but many birds refuse to eat them at first. Introduce them slowly, by adding them to your bird's regular meals.
5. Never give your bird junk food, chocolate, alcohol or scraps of food you wouldn't eat. Fruit cores and pits are especially dangerous because they contain pesticide residues.
6. Attach a cuttlebone to your bird's cage. It provides calcium and other minerals.
7. Sprouts are a super addition to a bird's diet.
8. Never try to starve a bird into trying something new. Birds aren't stubborn about trying things, but they are genetically programmed to be cautious. If they don't recognize something as food, they won't eat it—and because they have high energy requirements, they can starve to death in no time.

Bonding with Your Bird

1. Give your bird at least 48 hours to settle in before trying to tame her. During that time, sit near her cage to read, write or watch TV; and take time to talk to her.
2. Birds communicate with us through body language.
3. Make sure your bird's wings are trimmed before taking her out of her cage.
4. Taming a bird takes lots of patience. Choose the right method for your bird and celebrate your progress one small step at a time. Never lose your temper and scream at your bird, or hit her. Birds are sensitive and their bones are delicate.
5. Teach your bird the "up" command and give her ladder lessons.
6. Always let your bird know when she does something right.
7. Knowing how parrots act and react in the wild will help you understand your pet. For example, wild parrots do not use their beaks as weapons unless their life is in danger. Biting is a learned behavior. We teach it to our birds by mistake.
8. Follow the head-to-heart rule with medium to large birds. Have your parrot perch on your hand (not your shoulder) and keep her head at about the level of your heart.
9. Birds behave best when they get enough exercise.
10. When teaching your bird to talk, speak clearly and use lots of expression.

In Sickness and Health

1. Bathing is important to your bird's physical and mental health. Some birds like baths, while others prefer showers with a plant mister. Use lukewarm water right from the tap, without any additives.
2. Most pet birds should have their wings and nails trimmed periodically. Try to watch an expert do it the first time.
3. "Toweling" is the best way to catch and restrain a parrot for grooming or first aid. Canaries and finches are best held in your bare hand.
4. Sick birds need an *avian* veterinarian.
5. It's important to recognize the subtle signs of sickness because the sooner treatment begins, the better the chance of recovery.
6. Birds instinctively want to look healthy, so they try to hide their illnesses and injuries.
7. During recovery, sick or injured birds need extra warmth, peace and quiet. Their favorite foods and fresh water should be within easy reach.

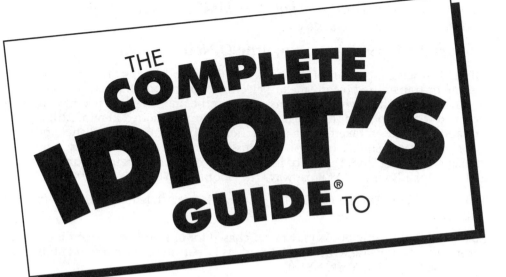

THE COMPLETE IDIOT'S GUIDE® TO

Bird Care & Training

by Jacqueline O'Neil

alpha books

A Division of Macmillan General Reference
A Simon & Schuster Macmillan Company
1633 Broadway, New York, NY 10019

To my husband, Tom, who got three birds as baggage when he said "I do," and adopted them instantly.

Copyright © 1998 by Jacqueline O'Neil

Macmillan Publishing books may be purchased for business or sales promotional use. For information please write: Special Markets Department, Macmillan Publishing USA, 1633 Broadway, New York, NY 10019.

International Standard Book Number: 0-87605326-6
CIP data is available from the Library of Congress.

00 99 98   8 7 6 5 4 3 2 1

Interpretation of the printing code: the rightmost number of the first series of numbers is the year of the book's printing; the rightmost number of the second series of numbers is the number of the book's printing. For example, a printing code of 98-1 shows that the first printing occurred in 1998.

Printed in the United States of America

Alpha Development Team

Publisher
Kathy Nebenhaus

Associate Publisher
Donald Stevens

Editor-in-Chief
Dominique DeVito

Editor
Beth Adelman

Marketing Brand Manager
Felice Primeau

Production Team

Production Editor
Lori Cates

Copy Editor
Nancy Sixsmith

Cover Designer
Kevin Spear

Photo Editor
Richard H. Fox

Photography
Tom O'Neil
Eric Ilasenko/Birdpix

Cartoonist
Kevin Spear

Indexer
Cheryl Jackson

Layout/Proofreading
Angela Calvert
Mary Hunt
Deb Kincaid
Julie Trippetti

Contents at a Glance

Appendices

Contents

Foreword

As I sit here at my computer, I can hear my cockatiels twittering in the living room. It's breeding season and they are saying sweet nothings to each other. It's quite romantic! I can also hear my neighbor's male canary. He is in his outside cage and he is singing wonderfully—a joyful expression of a summer day. A couple of houses away a conure is squawking; he is enjoying the summer weather, too.

No matter what their song, I enjoy listening to the birds. Their chorus, especially when added to the wild birds that come to my feeders, is a wonderful background to daily life. It's a touch of nature in a sometimes much too civilized world.

I grew up with budgies (called parakeets then). When I left home at 18 I took my parakeets with me. They were followed by conures, finches and cockatiels. My husband and I took in a rescued african grey parrot that had been terribly neglected, and a lesser sulfur crested cockatoo that had been attacked and horribly maimed by another bird. Over the years, these and other birds have been an important part of our lives. Their companionship, songs and behaviors have taught us a lot about them and their world.

When I had my first budgies, the only books I could find were either very simple, basic pet guides or extremely technical, difficult-to-understand veterinary texts. There didn't seem to be anything in between. In addition, very little was known about avian nutrition, medicine or behavior. Bird ownership was very much "fly by the seat of your pants!"

However, in the past decade or two, our knowledge has increased tremendously. We now know that those all-seed diets we used to feed are severely lacking in many essential nutrients. We know that many species of birds are much more intelligent than we gave them credit for, and that to house them alone in an empty, sterile cage is cruel. We can also treat many health problems now that used to be an automatic death sentence. Captive breeding is producing thousands of healthy, well-adjusted birds that are thriving as pets. We, and our avian friends, have come a long way.

This book, *The Complete Idiot's Guide to Bird Care & Training,* will be a wonderful reference for you. The information here will help you choose the right bird for your life—because all birds are not the same. You will also learn how to care for your bird, how to choose the right cage and toys, when to call the veterinarian and even how to play with your bird.

Many people, including some bird owners, don't realize how important our birds are to us. One day my husband and I were out in our front yard. My husband was working on one of the cars and things weren't going well, so the atmosphere was tense. A neighbor came over and was quite upset. "My birds are gone," he said. I didn't realize he owned birds, so I asked him what kind he had. "I have two budgies," he answered. He had set their cage outside so that they could enjoy the summer weather, then gone to church. When he came home the cage was still there, the door was open and the two budgies were gone.

I gave him some ideas about how to look for the birds, where to put up flyers and told him I would tell the neighbors on our street to keep an eye out, but that he should go to the street behind his house. About an hour later he came back, his face beaming. "I found them and they came to me," he said. "They were in a tree in the yard behind our house." When I congratulated him, he said, "I didn't realize how much I liked those birds. My wife brought them home and I always thought they just made a mess. But when I found them gone I almost cried. Me, 64 years old, crying about two budgies." He shook his head, "I don't know. But I have them back, and I'll make sure their cage door is locked next time." As he turned to walk back home, he said to me, "I knew you would understand why they were so important. Thank you for your help."

The lesson here is love your birds, even if people with no birds don't understand!

—Liz Palika

Liz is an award-winning writer. Her pet books include The Consumer's Guide to Feeding Birds, *as well as* The Complete Idiot's Guide to Turtles & Tortoises and The Complete Idiot's Guide to Reptiles & Amphibians.

Introduction

My first job out of college was with a newspaper in Davie, Florida, and I lived just outside of town with my dog and the horse I bought with my graduation gift money. While currying my horse one day, I was startled by a voice calling, "Hello Elaine, hello Elaine." Since my name is Jackie and I wasn't expecting anyone, I rushed back to the house and opened the door so Lobo, my protective Alaskan Malamute, could join me outside. But he wasn't the least bit worried, not even when the invisible voice said "Hello Elaine" three more times.

With Lobo beside me, I realized the voice came from above, in the direction of the avocado tree. Beneath the branches, I was greeted by several wolf whistles. The colorful chorus helped me locate a yellow head atop a green body that blended into the leaves. My visitor was a parrot!

It took two hours to bribe the bird down to where I could reach it. Finally it came close enough to take a cracker from my hand. As it held the treat in one foot and prepared to take a bite, I made my move and grabbed the parrot in both hands. Three puncture wounds later, the bird was safely perched on my mantle.

That evening I tried to locate "Kelly's" owner. There was nothing in the lost and found section of the local newspapers, and none of the humane shelters, radio or TV stations had received a call about a lost bird.

I had "Kelly" for two weeks and was hopelessly in love when a friend from Miami said she remembered seeing something about a lost bird in the classifieds some time ago. I called the Miami newspapers and sure enough, someone from South Miami, a good hour's drive from Davie, had advertised a lost double yellow-headed amazon parrot six weeks earlier. With shaky hands I dialed the number. The woman's voice was guarded. "Yes, I lost my bird Hank," she said in a monotone, "but it was so long ago I'm sure he's dead."

"Did your bird talk?" I asked.

"He didn't know a lot of words," she answered, "but my name is Elaine and he could say, 'Hello, Elaine' very clearly."

An hour later, when Handsome Hank stepped from my hand to Elaine's hand, we both cried. The next day I filled the empty spot in my heart with my own cockatiel.

Thirty years have passed, but I still remember Hank because he gave me a great gift. His brief visit introduced me to the intriguing world of birds. Since then, no matter where I lived or what I was doing, there has always been a bird in my life.

Through this book, I want to give the same gift to you. *The Complete Idiot's Guide to Bird Care & Training* was written to make living with a bird easy and fun. It will guide you through choosing your first bird and help you develop a better relationship with your birds, even if you already have five at home. It will simplify daily care, help you handle your birds with confidence, and tell you everything you need to know about keeping your bird healthy and happy. Whether you're a new owner or have enjoyed the companionship of birds for years, this book's quick and easy training techniques will bring back the hope, the anticipation, the excitement you felt the day you brought home your first bird. May you always enjoy the gift of a bird in your life.

Extras

The pages of this book are peppered with Bonus Boxes. Besides adding spice, they give you a quick bite of bird information. Here's what you'll find:

Avian Adventures

These big boxes are full of true stories, exceptions to the rules, fun facts and even a little trivia.

Bird Brainers

Most of these boxes contain tips, training techniques and shortcuts. A few have information specific to certain species and temperaments.

Squawk!

Whoa! Think of these boxes as flashing red lights. They will keep you from plunging into common, but potentially dangerous, mistakes.

Polly Sez

Every hobby has its own language. These boxes define the terms bird owners should know.

Acknowledgments

My editor, Beth Adelman, gave me the opportunity to write this book and enhanced it with her creative spirit.

My husband, Tom O'Neil, took several photos for this book—then took them again when the originals were stolen (along with the camera) during a trip to Mexico.

My stepdad, Needham Parrish, helped with the research by sending enough bird books and magazines to fill one whole level of a long bookshelf.

My cousin, Barbara Furman, helped me proofread when she was supposed to be vacationing.

My vibrant birds, Rooster, Sugar, Pinto and Bluebell, provided inspiration (read laughs). So did Cuka and Omelet. Those two old friends are gone now, but will always live in my heart.

Part 1
Before You Choose a Corner for the Cage

You've got the urge to get a bird. But with so many to choose from, finding the right bird may seem overwhelming. This part of the book will change all that. First, it will help you decide if bird ownership suits your lifestyle. Then it will give you the upside and downside of every popular species, so you'll be able to match your pet to your personality. Finally, it will help you find a healthy bird with a delightful disposition. After all, I want you to choose an avian amigo you'll love for years and years.

Wait! Don't skip this section just because you already have a bird or two. Learning how to recognize a healthy bird will help you catch minor health problems in your pets before they become serious. And, on a lighter note, I'll tell you the best way to enjoy bird parks on your next vacation.

Ready? Then let's take a look at birds and find out why so many people share their space with them.

Chapter 1

Why Be a Bird Owner

> **In This Chapter**
>
> ➤ The pet of the future
>
> ➤ Ancient aviculture
>
> ➤ Why people want pet birds
>
> ➤ Should feathers be part of your future?
>
> ➤ How much is that birdie in the window?

Do you want the pet of the 21st century? Then you're in the right place. Birds have become our nation's second most popular pet (cats are first and dogs are third). A study by the American Veterinary Medical Association estimates that there are 56 million cats, 53 million birds and 52 million dogs in American homes. Surprised? That's because you're used to seeing dog owners walking their dogs and cats running loose (unfortunately), but you seldom see birds unless you go to the pet store, because most pet birds are cage potatoes.

In this chapter, you'll learn how bird-keeping began and why it keeps growing. After that, it's self-evaluation time. Let's find out if bird ownership will be fun for you and if this is a good time to go for it.

Early Bird Owners

Appreciating birds for their companionship and beauty puts you in illustrious company. Getting a bird may be new to you, but people have cherished pet birds for thousands of years. In fact, birds were probably ancient peoples' first pets. Dogs and cats were originally domesticated for utilitarian purposes such as hunting, herding or rodent control, but birds were brought into homes just for enjoyment.

Queen Hatshepsut of Egypt was the first bird-keeper in recorded history. In 1500 B.C., she sponsored an expedition to collect falcons and hawks for the royal zoo.

Alexander the Great introduced aviculture to the Western world. Enthralled by the peacocks and tame parrots he saw in India, he had several of each shipped home to his native Greece. Later, he enacted a law prohibiting the slaughter of peacocks for food. Alexander also discovered the ring-necked parakeet and brought it to Europe, where it was renamed the alexandrine parakeet.

Perhaps Alexander developed his love of birds during his youth. His tutor, the philosopher Aristotle, was one of the first known bird writers. Aristotle's prolific works include stories about his own pet bird, Psittace. Later, the name was incorporated into the scientific name for the parrot family—Psittacine.

Avian Adventures

"You came out of an egg," was a compliment in ancient Greece. It meant that you were very handsome or beautiful, depending on your gender. No doubt it evolved from the myth of Leda. After her affair with a swan, who was actually the god Zeus in disguise, Leda laid two eggs. The lovely Helen of Troy hatched from one of the eggs, while Castor and Pollux, the handsome twins of mythology, hatched from the other.

During the heyday of the Roman Empire, it took plenty of pet birds to keep up with the Juliuses. Talking parrots were status symbols, and it was fashionable to wear a live bird or two as jewelry. Some wealthy Romans kept a hundred or more and built great aviaries out of precious metals to house them. Raising pigeons was also popular. The Romans are believed to be the first bird traders, credited with introducing a variety of pet birds to the rest of Europe.

By the early 18th century, bird-keeping was a popular pastime for the leisure class in Europe, and many of the finest homes featured large aviaries filled with a variety of splendid species. Birds became popular pets with the working class during the middle of the 18th century, about the time of the Industrial Revolution. The Avicultural Society, a club of fine bird breeders, was founded in England in 1894.

Although early parrot owners in America included Martha Washington, Dolly Madison and Andrew Jackson, pet birds weren't prevalent in the States until the budgie (parakeet) became popular during the 1950s. By the 1970s, wild parrots caught in faraway places appeared in pet shops and were considered unique and exotic acquisitions.

Avian Adventures

Some historians believe that Christopher Columbus introduced amazon parrots to Europe. They say he captured a pair of Cuban amazons in the New World and gave them to Queen Isabella when he got back to Spain.

Your Place in History

Bird ownership has increased more than 20 percent since the early 1980s, and the rise is probably due to the availability of better birds. No, birds haven't undergone genetic engineering, but today they are raised in the USA and are available in greater numbers and more varieties than ever before. Only three decades ago, most of the larger pet birds (amazon parrots, conures, cockatoos, macaws and the like) were caught in distant jungles or rain forests and imported to our country. Terrified, alienated and wild, many of them were too defensive or aggressive to make good pets. Today, most of the better pet stores offer hand-raised birds. Already bonded to people, these silly-sweet youngsters make marvelous companions. So where are you in bird-keeping history? You're in the best place at the best time to get the best possible pet bird.

Polly Sez

Parakeets, also known as *budgerigars*, a.k.a. budgies, are the most popular pet birds in the world. Which name is correct? All of them. But serious bird breeders and enlightened owners use *budgie* because budgerigar is too darn long and the term parakeet describes any long-tailed member of the parrot family.

Why People Want Birds

Social, beautiful and relatively low maintenance, birds come in assorted colors and are available in small, medium and large. They liven up a home by singing, chattering, whistling, squawking, laughing or even talking, and sometimes all of the above. Some are sort of quiet, while others are noisy. Some are affectionate, even cuddly. Others do just fine with another bird for a buddy.

Birds fit in homes that may be too cramped for a dog or cat. In fact, many landlords and condo associations allow feathered, but not furry, pets. Birds also fit in with other companion animals. Sixty-five percent of bird owners have a dog, 47 percent have a cat, and although I've never seen the statistics on how many bird owners have both dog and cat, I'm sure there are thousands of us.

Avian Adventures

During the 15th century, Portuguese sailors captured songbirds on the islands off the coast of Morocco so they would have music on their long voyages. Today, those islands are called the Canary Islands and the sailors are credited with introducing the canary to Europe. Particularly prized in Holland, Italy, Belgium, Germany and England, the canary was soon domesticated, and selectively bred to enhance both its beauty and its song. Paintings from the period often show a canary perched on the graceful fingers of a fashionable lady.

Birds are responsive pets and make people feel good. That's me with two of my friends.

Birds are also ideal pets for working families. After all, you don't have to walk Polly during the morning frenzy of getting the kids off to school and yourself off to work. And you don't have to worry about what she's doing while everyone is away for the day. She won't be using the sofa for a scratching post or redesigning the antique rocker (unless you left the cage door open, but that's another story).

It's a scientific fact that playing with a pet relaxes the mind, lowers the blood pressure and is just plain good for people. So what are you waiting for? Let's find out if a bird is the right pet to lighten up your life.

Bird Owners Rate the Benefits and Drawbacks of Having a Pet Bird

Benefit	% of Owners Who Agree
Entertaining, fun to watch	90
Companionship, company	82
Convenience, easy to maintain	61
Conversation piece	52
Appearance	47
Relaxation	45
Good for kids, teaches responsibility	36
Educational	27
Hobby	22
Good for health	19
Sings, chirps, cheery	8
Competitive hobby	4
Affectionate	2
Enjoyment, pleasure	2

Drawback	% of Owners Who Agree
Cleaning up	59
Finding care when away from home	46
Noise, chirping	27
No drawbacks	16
Cage odor	10
Cost of food, care, medicine	8
Health (sanitary conditions of home)	7
Family member allergy	5
Vet not knowledgeable	5
Too great a responsibility	5
Other	4

Source: The American Pet Product Manufacturer's Association

Is a Feathered Friend in Your Future?

While most bird owners are crazy about their pets, a few wish they had never brought a bird home. These disillusioned owners consider their pet a burden or a nuisance, yet they must have thought they wanted a bird at one time or they wouldn't have one. What went wrong, and how can you keep it from happening to you? Asking yourself the following questions will help.

Why Do I Want a Bird?

Ideally, birds fascinate you and make you feel good, and you can't pass a pet shop without visiting every critter in feathers. However, your reason for buying a bird may be less than ideal, yet work out well anyway. For example, are you bored and believe a bird will add gusto to your life? A few feathers wrapped around a pleasant personality will spice up your spirit if you let it. But unfortunately, birds bought to relieve monotony are usually ignored once the novelty wears off.

Before buying a bird, decide if you will always appreciate your pet or if you just crave some instant entertainment. Still not sure? Ask yourself this: Am I ready to care for a bird for the next 10 years or more (maybe much more), or would two weeks in Tahiti be just as effective for banishing my boredom?

Polly Sez

Scientific Class *Aves*, which is birds, is divided into 28 Orders. Almost all the birds kept as pets are members of either the Order *Psittaciformes*, which includes all the parrots; or the Order *Passeriformes*, which is made up of perching birds, and includes canaries and finches as well as the songbirds in our backyards.

Is This a Good Time to Get a Bird?

Sometimes timing is everything. People often become impatient and acquire their bird too soon—before they have the stability and time to enjoy it. Bad timing is one reason why many lonesome doves are relegated to a quick feeding, a change of water and little else. Before deciding what kind of bird you want, ask yourself whether owning any bird fits into your life right now—and still will in the foreseeable future. If you're still in school, starting a new job, getting married or getting divorced, it may be best to put off getting a pet until you are somewhat more settled.

Will I Enjoy a Bird's Dependence?

Unlike kids (well, some kids anyway), birds don't grow up and become independent enough to make their own meals or clean their own cages. That's not a problem for most owners because they enjoy daily bird care and find it relaxing. They talk to Polly while changing the cage paper and are entertained by her reactions to food and treats. Will you get a kick out of caring for your bird? Daily bird care only takes a few minutes, but if years of caring for a dependent bird sounds like a drag, that's exactly how it will feel.

Am I Being Pressured into Buying a Bird by My Kids?

If you're thinking about getting a bird because your kids want one, I'll bet they promised to do all the feeding, water-changing and cage cleaning. Don't believe it. While caring for a pet does make kids more responsible, they shouldn't be left totally in charge. Ideally, bird care should be a family affair, with other family members willing to feed Polly and change the cage papers if Junior went to a friend's house after school. The bottom line is that someone does have to take overall responsibility to make sure Polly is fed, watered and has a clean cage. Since *you* are the one reading this book, I'll bet you'll be that someone. Will you relish being parent to a parrot?

Polly Sez

When we call a plane a "bird" or a helicopter a "whirleybird," we're not just using slang; we're being intellectual. *Avis*, the Latin word for bird, is the root of aviation, aviator and several other words. For example, *aviculture* is the care and raising of birds, anything having to do with birds is *avian*, and an *aviary* is a large home for birds.

Can I Afford a Bird?

Bird prices vary between species, and you have to include the cost of a cage, cage toys and possibly a playpen when tallying the initial expense. Ongoing expenses include food, cuttlebones, stimulating new toys, and perhaps specialized perches and a cage-top gym. Veterinary expenses include a yearly examination. If none of those items scare you off, ask yourself if you could afford emergency treatment if Polly has an accident. Think priorities. If Polly's problem puts you on a budget of beans for a month, would you (or your family) beef about it?

Dollars and Sense

The major factors affecting the price of birds are the rarity of the species and the tameness of the bird. In general, hand-fed babies cost more than untamed adults of the same species. Other than that, price reflects rarity and has nothing to do with how good a pet a bird will be. For example, the rarer rose-breasted cockatoo may command $2,200, while the more common umbrella cockatoo sells for around $1,200, even though umbrella cockatoos are usually better pets.

Although prices vary considerably in different parts of the country, the following table represents the approximate cost of several popular pets:

Typical Prices for Popular Birds

Type of bird	Price
Finch	$10–16
Budgie	$12–18
Love Bird	$50–70
Canary	$50–100
Cockatiel	$50–100
Conure	$300–500
Amazon Parrot	$500–1,000
Cockatoo	$700–2,200
African Grey	$800–1,100
Macaw	$900–2,500

Bird Brainers

According to a survey done by the American Pet Product Manufacturer's Association, 42 percent of bird-owning households have children living at home.

Squawk!

Don't rush out and buy a bird just because you're satisfied with your answers to these questions. Instead, keep reading. A pet that matches your personality is the most fun, and the next few chapters will help you find out what type of bird will be your best buddy. After all, you can't be roommates with just anybirdy.

Will a Bird Blend into My Home, Family and Lifestyle?

Your spouse's opinion, your children's ages and allergies and a compulsion for an immaculate home are all major considerations when deciding whether to make a bird part of your family. Bringing home a bird even though your spouse doesn't want one is unfair to everyone. Sure, there are exceptions where the reluctant spouse learned to like the bird, but more often than not the unwilling partner never comes around. Defending your bird on a daily basis gets old real fast. (Listen up. This is the voice of experience talking. My ex complained about my parrot for 20 years!)

Are your children still babies or toddlers? If so, do yourself a favor and wait a few years before getting a big bird. Youngsters can be hurt by large hookbills, so their time together should always be supervised. We'll talk more about the child-bird combo in Chapter 6, but you should know up front that when small children are involved, you'll have to take pains to keep both kids and birds safe. Older children, provided they are patient and respect animals, are often good with birds. In fact, some teenagers seem to be naturals when it comes to bird handling.

What kind of housekeeper are you? Is your home casual and relaxed, the kind of place where friends gather and eat popcorn while watching videos? Or is your home so spotless that family members remove their shoes before stepping on the cream-colored carpet? Birds are messy little critters, and no matter how hard you try to prevent it, some of their food and a few feathers always end up on the floor. A cordless vacuum cleaner cleans it up instantly, but a few people are just too uptight about keeping house to enjoy keeping a bird.

Do you live alone and travel often? Unless you have friends or relatives who are willing to bird sit, consider the expense of boarding your bird when you are away. Prices vary across the country, so call a couple of local pet shops and ask about boarding fees *before* you decide to get a bird.

You're Probably Going to Be a Bird Owner if You:

➤ Visit pet shops just to look.

➤ Know any of the pet shop birds by name.

➤ Feel yourself smile when you talk to birds.

➤ Scan the pet column in the classifieds just to see what's there.

➤ Know all your friends' birds by name and species.

➤ Have already decided where you'd put the cage.

The Least You Need to Know

➤ Birds have been prized as pets throughout history, and come in many sizes and colors.

➤ Although birds are relatively low-maintenance pets, they all need daily care.

➤ Be sure a bird will blend into your life before buying one.

Chapter 2

Making a Match

In This Chapter

➤ Looking, listening and learning about birds

➤ What qualities do you want in a pet?

➤ Who's noisy and who's not?

➤ The benefits of hand-fed babies

There's something about birds that attracts you, or you wouldn't be reading this book. Maybe you're turned on by watching fleet finches hop, sparrow-like, about their business. Or perhaps it's a big parrot, standing on one foot while munching corn on the cob out of the other, that makes you smile. Do you admire the cockatiel's crest? The budgie's lively chatter? Maybe, like me, you appreciate them all. But few of us can have them all, and even if we could, we wouldn't be able to give that many pets enough individual attention to keep them happy. So it all comes down to decisions, decisions.

If you haven't decided which species you want, a world of fun awaits you. It's time to observe birds. The more you see, the more confused you'll be at first, but don't let that bother you. Instead, savor the sounds and colors while finding out who's who in the bird world. Soon certain traits, both appealing and unappealing, will stand out and help you narrow down your choices.

Here's Looking at You, Feather Face

When observing birds in pet stores, take your time. Don't approach them fast enough to frighten them and don't try to interact with them. Stand a couple of feet away from their cages or perches and just watch. You're not choosing an individual yet. You're just trying to decide which birds you like best.

While watching, ask yourself questions that help you become aware of your preferences. For example, are you bored with the fluttering finches but attracted to the silly cockatoo who hangs upside down by one leg while screaming for your attention? Does the parrot's shrill squawk make you wince, while the melodious canary sings away your tension? Do you spend most of your time admiring the multicolored lovebirds, or were you so smitten when the grey parrot said "Hello" that you never noticed another bird?

Avian Adventures

While budgies (parakeets) that talk fluently are engaging exceptions rather than the rule, a budgie named Puck from the United States holds the Guinness World Record for having the largest vocabulary of any animal, with 1,728 words. Another budgie, Sparkie of Great Britain, held the record during the 1950s and '60s. In 1958 he won the BBC's Cage Word Contest by reciting eight nursery rhymes without stopping. Sparkie's vocabulary was estimated at 531 words and 383 sentences.

Analyze your reactions every time you watch and listen to birds. Soon you'll know if you are attracted to song, speech, hilarious behavior, sweet personalities or certain colors. You'll also discover whether you can live with occasional loud screeches and squawks, or would trade the possibility of speech for a quieter pet. Most birds capable of speech are also capable of screech, but there are exceptions. Some budgies (parakeets) and cockatiels learn to talk, and they don't have particularly shrill voices. Also, a few parrot species are quieter than others.

Hanging Out in Pet Shops

One of the easiest places to observe birds is at your local pet shop. If there are several in your area, try them all. While most of them will have a variety of finches, canaries, budgies and cockatiels, they may not have a lot of large birds because big birds are a big investment. Most pet shops have a few parrots and conures, but one store owner may have invested big bucks in a macaw or two, while another shop features cockatoos. The more stores you visit, the more species you'll see. There are exceptions. Some specialty bird stores feature a fabulous selection under one roof.

Expect to be a magnet for salespeople and don't hesitate to tell them the truth. You're interested but just looking, because you're not ready to decide. Some (but not all) pet shops put a tag on each bird's cage with the species (african grey, umbrella cockatoo, etc.) and sometimes the price. Bring a notebook to help you remember which birds you liked best. If you're observing birds in a store without cage tags, ask the salesperson about the ones you find most appealing. Salespeople in the better bird stores will be knowledgeable about the species on display and glad to answer your questions.

While budgies, canaries, finches and other small birds will almost always be displayed in cages, some pet shops exhibit their larger birds out in the open—on T-stands or intricate bird gymnasiums. These birds are usually so well socialized that some of them even bow their heads and fluff their neck feathers for petting, so approach slowly and talk to the bird. If it stretches, wags its tail, or fluffs and bows, chances are it wants you to come closer. But if it squawks, snaps in your direction or backs away, respect its request to be left alone. Also, no matter how inviting a bird appears, obey any sign that says "Do Not Touch. "

Polly Sez

T-stands are bird perches shaped like a capital T. You'll hear more about them later, because they are handy for taming, training or taking your pet from room to room with you.

Polly Sez

People who selectively breed and raise birds in an effort to produce exceptionally fine specimens for exhibition are called bird *fanciers*. They are part of the bird *fancy*, which includes breeders, exhibitors, judges and those who frequently attend bird shows.

Meeting Bird Breeders

The best way to meet flocks of bird breeders is to attend a bird show. The breeders are accessible because they stay near their birds, and most of them are happy to answer questions. Best of all, you'll see many magnificent birds in perfect condition.

Most of the magazines devoted to pet birds (see Appendix A) announce upcoming bird shows across the country and contain classified ads for hundreds of breeders. *Bird Talk* magazine, for example, has a Show Calendar and an Avian Directory. It also runs the breeders' ads by state, so you can easily find the ones closest to you.

Bird breeders and fanciers watch the judging at a bird show. The walls are lined with birds in their special show cages.

Talking Bird with Your Buddies

Tell your friends at work you're thinking about getting a bird and mention it at club meetings, the gym, parties and wherever your life takes you. Chances are, someone in your circle of friends has a bird or two. Bird owners love to talk about their pets, and may invite you over to meet pretty Polly. Accept the invitation and you'll see a slice of life with a bird. Even though every species is different and every individual bird within a species is unique, you'll still come away with an overall impression of whether or not having a bird in your home appeals to you.

If you have access to the Internet, you'll find plenty of owners eager to chat and answer questions about their favorite species. Just keep in mind that bird owners are their own birds' biggest fans, and what one person finds appealing, another may find appalling. Don't select and send away for a species on someone else's say-so. Meet at least one bird (more are better) of a species before buying.

Squawk!

Some breeders ship birds by air. While the transfer usually goes off without a hitch, sometimes it doesn't and a bird can get sick. Besides, it's better to buy a bird you have already met. There should be some chemistry between you.

Visiting a Bird Park or Zoo

Visiting bird parks, theme parks or zoos with exotic bird displays is an exciting way to see a variety of species. Some of them even allow visitors to interact with the birds.

Avoid the maddening mob by visiting bird displays during the week if possible, rather than on a weekend. The handlers may have time to talk, and you'll also have a better view and more possibilities of interacting with the birds. Parks with exceptional bird displays, such as Busch Gardens and Parrot Jungle, offer shows with trained birds as the stars. Show times are posted.

Birds just being themselves in beautiful surroundings are also a spectacular sight. They are most active early in the morning and late in the afternoon, because that's when they would feed and socialize in their natural habitats. From late morning through early afternoon they tend to tuck their heads under their wings and take siestas, no matter how many visitors whistle at them. And we call them bird brains!

Ready to plan an outing but don't know where to start? Start by turning to Appendix B. It lists some of the better bird displays across the country.

Avian Adventures

If you're vacationing in Florida, don't miss Parrot Jungle in Miami. Besides seeing myriad species on display, the show includes cockatoos riding scooters and cycles; and macaws who count, skate and drive trucks. My favorite was a macaw named Kitty. She slid down a pole, "rode to the moon" in a space ship and returned to Earth in a parrotchute.

Making a Match

Bird shopping is a lot like life. Most of the time we get into a lot less trouble if we spend a moment admiring an attractive item that was never meant to be ours and then move on. By now you may have seen several species, but picking a bird buddy on looks alone is about as smart as making a long-term commitment to a cute guy or gal you just met. An array of colorful characters are waiting for the curtain to raise on Chapter 3. While every one of them is the ideal pet for some bird lover, that someone isn't necessarily you. The right bird will fit into your time and space, need as much attention as you want to give and make as much noise as you find amusing. So, before we meet the characters waiting behind their wings, I'm going to present you with a few problems "for your own good," as my mother would say.

Your Space and Time

In Chapter 1 you decided whether a feathered friend should be in your future. You're still with me, so the answer must be "yes." Congratulations! You're going to love having a bird. Now let's start finding the best bird for you by whittling down your choices. Then you can focus on a narrower field of feathers and see which species suit your style.

How Big Are Birds?

Bird	Size (in inches)
Finch	4
Canary	5 to 7
Lovebird	5 to 7
Brotogeris (Pocket Parakeet)	7 to 8
Conure	8 to 18
Pionus	9 to 12
African Grey	9 to 14
Amazon	10 to 18
Cockatiel	11 to 14
Cockatoo	12 to 28
Macaw	12 to 40

Sound Judgment

Just how much noise can you handle? Will chattering budgies amuse you? Will a canary's song soothe you? Do shrill sounds get on your nerves, or will your parrot's squawks be the lively background music that makes your house feel like home? Sometimes parrots are moody. Will everyone in your family keep their cool when Polly has a bad feather day and screams her frustration to the skies? You'll have to know the answers to these and other questions before choosing a species and doing any serious shopping.

One of the reasons parrots are so popular is that they are sociable pets who connect and communicate with their owners. The downside of this charming connection (for some) is that they sometimes communicate with shrill whistles and occasional screams. Talking parrots may shout their repertoire of words and phrases when they want to attract attention, and most parrot owners applaud and encourage this behavior. But music to one

Squawk!

Don't make a snap decision and bring home a bird on a whim. Instead, know the pros and cons of each species you are attracted to before making your selection.

ear may be maddening to another, especially when that ear belongs to a neighbor who doesn't even like birds. Making noise is a parrot trait. That's why the amount and type of noise you can tolerate, and the distance to your nearest neighbor, should be considered when selecting a species. Who, besides you, will live with your pet? Who will hear your bird when you're not there?

Birds in the wild are most active at sunup and sunset, so every member of the parrot family turns up the volume when greeting the dawn and the evening star. This trait doesn't disappear with domestication, but there are over 350 different species in the parrot family alone, and voices and volume vary considerably among them. In general, little birds like budgies and cockatiels have much smaller voices than larger parrots, and aren't loud enough to bother most neighbors. At the other end of the spectrum are macaws, cockatoos and some conures. Some of their screams could awaken a hearing-impaired neighbor three houses away!

Who Whistles, Who Peeps, Who's Quiet and Who Shrieks?

These birds are best bets for apartment and condo dwellers:

➤ Finches

➤ Canaries

➤ Budgies

➤ Cockatiels

➤ A single lovebird

➤ Most single pionus parrots

These birds are fine if you live near your neighbors, but are separated by more than just a wall:

➤ A pair of lovebirds

➤ A single pocket parrot

➤ A single pionus parrot

➤ Some single eclectus parrots

➤ An occasional African grey parrot

These birds do fine in developments with single-family homes:

➤ African grey parrots

➤ Amazon parrots

➤ Some lories and lorikeets

➤ Mynah birds

➤ Some conures

continues

continued

Plenty of space between you and your nearest neighbor is the best bet with these birds:

➤ Some conures

➤ Some lories and lorikeets

➤ Cockatoos

➤ Macaws

Do You Want a Talking Bird?

Even if your answer is a resounding "yes," I can't guarantee you a talking bird. Every bird is different, and some individuals communicate in other ways, even though they are members of a species known for its talking ability. Birds are great communicators, with or without words, but if owning a talking bird is important to you, make it happen by buying an older bird who already says some words, instead of a baby.

Bird Brainers

There are more than 350 species of parrots, and about 280 of those species are kept as pets.

If you prefer raising a youngster, and will love it whether or not its gifts include gab, here's a list of popular species that are widely believed to be reliable talkers. Many other species are also capable of becoming super speakers, so check out the cast of characters in Chapter 3 before making a decision:

Popular pet birds that often become excellent talkers:

➤ African grey parrot

➤ Greater hill mynah

➤ Yellow-naped amazon parrot (male)

➤ Double yellow-head amazon parrot (male)

➤ Yellow-fronted amazon parrot

➤ Blue-fronted amazon parrot (male)

➤ Quaker (monk) parakeet

➤ Blue and gold macaw

How Much Time Will You Spend with Your Bird?

Different species make different demands on your time. Some are happiest if you disappear after filling their dishes, while others thrive on your attention. Are you content to sit back and observe birds from a distance, or are close encounters of the bird kind what you have in mind?

How much attention do birds need? In general, the tamest and best-trained birds need the most. A bird trained to talk or do tricks has learned to expect attention, and may change from sweet to snappish if it feels abandoned. Even a trusting, hand-fed baby parrot will revert to a wild animal if no one handles it. When suddenly neglected, a nice bird becomes a candidate for a variety of problems, including nervous disorders and a troublesome temperament.

Certain parrot species, such as amazons, african greys, cockatoos, cockatiels, conures and macaws, are prized for their sociability. They want and need human attention. In fact, relating to their owners is a delightful part of their personality. Although you may have enough time to play with a sociable bird now, consider the future before choosing a species. Do you have a demanding career? Yanking yourself up the corporate ladder might mean working such long hours that a needy bird awaiting your homecoming feels more like pressure than play. No fun for you. Unfair to your friendly bird.

Do you have a history of giving new things lots of time and attention at first, then ignoring them when the newness wears off? What's hidden in your closet? Is a tennis racquet, golf clubs, a guitar or in-line skates squirreled away where they can't make you feel guilty?

If there may be long periods of time when the only attention your bird gets is basic care, consider buying a pair of small, active birds. Budgies, lovebirds and finches are all fun to watch. Finches don't want human attention, but must have the company of another finch to thrive. A single budgie or lovebird, on the other hand, would literally do acrobatics to attract your attention. But if you don't have time to love your lovebird or budgie consistently, buy a pair. The twosome will play together and won't care if you join in or not. With a pair of finches, budgies or lovebirds in your home, an amusing bird show will be playing whenever you want one. And when you don't, there's no need for guilt. Twosomes always keep each other entertained.

Squawk!

Neglected birds can become dangerously depressed and take their distress out on themselves. Some even pull out their own feathers.

How Much Space Can You Set Aside for a Bird Cage?

Every bird needs a cage large enough so it can stretch its wings and flap them without hitting the bars. Cage size usually corresponds to bird size, but there are exceptions. For example, a pair of finches requires a rather large cage because they need a roomy area for exercise, and some smallish birds need tall cages to accommodate their incredibly long tails. The following table gives you minimum cage sizes for several species, so you can figure out what type of bird will fit in your home. For details on cage selection, see Chapter 5.

Minimum Cage Sizes

Species	Minimum cage size (in inches)
Canary	16L × 12W × 15H
Budgie	15L × 15W × 18H
Canary-winged or other small parakeet or lovebird	18L × 18W × 18H
Cockatiel	18L × 18W × 24H
Alexandrine or other long-tailed parakeet or small macaw	24L × 18W × 30H
African grey, amazon or pionus parrot	24L × 16W × 28H
Conure (small)	20L × 18W × 24H
Mynah	24L × 18W × 30H
Conure (large) or cockatoo	24L × 24W × 36H
Pair of finches	30L × 18W × 20H
Toucan	60L × 36W × 48H
Macaw (large)	60L × 36W × 60H

When it comes to cages, bigger is always better. A spacious cage encourages exercise and lets your pet perform acrobatic feats that are impossible in smaller quarters. The sizes given in the table are sufficient if you lack space. But buy a bigger cage if you have enough room. (Except for finches, these requirements are for one bird. A pair will need larger accommodations.)

Polly Sez

The terms *hand-raised* and *hand-fed* baby birds are used interchangeably. They refer to a bird that was taken away from its parents soon after birth and raised by a person. The result is a tame young bird who not only doesn't fear people, but identifies with them and depends on them.

Is Petting Important?

Whenever you see a bird sitting on someone's hand or bowing its neck and fluffing its feathers in hopes of having its head scratched, you can be sure someone spent time socializing it so it would crave human contact. Some socialized birds absolutely adore their owner's touch. These affectionate feather balls love to be petted and are sometimes referred to as "teddy bear parrots" because they're so cuddly. Get a species that could become a "teddy" only if you plan to play with your bird often. Rejected teddys soon become dejected teddys, and may take their stress out on themselves.

The following is a list of popular species that especially enjoy being petted and held. Individuals from many other species have become "teddys," too, so check out the characters in Chapter 3 to find out if your favorite is a good candidate for a neck rub.

➤ Cockatoos

➤ Most pocket parrots

➤ Green-cheeked amazon parrot (a.k.a. mexican red-head)

➤ Mealy amazon parrot

➤ Some pionus parrots

➤ Jardine's parrot

➤ Many african grey parrots

➤ Some lovebirds

➤ Some quaker (monk) parakeets

➤ An occasional cockatiel

➤ An occasional budgie

Some birds, like Rooster the mexican red-head, bow their heads and beg to be petted.

Does Messiness Matter?

I already admitted that all birds are somewhat messy when they eat and play, but a few species deserve Master's Degrees in messiness. Lories and lorikeets lead the list in one respect. They are nectar sippers and fruit eaters in the wild, and require a softer diet than other parrots. That makes their droppings loose. If their eliminations simply fell to the bottom of the cage, it wouldn't be much of a problem. But these acrobatic birds often cling to the cage wires and squirt their droppings several feet into the room. On the other hand, they are among the cleanest birds when it comes to airborne feather dust or dander, making them prime pets for people who have allergic reactions to other birds. If you are allergic to feather dust, or just want a gorgeous and rather rare bird, don't let a lori's soft stools stop you from enjoying its lively company. Many people swear by (not at) their lories and lorikeets. They simply keep them in specialized cages or outdoor aviaries.

Do lots of things make you sneeze or wheeze? Then don't consider a cockatoo. Cockatoo feathers produce a fine white, powdery dust, and people prone to allergies may react to it.

Avian Adventures

Some birds carry I.D. all the time, in the form of a metal band around their leg. That's because most breeders use bands to help identify their stock. Also, in an effort to reduce the number of birds smuggled into the U.S., some states require that certain species be banded with traceable numbers. Closed or seamless bands indicate a bird bred in the United States. Open bands have a small break in the ring and indicate a legally imported bird that was banded while passing through federal quarantine.

When it comes to eating and playing, who's the messiest parrot? Rooster, my mexican red-head, is sitting on the T-stand munching a piece of celery as I write this. He's wearing celery from the tip of his beak to the top of his head. There's celery on the screen, the keyboard and the mouse pad, and I just drank a small chunk along with my iced tea. So is Rooster the messiest parrot? Not by a long shot. The red-head is one of the smaller amazon parrots, and as a general rule, the larger the bird, the bigger the mess it can make. Of course, it's all controllable. The celery silliness was my fault. I know better than to let Rooster play with celery when he's out of his cage, but I did it anyway. Instead, I should have given him a piece of wood or an almond to keep him occupied. Then he wouldn't have got his beak messy, which made him shake his head, which made so much celery take flight in the first place.

Do You Have Other Pets?

Cats and dogs are both predators, so rather than blaming them for being what nature made them, take a few precautions and don't give in to your urge to experiment. A dog, a cat and four birds share our home, and we are far from unique. The key to success in multiple pet situations is to play it safe and sensible. Chapter 6 details the dangers and how to avoid them. In the meantime, here are the basics.

Cats are most dangerous to small birds because they are attracted to fluttering and quick movements. Large birds are less enticing because they move more slowly, and some cats are even slightly scared of them. Your cat may be bold, so don't take chances. Be certain your bird's cage is so secure that it can't be knocked down or opened by even the most determined tabby.

Dogs usually aren't intimidated by birds, no matter how big, and can kill even a large macaw in a heartbeat. While it has happened, it's rare for a dog to knock down a bird cage and kill the occupant. Most bird deaths by dogs occur when the bird and the dog are both loose and on the floor. Most often, they are accidents—a frisky dog gets too excited, and the bird doesn't survive the game. While some bird deaths result from dog-bird experiments ("Polly has been here a couple of weeks, so let's see if Sparky is used to her yet"), others occur when a peaceful old dog gets his nose pinched by an inquisitive bird.

Imagine That!

Now that you've observed some birds, close your eyes and imagine one in your home. How big is the bird and what is it doing? Is it singing sweetly? Wolf whistling as you walk by? Saying its first word? Will it transport you to a distant jungle with the squawk of the wild? Will it perch on your finger? Eat out of your hand? Bow its head and lean into your hand for petting? Show off by hanging upside down from the top of its cage? Or is your imaginary bird actually a colorful pair of birds who don't need your attention (except for daily care), but are affectionate toward each other and fun to watch?

Can one bird be all of those things? In a word, no. Birds are specialists. Some learn to talk more easily than others, and some don't talk at all. Some are affectionate and enjoy handling, while others never bond to anything but another bird. Some sing, others chatter, and most of the big boys squawk or shriek—at least sometimes.

Choosing the right bird becomes easier once you know who does what. Now that you've seen some birds and know which traits you like, come with me to Chapter 3. It's time to find out the facts about several intriguing species.

The Least You Need to Know

- ➤ Spend some time observing birds before selecting a species.
- ➤ Pet shops, bird shows, zoos and bird parks are good places to observe birds.
- ➤ Choose a species that matches your personality and fits into your lifestyle.
- ➤ No pet is perfect. There is an upside and a downside to every species.
- ➤ If this is your first bird and you want a medium to large one, your best bet is a hand-fed baby.

Chapter 3

Here Come the Characters

In This Chapter

➤ Getting to know birds

➤ The characteristics of several popular species

➤ Upsides and downsides of each species

In this chapter you'll meet several species that would add to your pleasure if they were in your home. Some would be happy to come out of their cages and join you for dinner or a night of television. Others will give you a good show, provided you keep your distance. Some are rather quiet. Others can be insistent squawkers. Since you won't be able to turn them off as if they were an irritating TV commercial, you should know who's likely to do what before buying any birds.

This chapter is your guide to the popular pet species. It will give you the upside and the downside of the birds you are most likely to encounter at the pet shop or through a breeder. In other words, it will tell you who talks, who peeps, who's quiet and who shrieks—and everything else you need to know to make an intelligent decision.

Canaries—Mini Music Makers

Latin Name: *Serinus canarius*

From: Islands off the northwestern coast of Africa; named the Canary Islands after the birds

Size: Between five and seven inches long

Talking Ability: None

Sexual Differences: Your eyes won't be able to tell the difference, but your ears will. The cock sings and the hen doesn't.

Usual Colors: Yellow, orange, red, white or variegated (yellow, orange, white or red base color; mixed with darker, usually brown, feathers)

Canaries are selectively bred to look or sing a certain way. The table lists some of the most popular varieties and what they are famous for.

Canaries' Claim to Fame

Canary Type	Claim to fame
American Singer	Song
Roller	Song
Norwich Fancy	Shape and plumage
Border Fancy	Shape and plumage
Gloster Fancy	Shape and plumage
Yorkshire Fancy	Shape and stature
Frills	Curly plumage
Red Factor	Color

Upside

The canary is a songbird. A male canary doesn't just chirp and peep. He breaks into complex melodies, complete with high notes, low notes and lots of lovely notes in between. Even a canary bred for shape, plumage or color will sing well, although not with the ideal tones of the song-bred bird. Female canaries make a little music too, but their voices sound more like a warble.

Canaries are attractive, active, relatively inexpensive, low-maintenance birds. They eat a simple diet, don't take much space and never develop a taste for the woodwork.

Polly Sez

Plumage is a fancy word for feathers.

Canaries can be tamed and taught to perch on your finger if you take the time, but it isn't necessary. Untrained birds don't develop bad habits because canaries don't need quality time with a human to be happy. If you have babies or young children, the canary is an ideal pet. Its cage can be hung high above your toddler's reach, and your child can enjoy watching and listening to the bird long before he or she is old enough to interact with an animal.

Canaries aren't all just yellow anymore.

Downside

While your canary may become tame enough to eat out of your hand, or sit on your finger or shoulder, it will not enjoy being petted the way some parrots do, and will not be interested in learning tricks. Although they are generally healthy, canaries must be handled with care because of their small size.

Some Significant Stuff

Is your main reason for wanting a canary its song? Then don't buy one until you hear it sing. If it sings a lovely song in the pet shop or its breeder's home, you'll know it's a male. If it doesn't sing before you buy it, don't take anyone's word that it will. Also, make sure you like a bird's singing voice before buying it. Different types of canaries have different voices, and there is considerable variation, even within the same variety. If the sound of one canary doesn't delight you, listen to other cocks until you hear notes that will be music to your ears every single day.

After you bring home the canary with the sound of an angel, it may be silent for several days. Don't worry. As soon as it feels secure in its new surroundings, it will tell you with a tune.

Finches—It Takes at Least Two

Latin Name: *Poephila guttata* (zebra finch) and *Lonchura domestica* (society finch) are the most popular.

From: The zebra finch hails from Australia. The society finch, also known as the bengalese finch, does not occur in the wild and may be the result of cross-breeding done in China centuries ago.

Size: Four inches long

Talking Ability: None

Sexual Differences: Zebra finch cocks are more colorful. Male and female society finches look alike, but the cock sings.

Here's a colorful male zebra finch.

Usual Colors: Zebra finches have bright coral-red bills. The cock is the most colorful. He has a flashy orange cheek patch, setting off a gray-blue head and neck; and gets his name from the dark, wavy horizontal stripes coloring his throat and upper breast. The cock also has an off-white belly and russet flanks, decorated with white spots. His wings and upper body are dark grayish-brown. The hen's colors are more muted and she lacks the orange cheek markings, zebra chest stripes and russet flanks. Both sexes sport black-and-white bands on their tails, red eyes, black vertical eye lines, and small white patches between the eye line and the beak. They also have orange feet, but the female's feet and beak are usually lighter than the male's.

Society finches come in a variety of warm brown shades, ranging from chocolate to honey colored, often mixed with white. They may have white markings in a variety of patterns.

Upside

Finches are small and colorful, and make a variety of attractive sounds, none of which are particularly loud. They are also entertaining, especially when the male dances and performs courtship displays for the female. Finches are low-maintenance birds and are not destructive. Their antics entertain young children while their cages can be kept safely out of reach.

Downside

Finches are social birds, but to each other, not to humans. While a few have become finger-trained, most of them won't want to perch on your hand and will be happiest if you give them daily care quickly and leave them alone. It's unfair to keep only one finch, because the sad little soul will suffer without a mate.

Some Significant Stuff

When visiting pet shops, breeders or bird shows, you'll see many finches in addition to the two varieties mentioned here. Gouldian finches, for example, are winged rainbows, but you may have to find the pot of gold to afford a pair. Some finches need live food as well as seeds and greens, which makes their maintenance more complex. Before falling for a beautiful pair, check on their dietary requirements.

Squawk!

When selecting a pair of finches, please honor their commitments and choose a pair that are obviously bonded to each other. Picking a cock from one pair and a hen from another is like breaking up two happily married couples.

Budgies—Bestsellers of the Bird World

Latin Name: *Melopsitt undulatus*

Also Known As: Parakeet, budgerigar

From: Australia

Size: Seven inches long

Popular Varieties: Budgie and english budgie. Although they are the same species, the english budgie is a bit bigger and more sedate than the common budgie.

Talking Ability: Good. Males make the best talkers. Pronunciation is clear, but words are often spoken so softly that they are hard to decipher.

Polly Sez

The budgie's *cere* is the area between the facial feathers and the beak, containing the nostrils.

Sexual Differences: In adult budgies, the male has a blue cere, while the female's cere is tan or brown. But baby budgies all have buff-colored ceres and look alike. Unless you have your heart set on a certain sex, you're best off buying a baby bird and letting it surprise you. By the time it's four months old, its cere will signal its sex.

Usual Colors: Green, blue, yellow, turquoise, white, or any combination of these colors, usually with dark stripes

Upside

Colorful, smart and brimming with personality, the tiny budgie can be as entertaining as its bigger cousins without being as noisy or expensive. Budgies are easily trained to perch on fingers and shoulders, are hardier than they look and love to play with their toys.

Downside

Most breeders let budgies raise their own chicks, so your new budgie will probably be wilder and more fearful than a hand-fed baby parrot. That means taming your bird will be a do-it-yourself project. Don't worry—budgies learn to like people in no time. You may get a nip or two in the process, but if you follow the suggestions in Chapter 13, you'll soon have a budgie on your finger.

Some Significant Stuff

Since baby budgies are the easiest to tame, you should know how to recognize one. A budgie under four months old has completely dark eyes and the stripes of dark feathers on its head reach all the way to the cere. Eyes and head feathers change as the bird matures. An adult budgie has a white iris surrounding its pupil and its dark stripes stop on top of the crown.

Cockatiels—Crested Comedians

Latin Name: *Nymphicus hollandicus*

From: Australia

Size: Eleven to fourteen inches long

Talking Ability: Fair for males; females seldom speak

Sexual Differences: Babies look alike, but a baby that is whistling or chirping is probably a male. At maturity, males usually have a darker orange cheek patch than females of the same body color. Mature gray and lutino females have light bars on the underside of the wings and tail. Adult pearl cockatiels are always female, because males lose their scallops and become solid gray before they turn two.

Usual Colors: Gray, with orange patches on the cheeks, and a crest of lighter gray or yellow. Cockatiels also come in pied mixtures of yellow, white and gray; lutino (white to yellow body with a yellow head); and a scalloped pattern called pearl. Most color combinations include sun spots on the cheeks.

Upside

The cockatiel is a smallish, attractive, intelligent bird with a long tail and a topknot or crest that may proclaim its mood. It can raise and lower its crest at will, and often holds it high when it is curious or excited. Female cockatiels are affectionate and quiet, with sweet dispositions. Males are moodier and generally less attuned to their owners, but are accomplished whistlers and sometimes learn several words. Both sexes love attention, are easily tamed and trained, and have a happy demeanor.

Squawk!

Before paying big bucks for a "rare" or "new colored" cockatiel, make sure the bird is healthy. Chapter 4 will tell you how. Occasionally a breeder is so concerned with color that he or she sacrifices hardiness.

Downside

If you don't have time to play with your bird, don't buy a cockatiel. It's full of personality and needs attention to thrive.

Some Significant Stuff

While you may pay a premium price for a pearl, white-faced or other unusual colored cockatiel, color is the only difference between it and a more ordinary colored bird. All hand-raised baby cockatiels have the potential to be charming pets.

Bird Brainers

Baby cockatiels are easy to tame, even if they weren't hand-fed babies.

This pied cockatiel is playing on a parrot-sized perch.

Lovebirds—One Will Do, You Don't Need Two

Latin Name: *Agapornis*

From: Africa

Size: Five to seven inches long

Popular Varieties: Peach-faced and masked

Talking Ability: Poor, but possible

Sexual Differences: Both sexes look alike in the common species, but males may be more gentle pets than females. In some of the rarer species, males and females have different colorations.

Usual Colors: The peach-faced lovebird is green with a striking peach face and throat, a blue rump, and an orange and black banded tail. The lutino version retains the peach face and throat, but has a bright yellow body and a white rump. Many other color combinations are available.

The masked lovebird has a green body, a black head with white eye ring, a yellow collar and breast, and a blue rump. The blue version of the masked lovebird also sports a black head and white eye ring, but it has an off-white collar and breast. Its body is shades of blue.

Upside

Lovebirds are small, gutsy birds that enjoy cuddling up in closed places. They like to crawl inside shirts, burrow into pockets or relax high up on shoulders, just under the hair. Although they like to chatter, lovebirds are not loud enough to annoy the neighbors. They are smart, and enjoy playing with toys and executing acrobatic feats in their cages. Hand-raised babies make affectionate pets, and some of them learn to do a few tricks. The most popular species are moderately priced.

Downside

Lovebirds don't stay loving unless you keep loving them. If ignored too long, even hand-fed babies turn nippy. They need to spend time outside their cages, perched on your hand or under your shirt. Like larger parrots (and people), they can be moody, stubborn and domineering at times, but these moods pass. Lovebirds need the stimulation of new toys and a spacious cage with a place to burrow, such as a nest box or an empty cardboard container. They whittle wood well for their size, and can be destructive when out of their cage without supervision.

Some Significant Stuff

The most important difference in lovebirds is between hand-fed and parent-fed babies. If you want a bird you can play with, not just watch, be sure to get a hand-fed baby— even if it costs more. Also, make sure you can handle the youngster before buying it.

If you're frequently going to play with your lovebird outside of its cage, buy only one. It will bond to you and become affectionate. But if you want to admire a lovebird, even though you don't have time to play with a pet, get a matched pair. They'll bond to each other and give you double the visual enjoyment. Since you won't be handling your birds, don't pay extra for a hand-fed baby. Parent-raised pairs are just as pretty.

Bird Brainers

To tell a baby lovebird from an adult, look at its beak. Baby lovebirds have black markings on their beaks that fade as they mature.

Perky Pocket Parakeets

Latin Name: *Brotogeris*

Also Known As: Brotogeris and bee bee parrots (though technically, they are parakeets)

From: South America and southern Mexico

Size: Seven to eight inches long

Popular Varieties: Gray-cheeked parakeet, canary-winged parakeet and orange-chinned parakeet

Talking Ability: Poor, but possible

Sexual Differences: None apparent to people

Usual Colors: Green body, often with blue on the wings, tail and head. Other coloration depends on the variety.

Upside

Affectionate and playful, hand-raised pocket parrots burrow in their owner's pockets and crawl up sleeves and down shirts. Most of them adore attention, and perform acrobatics and other antics just to make their owners laugh. Many learn tricks, and some have mastered a few words. A wonderful choice for those who want a parrot but lack the space or the finances. The most popular brotogeris parakeets are moderately priced and can be kept in a large budgie or cockatiel cage.

Downside

Pocket parrots are loud for their size. Although they can't turn up the volume like a big parrot, they have a harsh voice that gets on some peoples' nerves. These little guys are gutsy, and whether that's a good trait or a bad one depends on how often you play with your pet. The gray-cheeked, in particular, will become nippy unless it is handled frequently, and pocket parrots have a surprisingly hard bite.

Some Significant Stuff

Several other varieties of brotogeris parakeets may be available through a breeder in your area. They all make marvelous pets.

What's Great About African Greys?

Latin Name: *Psittacus erithacus*

From: Africa

Size: Twelve to 14 inches for the congo, and nine to 11 inches for the timneh

Popular Varieties: Congo and timneh

Talking Ability: Excellent

Sexual Differences: None apparent to people

Usual Colors: Congos are silver to dark gray with a red tail. Timnehs look the same, except they have a maroon tail.

Upside

The amazingly intelligent african grey is capable of developing a large vocabulary. Some even use words and phrases in the right context, such as asking, "Did you feed the parrot?" when the family sits down to dinner. Greys are curious, enjoy socializing with their favorite people and like to play with toys. Since their loudest sound is a shrill whistle, most of them are not nearly as noisy as other parrots of comparative size. Many experts consider greys the ideal pet parrot (provided they have ideal owners). One of our nation's most popular parrots, greys are readily available as hand-fed babies.

Downside

With high intelligence comes sensitivity. Although handling and cuddling are not among their favorite things, greys need regular attention. Vocal communication and just being near you make them happiest. When emotional fulfillment is lacking, some greys bare their bodies. They become feather pluckers, pulling every feather they can reach right out of their skin until only their head is covered.

Sometimes african greys are too smart for their own good. They learn to open cage doors that most other birds find impossible, so experienced grey owners often use a lock. Greys need a slightly more specialized diet than amazon parrots (see Chapter 10), and tend to be somewhat nervous and high strung. An angry or frightened grey can emit a growl that puts a Doberman Pinscher to shame. Although they love toys, greys sometimes panic when something new "invades" their home. It's best to place a new toy beside a grey's cage for a day or two before placing it inside.

Some Significant Stuff

In every important way—intelligence, talking ability and personality—the congo grey and the timneh grey are identical. But the timneh often costs less than the congo because it's smaller and its tail isn't as bright.

How will you know if a grey is a baby? Look into its eyes. If the whole eye is dark, it's a youngster, even if it appears full grown. But if the iris (the part surrounding the pupil) is bright yellow, the bird is mature. Also, the tail feathers on a baby congo grey are blackish red, not bright red like the adult.

Bird Brainers

The ghana grey looks and acts like the congo grey, but is slightly smaller. Is it just a small congo or is it a subspecies? The debate continues.

African greys are terrific talkers.

Those Amazing Amazons

Latin Name: *Amazona*

From: Mexico, Central and South America, and the Caribbean

Size: Ten to 18 inches long, depending on the variety

Sexual Differences: None that are obvious. Some believe male amazons bond best to women, and female amazons to men.

Usual Colors: Bright green bodies with lighter green on the stomach. Colors of the head, neck and wing tips may be yellow, red, blue or white, depending on the variety. Since they all have green bodies, head color is the best indicator of variety in amazon parrots. The table shows the colors and talking ability of the most popular amazons.

Color and Talking Ability in Amazon Parrots

Amazon parrot variety	Color	Talking ability
Blue-fronted	Blue on forehead, sometimes with yellow and white	Fair to good
Yellow-nape	Dark beak, yellow on back of head extends down the neck as the bird matures; may have yellow feathers above the nostrils	Excellent
Double yellow-head	Whole face and head are yellow; white eye ring; babies have yellow speckles on their heads	Good
Yellow-fronted	Splash of yellow on the head	Fair
Mealy	White eye ring and black beak; some have a few yellow feathers on the forehead and/or blue on the crown	Fair
Mexican red-head or green-cheeked	Red crown with small blue-violet line just behind the eyes; cheeks lighter and brighter green than the body	Fair

Upside

Bright, playful and packed with personality, the amazon is a big pet in a parrot-sized package. A good parrot for those who admire an opinionated pet, the amazon will let you know when he's happy, when he isn't and what you should do about it.

Is your home animated with lively, sometimes loud conversation? Do kids practice the latest dance steps or play musical instruments? An amazon will love living with you. Rowdy, curious and comical, amazons are good-time birds. They like playing with toys and listening to lively music. Some even dance with the beat. Provided they receive sufficient attention, many blue-fronts, mealys and red-heads become affectionate enough to enjoy daily petting and cuddling sessions.

Yellow-napes are the top talkers of the amazon world. Their ability to mimic speech is so good that they often learn words just from listening to their owners, without being taught at all.

Downside

Amazons can be bullies. The yellow-nape, in particular, may grow out of its youthful gentleness and become a biter if not consistently handled. Moodiness is part of the amazon personality. Within the space of an hour, the same bird may be loving, independent, comical and angry.

Amazons tend to be noisy and somewhat demanding. Shatter their expectations and they will nag you nonstop. For example, if you always give your amazon a taste of your dinner (and you should), your pet will holler if you ever forget him. Adult amazons have a tendency to become one-person birds unless trained otherwise. Once bonded to a family member, they are jealous when "their" person shows affection to other members of the family.

Amazon curiosity knows no bounds, and no matter how many chew toys an amazon owns, he'll always have an urge to whittle the woodwork.

Some Significant Stuff

Although every amazon has a unique personality, some traits are common to most. When excited, whether due to delight or anger, the amazon spreads his tail into a fan and dances on his perch. He also flashes or "pins" his eyes. The pupils dilate and contract rapidly, and the sight is absolutely awesome until you get used to it.

There are several rarer but equally fascinating types of amazon parrots. All of them make super pets, especially if they began life as hand-fed babies.

Avian Adventures

Rooster, my red-head, fans his tail and flashes his eyes when he meets someone he likes or someone he doesn't like. How can I tell the difference? When he likes someone, he also bows his head and ruffles his neck feathers for petting. When he's trying to chase someone away, he ruffles his feathers to make himself look bigger and tougher, but doesn't bow his head. Instead, he makes growling noises and snaps at the air in the direction of the human he hates.

The Pleasant Pionus

Latin Name: *Pionus*

Also Known As: One species is nicknamed the blue-headed parrot.

From: Central and South America

Size: Nine to 12 inches long

Popular Varieties: Blue-headed and white-capped

Talking Ability: The blue-headed is fair to good, while the white-capped is fair.

Sexual Differences: None visible to people

Usual Colors: Most popular varieties have green bodies. Every variety has bright red feathers on the underside of the tail. The blue-headed has a blue head and neck, and a green body. The white-capped has a green body, a white cap on the head merging into blue, a white upper chest with a touch of pink, and bronze and blue wings.

Upside

If you are intrigued with amazons and wish there were a more subdued parrot with similar characteristics, the pionus might be perfect for you. Pionus parrots are good-natured, affectionate, and respond well to attention and training. They are often touted as the ideal apartment parrots because they are less active, quieter and much less destructive than other parrots of similar size, and can even get by with a smaller cage. If you enjoy preparing food for appreciative eaters, many pionus parrots have a trait you'll find charming. Instead of taking food for granted, they dig in and pig out with obvious relish.

The blue-headed is the ideal parrot for someone who travels often and has to board their bird. He tends to stay cuddly and loving, even during periods when he has little individual attention. Another plus for the pionus is his ability to bond with several family members, provided they all give him attention.

Downside

"Quiet parrot" is an oxymoron, so don't think a pionus isn't going to make a peep. An occasional racket is always possible with a parrot. Some pionus are nervous and high strung. When fearful or suffering emotional upset, a pionus may wheeze as if it's gasping its last. But since the asthmatic episode comes from the mind, not the lungs, reassuring words and gentle handling soon bring the bird back to regular breathing. The white-capped may be a bit bossy and is the most moody pionus.

Bird Brainers

Don't walk by a dull green and brown bird with hardly any color too quickly. It may be a maximilian pionus, one of the sweetest parrot personalities in the world.

The blue-headed pionus combines beauty and a pleasant personality.

Some Significant Stuff

If a pionus looks plain to you, ask to look at it in different, preferably natural, lighting. When kissed by the sun, pionus plumage becomes iridescent and practically glows.

There are six other species in the pionus family, and every one of them makes a delightful pet.

Conures Are Cuddly Charmers

Latin Name: The five genera of conure are *Aratinga, Nendayus, Pyrrhura, Enicognathus,* and *Cyanoliseus*

From: Central and South America, Mexico and the Caribbean Islands

Size: Eight to 18 inches, depending on the species; most popular varieties are between 10 and 12 inches long.

Talking Ability: Fair to good. Of all the popular conures, the blue-crowned has the best gift of gab.

Sexual Differences: No visible differences in the popular species

Usual Colors: It depends on the species. The table lists the most popular conures and how to recognize them.

Popular Conures and How to Recognize Them

Conure	Color
Sun	Yellow with deep orange, red and green markings
Jenday	Yellow and orange on the head, neck and belly; wings and tail are green, tipped with blue and black
Nanday	Green body; nearly black face; touch of blue on the throat, breast and flight feathers; red thighs
Halfmoon	Green body; orange marking above the beak blends into blue behind the head
Blue-crowned	Green body; blue blush on the face
Dusky-headed	Green with a bluish-gray head
Maroon-bellied	Green body; reddish-brown feathers on the belly, wings and tail
Cherry-headed	Green body; mostly red head; and large, horn-colored beak

Upside

How about a bird that will lie on its back in your hands? Or learn to do tricks, like standing on its head? A hand-raised conure can learn all that and more. Besides, he'll beg you to bring him out of his cage so he can entertain you. Conures are affectionate, smart and puppylike in their playfulness. Some of them even turn into little puffballs when you pet them, fluffing their feathers to signal their enjoyment. They love toys, especially wooden ones made to be destroyed.

Many species have spectacular colors, but if you're looking for a pet more than a showpiece, don't pass up the plainest ones. The dusky-headed conure is one of the most loving birds imaginable, and isn't loud like his prettier cousins.

Bird Brainers

Baby cherry–headed conures are plain green. After the first molt, a bright red mask covers their face and head and remains for the rest of their lives.

Downside

Most conures (with the exception of the dusky-headed and some blue-crowns) are loud, and some (especially the nanday) are so shrill that you'll fear for the family crystal. Conures are speed demons when it comes to working with wood, and need lots of chewable toys to keep them occupied and happy. Free from supervision, they can turn a chair leg into splinters before you realize you forgot to close the cage door. Some conures become nippy during adolescence, even though they were hand-fed babies. Most, but not all of them, outgrow it.

Some Significant Stuff

If you are fascinated by macaws but fear their formidable beak, or don't have room to house a really big bird, a conure might be the answer. Conures resemble macaws in personality and body shape, but are pint-sized by comparison.

Cockatoos Hide a Heady Surprise

Latin Name: *Cacatua*

From: Australia, Indonesia, Moluccas, New Guinea and the Phillipines

Size: Twelve to 28 inches long, depending on the variety. Those commonly kept as pets are in the 12- to 20-inch range.

Talking Ability: Fair to good. The best cockatoo communicators are the bare-eyed and the goffin's.

Sexual Differences: None you can see in the popular species, but some say males are louder.

Usual Colors: Predominantly white; or white with shades of salmon, yellow or orange, most often in the crest.

The Most Popular Pet Cockatoo Varieties

Larger varieties (17–20 inches)	Description
Umbrella	White with large white crest; yellow under the wings and tail
Moluccan	Shades of pink and peach with large salmon crest
Greater sulphur-crested	White with large yellow crest and yellow on cheeks; some yellow under the wings and tail

Smaller varieties (12–16 inches)	Description
Lesser sulphur-crested	White with large yellow crest and yellow on cheeks; some yellow under the wings and tail
Bare-eyed	Mostly white; a bit of pink on the face and yellow under the wings and tail; small crest; big bluish eye ring makes this cockatoo look as if it just lost a fight.
Goffin's	Almost all white, with a bit of salmon on the face and yellow under the wings and tail; small crest

Upside

Cockatoos are beautiful birds, and some have astonishing crests that they can raise and lower at will. Hand-fed cockatoos love to cuddle. Eager to give and receive affection, they like to be part of whatever is happening at home, even if it's just sitting on your lap watching television.

Cockatoos never cease to entertain. All of them are good mimics, and most of them showcase their ability by copying household noises and the voices of other pets. While their talking ability doesn't rival the african grey and some amazon parrots, cockatoos have been known to use words in context with what is going on around them. Besides being intelligent, cockatoos seem to be mechanically inclined and can solve simple puzzles. Some even learn to open locks.

While they love playing with toys, they are most content when interacting with their owners. If you have time on your hands and want to fill those hands with a bundle of friendly feathers, a cockatoo could be the bird for you.

Avian Adventures

Remember Fred on the TV show *Baretta*? He was a greater sulphur-crested cockatoo.

Downside

Owning a cockatoo can be compared to having a toddler, except that kids grow out of the terrible twos and cockatoos don't. A cockatoo demands attention and may scream until someone notices him. If routinely neglected, he may even pluck out his own feathers. Happy cockatoos do some screaming too, and their voices are loud.

Besides needing more time with their owners than most other parrots, cockatoos require considerable space for playing and a variety of toys, especially the type meant for chewing. Cockatoo beaks can make toothpicks of table legs in less time than it takes you to go to the movies and come home again. Put a lock on the cage door if you get a cockatoo—crested Houdinis have figured out combination locks.

If you or anyone in your family has respiratory allergies, beware of the cockatoo. They have powder down (read: feather dust) that people with allergies may react to.

Some Significant Stuff

Cockatoos are amenable to learning good habits, but their strong beaks and loud voices may intimidate first-time bird owners. If you want cockatoo cuddliness and charm in a more easily manageable pet, consider the bare-eyed variety.

Eclectus Parrots Parade Electrifying Colors

Latin Name: *Eclectus*

From: South Pacific Islands, from Indonesia and New Guinea to Australia

Size: Twelve to 14 inches long, depending on the variety

Popular Varieties: Solomon island, vosmaeri, grand and red-sided

Talking Ability: Fair; females seem to talk more than males.

Sexual Differences: Females sport brighter colors. They are also more aggressive than males and may be better talkers.

Polly Sez

Dimorphism means differences between the sexes. In eclectus parrots, the sexes are so distinctive that males and females were once believed to be separate species.

Usual Colors: Males are bright green at first glance, but hide a showy surprise: The underside of their wings is scarlet, trimmed in turquoise and blue. Even so, females are the most eye-catching. They are brilliant red, trimmed in blue and violet.

Upside

The eclectus is one of the world's most beautiful and unique parrots. Because of its feather structure, it appears to be covered with shiny soft fur, especially on the head and neck. The eclectus is friendly in a laid-back way. It likes to be near its favorite person (and may prove it by following its owner from room to room like a puppy), but most eclectus do not enjoy being petted or cuddled.

Considerably quieter and less destructive than most parrots, the eclectus seldom screams and isn't driven to redesign the woodwork. It's a good parrot for people who want a friendly pet near them, but not in their face all the time.

Downside

Even the friendliest eclectus won't enjoy petting the way many other parrots do, but these birds still need plenty of attention and toys. If ignored, they may become bored and pull out all those fabulous feathers. While the male is usually more loving than the female, he may be somewhat shy.

If yours is a home where teens practice cheerleading and budding musicians jam with their friends, the activity level and the steady stream of people coming and going may be more than an eclectus can handle (although most amazons would be in heaven). The eclectus does not love drama the way an amazon does. Some have been known to withdraw and detach themselves from their surroundings if their environment shatters their nerves. After a few weeks in a more tranquil home, they slowly start responding again.

Avian Adventures

In the jungle, the female eclectus has to be aggressive for the species to survive. She stays in the nest and protects the eggs and chicks by fending off snakes, bigger birds and other predators while the male brings home the groceries. The male therefore mates with the toughest female he can find.

Some Significant Stuff

The eclectus needs a larger cage than an amazon of similar size, or plenty of time on a cage-top play gym to keep it active and involved.

The exquisite female eclectus is more moody than the plainer male, and must be understood to be appreciated. Many people prefer males as pets because they are gentler and more predictable. If this will be your first bird, don't buy a female eclectus. Admire her, drool a little if you must, then walk away. But if you are an experienced bird owner, the beautiful bitch of the bird world might become your best buddy.

The female eclectus is brighter in color, but can be moody.

Lovely Lories and Lorikeets

Polly Sez

Lorikeets are like lories, but have longer, pointed tails. Lories have rounded tails.

Latin Name: *Loriinae*

From: Australia, Indonesia, Solomon Islands and other South Pacific islands

Size: Five to 13 inches long, depending on the variety

Talking Ability: Fair

Sexual Differences: None are apparent to people

Usual Colors: A magnificent mix of hues. The following table details some of the most popular varieties.

Popular Varieties of Lories and Lorikeets

Variety	Description
Blue mountain lorikeet	Violet-blue, red, yellow and green
Rainbow lory	Red, blue, green and yellow
Red lory	Vibrant red
Dusky lory	Olive, brown, gold and red
Chattering lory	Mostly red, with olive and yellow
Blue-streaked lory	Red, with a purplish streak running from the eye to the neck; red and black wings and black tail

Upside

Which birds have the most fun? Lories and lorikeets, according to some. These clowns play nonstop and can entertain you (and themselves) for hours, provided they have a large cage and plenty of props in the form of assorted perches and toys. Upbeat birds with cheerful dispositions, most lories are also aerial acrobats. Some swing all the way around their perch over and over. Others lie on their back with a toy in their claws and wave it around in a bid for attention.

The only pet livelier than a lory is two lories. A pair will invent games of tag and chase, and seem to compete in swinging and climbing contests. Besides being fun to watch, lories are strikingly beautiful and quite intelligent. They tame easily, enjoy interacting with their owners and seldom become one-person birds.

Downside

Lories have a shrill, high-pitched call and an especially sharp beak. They are less aggressive than most parrots, but if one does happen to bite, it really hurts, even though the injury isn't serious.

Lories (and lorikeets) need a diet high in fresh fruit and nectar, but feeding them isn't the problem. Formulas created especially for lories are readily available and simulate the nectar in their natural diet. The problem is that what goes in has to come out, and since it went in soft and sticky, it comes out—well, you get the picture. Here's a worst-case scenario: An active lory is climbing his cage wires when his dinner comes through. And I do mean "comes through." Right through the opening in the wires it flies, until it finally splatters on the floor a good three or four feet from the cage!

There are solutions, of course. Some lory owners keep easy-to-clean plastic runners on the floor around the cage. Others buy cages built especially to house lories. Even so, no matter how you choose to house and clean a lory, it will still take more cleanup time than almost any other bird.

Squawk!

Recently some manufacturers have been marketing dry diets to make lories' droppings more manageable. Buyer beware! While these formulas are nutritious, it's too soon to know what their long-term effects will be on birds that are especially equipped by nature to be nectar sippers and fruit eaters.

Some Significant Stuff

If you're planning an outdoor aviary, consider lories and lorikeets. Their beauty and activity level make them ideal inhabitants, and they have no downside when housed outdoors.

Magnificent Macaws

Latin Name: *Ara*

From: Mexico, Central and South America

Size: Up to 40 inches long for the largest macaws; mini macaws range from 12 to 18 inches. All have long tails ending in a point.

Popular Varieties: The large macaws most often seen as pets include the blue-and-gold, green-winged (red body with green and blue on the wings) and scarlet (red body with gold and blue on the wings). Among the most popular small macaws are the severe (mostly green) and the yellow-collared (green with a yellow nape).

Talking Ability: Fair to good

Sexual Differences: None you can see in the popular species, but some say males are louder and more active than females.

Usual Colors: From glossy green to stunning hyacinth, macaw coloration varies with the species and includes vivid reds, golds and blues. Many varieties have a large patch of white skin covering the cheek and eye area. Fascinating feather lines cross this area like a highway map on some species.

Some macaws have fascinating feather lines on their faces.

Upside

Regal and royally robed, the macaw is one of our most fabulous feathered creatures. Affectionate and gentle, a macaw may lean into your hand for a cheek rub, or mutter sweet nothings in your ear. Though able to crack a Brazil nut with a single squeeze, macaws are well aware of their strength, have excellent control of their beaks and usually handle their owners' wrists and fingers with care.

Macaws are exceptionally intelligent and like working with rather intricate objects. They can learn simple puzzles and difficult tricks, including riding bicycles or pushing wheelbarrows created especially for parrots. That's why they have star billing at many shows in bird parks.

Bird Brainers

Some parrots blush when they're embarrassed, just like people do. How do we know? The blush is visible in the white patch of skin covering a macaw's cheeks.

Macaws have playful personalities and love to show off. When outside their cage in a play area, they may hang by their beaks, stretch out their wondrous wings or do head-bobbing dances with energy even a rock star would envy. While they seldom develop a large vocabulary, macaws talk loudly and pronounce words well.

Downside

Macaws make more demands than toddlers and can be noisy nags. The large species are big all over. They have loud voices, huge personalities that demand lots of attention and powerful beaks that could be downright dangerous if used against you.

Macaws need large cages, as well as space outside the cage for exercise and play. They have a need to chew, go through lots of toys and make major messes. Mischievous and destructive, they can wreak havoc when out of their cages, unsupervised.

Macaws are intelligent enough to be manipulative, and because they are potentially intimidating, a large one is not a good choice for a first bird. Especially avoid the scarlet macaw. While it makes an excellent pet for an experienced bird handler, its disposition is too unpredictable for a beginner. For the fun and intelligence of a macaw in a more manageable bird, consider a smaller species like the severe or the yellow-collared. Some say the little yellow-collared is one of the best talkers in the macaw family. While large macaws tend to be active and noisy, the green-winged is considered the most sedate.

Bird Brainers

Would you like a macaw but only have room for a parrot? At only twelve inches, the noble macaw (mostly green, with a bit of blue and a touch of red) is amazon-size and prized for its gentle disposition.

Some Significant Stuff

I didn't include the hyacinth as a popular variety because it can cost more than a reliable set of wheels. Do try to see one, though. Not only is the hyacinth stunning, but it tends to be a gentle giant and makes friends easily.

Toucans Can Be Terrific

Latin Name: Popular species seen as pets include *Ramphastos toco* (popular name toco), *R. tucanus* (red bill), *R. sulfuratus* (keel bill), and *R. vitellinus* (channel bill)

From: The rain and cloud forests of Central and South America

Size: Six to 22 inches long, not counting that big bill

Popular Varieties: Toco, red bill, keel bill, channel bill

Talking Ability: None

Sexual Differences: Only another toucan (or a trained avian veterinarian or breeder) knows for sure. Some say males are louder and more active than females.

Usual Colors: Black bodies and blue eye rings; with contrasting large bibs of white, yellow or a combination of white and yellow with a touch of red below, depending on the species. The ample bills may be orange, tipped with black (toco); red and black (red bill); yellow and light green, tipped with red (keel bill); or black with a blue band (channel bill).

Upside

Hand-raised toucans make affectionate pets and sometimes signal their happiness with a purring sound. They are smart, enjoy human contact and are more than willing to learn tricks and perform them for your friends. Toucans don't squawk, scream, remodel your woodwork or use their big bill as a weapon against you. They won't dust your home with feather dander either, so people allergic to other birds might be able to live with a toucan.

Downside

Toucans are large and active, and need housing to match. A cage meant for a large macaw will do, provided it's at least 4 feet long. Toucans are a high-maintenance species.

Some Significant Stuff

Toucans have a number of dietary cautions. Check Chapter 10 before deciding if Mr. Bountiful Beak is the right bird for you.

More Characters Worth Meeting

The following birds make fine pets and aren't particularly pricey, but some may be hard to find in your area.

Mynah Birds

Once a popular feature in pet shops, the mynah (*Gracula*), a black bird with a yellow wattle (an area of featherless skin) on its neck and a pointed beak, is less available and more expensive than it was a couple of decades ago. An Asian species, mynahs were once imported by the thousands. They are rarer today because most of them are domestically bred, and they don't breed well in captivity.

If parrots don't appeal to you but you'd love to have a talking bird, maybe you'll get lucky and find one of the baby mynahs that are occasionally offered for sale. Mynahs rival the african grey in talking ability. They mimic their owner's voice, and some of them speak in sentences and sing entire songs. But they aren't perfect. They are messy eaters, are often noisy and are not cuddly or demonstrative in their affection, although they will become quite friendly.

Bird Brainers

Technically, the parrot family includes birds ranging from tiny budgies (parakeets) and cockatiels to huge macaws. That's because all of them share the same basic traits. A parakeet, a macaw and every other bird with similar traits is a *species* of the parrot family.

Jardine's and Senegal Parrots

The jardine's and senegal parrots are both smallish parrots from Africa. The jardine's is eleven inches long, with yellowish-green scallops setting off its shiny dark feathers; and the senegal is nine inches long and mostly green, with a dark mask over its whole head and a golden-orange belly. The Latin name for both is *Poicephalus*.

The jardine's is a good mood bird. Friendly and steady with an affectionate personality, it's almost always in a pleasant frame of mind, and its unique habits will keep you happy, too. The jardine's doesn't announce dawn and dusk with the scream of the jungle. Instead, its natural notes are soft, pleasant and musical. Not only that, but it is an intelligent bird and can learn to talk. When a jardine's becomes upset, which won't happen often, it will tell you about it with a growl rather than a squawk.

The senegal parrot is small enough to fit in a studio apartment, but is active and needs plenty of time on a play gym. It is curious, intelligent and can learn to talk, but tends to become a one-person bird unless every member of the family interacts with it often. While your young senegal may go through a nippy stage, with proper handling it will grow into an affectionate companion.

Not as easy to locate as the more popular parrots, hand-fed jardine's and senegals are worth looking into if they are available near you.

Quaker (Monk) Parakeets

Although it's as much fun as it ever was and is easily one of the top ten talkers, the noisy and naughty but charming quaker parakeet is less popular as a pet than it used to be. That's because escapees have set up colonies from Florida to Chicago to California, and authorities, fearing the species will displace our native songbirds, have banned them as pets in a few states.

The quaker (*Myiopsitta monachus*) hails from South and Central America. It is a smallish, stubborn, strong-willed scold, yet a hand-fed baby makes a fabulous pet in the hands of the right owner (someday I'm going to get one). If the quaker is legal in your state and you see one in a pet shop (green on top, gray on the bottom), take the time to find out if you like each other.

Bird Brainers

The quaker is the only member of the parrot family that builds a nest. The others are cavity breeders. That means they hole up in a hole in a tree to raise a family.

Ring-Neck Parakeets

There are many species of ring-neck parakeets (*Psittacula*), ranging in the wild from India and Africa, and they come in an array of colors from watercolor-like pastels to dramatically deep hues. They are big at both ends, with exceptionally long tails, large heads and powerful beaks. Ring-necks have talking ability and tend to be friendly, although they are not as affectionate as many other species. They need large cages to accommodate their terrific tails, and are popular in outdoor aviaries.

The Least You Need to Know

➤ Pet birds that suit almost any lifestyle are available, so learn all you can about a species before buying it.

➤ All pet birds require some care, but some need a lot more attention than others.

➤ What one person considers the downside of owning a certain species may be another person's reason for wanting that bird.

Say "Aaawk!"

After reading the first three chapters, you've probably pared down your choices to a few species. Now it's time to meet some of those birds up close and personal. Let's go shopping together. Whether you decide on a $15 budgie or a $1,500 macaw, I'll help you find a healthy bird with a pleasing personality.

What's Good and What's Not at Your Local Pet Shop

One of the biggest advantages of buying a bird from your local pet shop is that it's close to home. When choosing a bird, it's best to observe it a couple of times over the course of a few days before making a decision, and that's easiest to do when the pet shop is convenient. Also, a good pet shop stands behind its birds and may even offer a short guarantee of good health—one that lasts long enough so you can take your bird to the veterinarian for an examination.

How can you tell if your local pet shop is a good one? Look at the bottom of the birdcages. Have they been cleaned regularly or is the poop piling up? Check the water and food dishes. Are they clean, or are the birds slurping poop soup? Is the diet just seeds, or are fruit and veggies also on the menu? (Birds eating pelleted diets may be getting complete nutrition, but a varied menu is still best.) What about cage size? Are the cages large enough for their occupants, or do the birds seem crowded or cramped? Sniff around. Does the place smell clean or do you detect *perfuma de barnyard*? Are the birds bored and the cages bare, or do they have toys? Are the floors swept and the shelves organized, or do they remind you of a teenager's bedroom?

Bird Brainers

Besides having a healthier start, a young bird that is used to a varied diet won't balk at eating his veggies when you get him home.

Bird Brainers

Do the priciest birds make the best pets? In a word, no. Price indicates how rare a species is, not its suitability as a pet. Species that breed easily in captivity, no matter how smart or sweet, cost less than rarer birds.

Knowledgeable salespeople with good attitudes are also important. After all, once you buy your bird, you'll be back now and again for food and toys. If anything about the store, its personnel or the condition of its livestock turns you off, leave. One of my most memorable pet shop experiences was when my husband Tom and I visited a brand new store. "What type of larvae is this?" I asked the saleswoman, as I held out a wiggly creature I had found in the hermit crab display. Never having seen hermit crabs eat anything like it before, I wondered what it would be when it hatched, which obviously was going to happen soon.

"Aiiiyeee!" the young woman shrieked, raising the gold ring in her eyebrow and giving us a full frontal view of her pierced tongue. "It's gross, oh it's so gross, oh no, it moved again, put it down, put it downnnn!"

"Do you mind if we take it home and hatch it?" I asked, trying not to laugh. "We're just curious about what it is." She wrinkled her nose, making its blue stud sparkle. "Sure, just get it out of here."

"Okay, thanks. But there's at least 10 more of them in with the hermit crabs," I pointed out. "For real? Oh, no, oh gross," she wailed.

As soon as the door closed behind us, Tom and I bent double laughing. "I couldn't look her directly in the face," I gasped. "Those piercings really got to me."

In case you're curious, two days later the larva became a medium-size, reddish-brown beetle. We continued doing business with our old pet shop—the one with the helpful employees who aren't afraid of wiggly critters.

Getting Acquainted with a Potential Pet

Some pet shops display their bigger birds on cage-top gyms or perches. Usually the cage doors are open and the birds can climb in and out whenever they want. A bird displayed this way is usually well socialized and quite tame, at least with people it knows—which isn't you, so don't push it. The bird may become frightened or aggressive if you try to pet it or entice it off its perch. Instead, ask a salesperson if you can handle the bird, then watch its attitude when the bird is offered a familiar hand. If it steps on the salesperson's hand easily, it may easily adapt to you.

Once the bird is on the salesperson's hand he or she should help you get to know each other, and within minutes the bird should be perched on your wrist or hand. If the bird seems comfortable being close to you, perhaps even offering its head for petting, consider whipping out your credit card—especially if you visited this bird once or twice before and always found it active and interested.

Squawk!

Not every baby bird offered for sale in pet shops was hand-fed. Ask before you buy. Parent-raised babies may be less expensive, but they are not tame. Although they can become good pets if you approach the taming process with patience, knowledge and a little courage, hand-raised babies are best for beginners.

On the other hand, if you can't handle a big bird in the store, don't buy it, even if the salesperson assures you it's the most amiable amazon ever. Some birds have preferences. They may like one sex better than another or distrust anyone with a certain hair color. If Pauly dislikes you in the store, taking him home may or may not improve his attitude, so make sure the chemistry is right for both of you.

Buying from a Breeder

Bird breeders advertise in magazines such as *Bird Talk*, in the telephone directory and sometimes in the classified section of the newspaper. If you check these sources and find a bird breeder near you, make an appointment to visit. Most breeders raise their birds at home and don't keep regular hours like pet shops.

Unless you are looking for show-quality stock (see Chapter 25), birds purchased from a breeder will probably cost less than the same bird would at the pet shop. That's because the breeder has less overhead. The downside is that while the breeder may give you the same guarantee as a pet shop, he or she may not be able to fulfill the guarantee (if necessary) as quickly as the pet shop would. For example, if a replacement is promised, the pet shop will usually be able to give you one sooner because it deals with several breeders. An individual breeder, on the other hand, may run out of young birds, so you'll have to wait until more chicks hatch.

Some people advertise as breeders but are really middlemen (or women). Make sure you are dealing with a real breeder by asking to see their adult birds. While they may

Squawk!

Don't buy from a breeder who won't let you look at adult birds, even from a distance. It could be because they have no breeding pairs and you are actually dealing with a jobber who buys baby birds for resale.

not allow you in their aviary (strangers could carry germs or be stressful to breeding pairs), they should at least allow you to peek in through a window.

Answering a Newspaper Ad

Newspapers and shopper-style tabloids sometimes carry classified ads with birds for sale. These are usually adult birds, often offered "with cage and accessories." Don't expect a guarantee because there seldom is one. Although it's possible to find a good buy on a fabulous pet, the classifieds are strictly buyer beware. Some of the pets will be tame, talking birds that their owners must give up for a valid reason, but people also get rid of nasty, noisy and even sick birds through these ads. The more knowledgeable you are about birds, the better chance you have of getting a good one no matter where you shop, but this is especially true when shopping the classifieds.

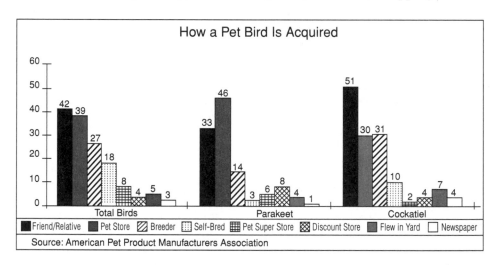

Signs of a Healthy Bird

A healthy bird will have every one of the following attributes, so don't settle for anything less:

➤ Alert attitude. A healthy bird is curious and interested in its surroundings. It plays, preens its feathers, vocalizes, stretches, flaps its wings, interacts with its cage mates and sometimes solicits human attention. Of course, it won't do all those things at once.

➤ The eyes have it. Check them out first. A healthy bird's headlights are clear and bright, with nothing oozing out of them. The skin or feathers around the eyes should be dry and clean.

➤ The nose knows. Breathing should be rhythmic and easy. Nostrils should be dry and unobstructed, and the feathers near the nostrils should be free of debris and dry.

➤ Bald is beautiful on my husband, but it's a bad sign on a bird. Birds should be thickly covered in shiny feathers.

➤ Peek at the feet. Look at them from underneath as well as topside (it's easiest when the bird climbs the cage wires). Pet bird species should have four toes on each foot, each ending in a toenail. The feet should be smooth and free of irritation, scabs, sores or swelling.

➤ Behold the beak. It should be properly shaped, with the top and bottom in alignment, and not encrusted with scales.

Bird Brainers

If you are able to hold the bird you are examining, gently feel its breastbone. In a healthy bird, it will be surrounded by muscle tissue. If it sticks out sharply, the bird is emaciated.

➤ Here's the poop. Droppings should have a solid section resembling a tiny green or brown worm. The colored part is partially surrounded by pasty white stuff and a little clear liquid.

➤ View the vent. It's the opening the droppings drop from. The vent should be dry and squeaky clean, and so should the feathers surrounding it.

Bright-eyed, alert and fully feathered with dry nostrils and a properly shaped beak, Sugar, the cockatiel is a playful, healthy pet.

59

Body Language of Responsive Birds

When shopping for Rooster, I didn't have a particular type of parrot in mind. I just wanted one that liked me and enjoyed being handled. Rooster and two other parrots were playing on their cage tops in a pet shop when I started talking to them from five or six feet away. All three parrots cocked their heads in my direction, but Rooster climbed down his cage, shinnied down the stand, waddled up to me and started chewing my shoelaces. As I slowly kneeled, he fluffed up his head and face feathers, and bowed for petting.

"How much is this one?" I asked the clerk, before allowing my heart to commit to something my wallet couldn't manage. Relieved that the bird was within my price range, I made a fist, offered my wrist, and said "up." He climbed on and I stood slowly, admiring the expressive red-head who had made my shopping expedition so easy by choosing me. One last test: Saying "up," I offered a vulnerable finger. The parrot climbed on and bowed his head again. Relieved, I gave a nervous laugh. Rooster raised his head, looked me straight in the face, flashed his eyes and mimicked, "Ha, ha, ha, ha, ha." Soul mates. I was so tickled that my hand shook with excitement when I signed the receipt.

Relationships work best when the chemistry is there, so when you find a bird that interests you, spend time watching it. Few baby birds step off their perch to pick a person (Rooster was a preowned young adult), but if the interest is mutual, a parrot's body language says so in several ways.

Stretching

Although healthy parrots stretch frequently, whether anyone is watching or not, stretching also indicates that a bird is at ease in your company or wants your attention. Since parrots often make snap judgments, don't be surprised if a bird you never met stretches when you walk toward it. What should you do if Pauly says, "Glad to see you," by shrugging his shoulders, or slowly extending a foot and a wing at the same time? Acknowledge his welcoming stretch with one of your own. Slowly shrug your shoulders or stretch an arm over your head while saying, "I'm pleased to meet you too." That will get your relationship off to a super start.

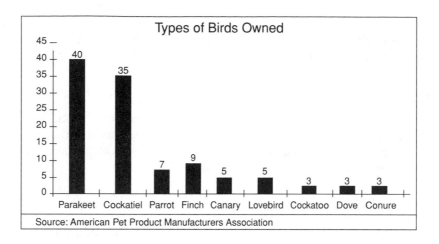

Types of Birds Owned

Parakeet	40
Cockatiel	35
Parrot	7
Finch	9
Canary	5
Lovebird	5
Cockatoo	3
Dove	3
Conure	3

Source: American Pet Product Manufacturers Association

Bowing

A fluffed, bowed head is a parrot's "come hither" look. When Pauly raises his head and neck feathers and tucks his beak into his chest, he's inviting you to pet the nape of his neck, and maybe even his cheeks. This is an excellent sign. Usually. Occasionally, a bratty bird uses this disarming gesture to lure in his next victim. If a sign on the cage says the bird bites, or a salesperson calls the charming con artist Dracula and tells you to be careful, heed the warnings and look elsewhere for a bird buddy.

When a bird fluffs his head and neck feathers, looks directly at you and uses his foot to scratch his own face or head, he's almost always begging to be petted. While it's smart to be cautious with a strange bird, this signal will be unmistakable once you and your own bird have bonded.

Preening

Healthy birds spend lots of time preening (grooming) their feathers, but if a strange bird starts preening as you come near, he feels comfortable in your company. He may even be showing off or trying to look his best for you. When a bird preens while sitting on your hand, it bodes especially well for bonding.

Tail Wagging

Tail wagging seems to have several meanings. It's often used to greet someone Pauly likes, and may accompany a stretch or a puffed head. Wagging may also signal the conclusion of an activity the parrot

Polly Sez

Birds in the wild, or living several to a cage, bond with a mate or friend and engage in *alopreening*, or mutual grooming. Since a bird can't reach all its own feathers, this buddy system helps it stay gloriously groomed all over. When your pet bird pecks at your hair or beard, it's accepting you as a partner by giving you a good grooming.

probably enjoyed—like lunch or a head rub. Sometimes, it's just a grooming device to put the tail feathers back in place. Consider a wag in the context of what's happening or has just happened to the parrot.

Begging

Parrots have a body position and expression so endearing that it can only be described as begging. When Pauly squats low on his perch with his body flattened and horizontal, his wings quivering and a pleading look in his eyes, he either wants your attention or your dinner. That's his way of saying "please."

Flashing or Pinpointing Eyes

Easily evident on larger, light-eyed parrots, flashing or pinpointing is when the pupils become smaller while the irises expand, over and over at a rapid rate. People who see a parrot do this for the first time often back up and make a nervous joke about the movie *The Exorcist*. But backing up isn't always necessary when a bird flashes. The two most common meanings of flashing eyes are "Wow! That's interesting," and "Back off, you're invading my space."

When teaching a bird to talk, pinpointing eyes are a good sign. They mean the bird is concentrating on the lesson. But flashing eyes are usually a sign of aggression when accompanied by a flared tail, wings held stiffly away from the body and an erect stance.

Beak Chattering

Some birds, especially cockatiels and cockatoos, open and close their beaks quickly several times in succession while moving their tongues in and out. Most bird behaviorists (yes, it's a business—no, I'm not kidding) say this means the bird either enjoyed what he just ate or likes the person he's looking at. Sometimes, the bird fluffs his feathers and/or wags his tail while chattering his beak.

Fluffed feathers, droopy posture and apparent exhaustion are all signs of sickness.

Features to Fret Over

The following traits mean trouble. Whether the bird is a bargain or a beauty, avoid it if it matches one or more of these descriptions:

➤ Don't buy a bird that shows no interest in you or its surroundings. Inactivity, drooping wings, constantly ruffled (puffed-up) feathers and a sleepy appearance are all signs of sickness. Many birds quiet down during the late morning and early afternoon, but a bird should still show interest when you talk to it.

➤ Don't buy a bird that looks like it spent the night at a Grateful Dead concert. Birds shouldn't have "sleep" in the corners of their eyes. Puffy or red eyelids, irritated skin in the eye area or any discharge from the eyes are often signs of sickness.

➤ Don't buy a bird with a breathing problem. Signs of respiratory trouble include rapid or open-beak breathing, a plugged or runny nose, sneezing, wheezing or a clicking sound and sticky or stained feathers around the nostrils.

➤ Don't buy a bird that looks like a reject from the rotisserie. An over-eager sales-person may assure you that the bird looks plucked in places because "it's just molting," but healthy birds lose only a few feathers at a time during the molt. They never lose so many that bare skin becomes obvious.

➤ Don't buy a bird with troublesome toes. Swelling, sores or scabs on the feet may all signal problems. A healthy bird will perch on one foot when relaxing, but shouldn't be reluctant to put the foot back down. When climbing or walking, the bird's weight should be distributed equally on both feet.

➤ Don't buy a bird with a prizefighter's schnozz. Bumps, lumps or any deformities of the beak are a bad sign. If you aren't sure how a particular bird's beak should look, compare it with another bird of the same species. Also, beware of scaly beaks, especially in budgies.

➤ Don't poop out before checking the droppings. A bird living alone in a cage should scatter its droppings all over the bottom. Poops piled up in one place may be a sign of an inactive, ill or depressed bird—unless the cage is too tiny for the bird to move around. Droppings should be on the solid side. Don't buy a bird that has diarrhea; or one with undigested food, blood or mucus in its stool. Exceptions are lories and hand-fed baby birds. Healthy lories have loose stools, and any species of hand-fed baby will have a wetter stool than a weaned bird, due to more liquid in the diet.

Bird Brainers

Are two birds of the same species better than one? It depends on how much time you can give your pet. A single bird will bond to you better, but will need regular attention. Two birds will bond to each other. They may still want to play with you, but they won't be as needy.

➤ Don't buy a bird that flares its tail or slaps its wings against its sides when you come near. As pretty as the tail may be, the parrot isn't showing off for you. Flared tails are a sign of extreme excitement—the type of excitement that often leads to aggression—and wing slapping often signals anger. Hostile birds may also flash their eyes while flaring their tails and slapping their wings.

➤ Be hard-hearted when choosing a small bird that is caged with several of its kind. Though it's tempting to pick a puny, picked-on bird to save it from its bolder cage mates, you'll be sorry later. A healthier, braver bird will make the best pet. Choose from birds that are playing, eating, preening or chattering to each other, and avoid the urge to rescue a sick, scared or sleepy one.

Why a Parrot's Wings Should Be Trimmed (Usually)

Veterinarians agree that most of the pet bird tragedies they treat could have been prevented by trimming the bird's wings. Pet birds flying free in the home crash into mirrors, windows and ceiling fans, and land in pots of boiling soup and sizzling frying pans. Some birds drown while sipping soda or water from a glass. Even though they may do it successfully many times, the final time they lose their balance on the slippery surface and slide in. Others lose their lives when they land in the toilet. It

Squawk!

Don't trim the wings on a canary or finch. They need to fly from perch to perch to get their exercise.

doesn't take much liquid to drown a bird. Falling into just half an inch can be fatal. Some birds never crash into anything, but end up just as gone. They simply disappear through an open door or window. Remember Handsome Hank from the Introduction? That's how he ended up at my house.

Properly trimmed (clipped) wings allow a bird to flutter to the ground safely if it falls or flies off a perch, but prevent it from taking off upward or flying fast. Besides keeping your bird away from a great many dangers, clipped wings are an important training aid (see Chapter 13). Parrots adapt easily to trimmed wings and don't seem to be adversely affected by losing their ability to fly.

Squawk!

Don't let a canary or finch fly free in your home. Keep it housed in a spacious cage for its own safety.

Before taking your Pauly home, ask the seller if his wings are trimmed. If not, request that they be clipped and watch the simple, painless procedure. I'll teach you how to do it yourself in Chapter 18 (feathers grow back and you'll have to trim them a few times a year), but it's best to have them clipped by an expert the first time. Confidence is important when building a bond with a new bird, and feeling like fumble fingers won't help.

If the pet shop employee or breeder is a bit behind the times, they may clip just one wing. If so, ask them to trim the other as well. Today, we know it's important to keep a bird balanced. With both wings trimmed evenly, your bird will be able to control his downward glide and land upright. A bird with only one wing clipped could crash land if he fell from his perch or tried to fly.

When *shouldn't* you trim your bird's wings? If you keep your birds in a spacious outdoor aviary, let them live as naturally as possible, and enjoy landing on the live trees and natural perches that are part of many outdoor bird displays.

Does Your New Bird Need a Veterinary Checkup?

It's a good idea to have your new bird checked by an avian veterinarian (one who specializes in birds). Although the bill for a thorough examination, complete with blood work and a stool culture, may be rather hefty ($75 to $125), it feels good to be assured that the newest member of your family is healthy. When considering an expensive bird without a health guarantee, having it examined before you buy will help put you at ease. If the owners won't allow it—even though they are invited to come along and witness the examination—go elsewhere to get your bird.

When buying a bird with a health guarantee, check the expiration date. Few guarantees last longer than the time it takes to make an appointment with your veterinarian and put the bird through a complete physical. For help in finding an avian veterinarian, see Chapter 20.

The Least You Need to Know

➤ Shop for your bird in places you trust.

➤ Choose a bird that shows signs of good health.

➤ Buy a responsive bird that seems to like you.

➤ The price of a bird reflects rarity, not how good a pet it will be.

➤ Have your new bird's wings trimmed by an expert and watch the procedure.

Part 2
Welcome Home, Feathered Friend

You've made the toughest decision—selecting a species—but you're not finished yet. Your bird needs a cage, complete with strategically placed perches, toys and dishes. Don't worry. There's no shortage of this stuff at the pet shop. The trick is knowing which items will be best for your new bird and how to use them. That's what this section is all about.

Chapter 5

Choosing a Cage

In This Chapter

➤ Cage sizes and shapes

➤ What a difference a door makes

➤ Safe bars

➤ Easy cleanups

➤ Outdoor housing

Cages can be confusing. They come in small, medium, large and several sizes in between. They may be rectangular, circular, square or even shaped like a pagoda. They are made of metal, wood, acrylic and bamboo, and are finished in black, white, gold or silver. They may stand on the floor, hang from a stand or sit on a tabletop. Their doors may slide sideways, up and down, open outward from the top like a drawbridge or swing open like a regular door when a connecting rod is removed.

Will Polly care which cage you buy? You bet she will! Some cages are designed to appeal to people, while others are created to be comfortable and safe homes for birds. Will you select a good one, even though you feel like an idiot when confronted with all those choices? Of course you will. No matter what kind of bird you have, this chapter will make it easy for you to pick your pet's new home.

Shapes, Sizes and Styles

Choosing your bird's cage is like buying a house. It's best to know exactly what features you want and why you want them before you begin. You wouldn't ask a real estate agent to find you any available house. Instead, you might ask to look at houses with three bedrooms, two baths, a roomy kitchen and a fenced yard, within a certain price range. That way, you wouldn't waste time visiting houses that didn't meet your basic requirements or were beyond your budget.

Your bird has basic housing requirements just like you do, but while yours may depend upon the size of your family, your bird's own size, tail length and exercise requirements determine the best dimensions for her cage. After you've narrowed your choices down to cages that are the right size for your bird, examine each one for safety, stability and convenience when cleaning.

Whether you have a canary or a cockatoo, the characteristics of a good cage are the same. Here's your shopping list. I'll explain each item a little later in the chapter, so you'll be able to customize it for your particular bird.

Ten Qualities of Terrific Cages

Going shopping for a cage? Take this list along. A good cage will have the following features:

✓ Big enough for your bird. Minimum dimensions are _____ × _____ × _____ (I'll help you fill in the blanks a little later in this chapter).

✓ A simple rectangular or square shape that accommodates your bird's length, wing span and exercise requirements.

✓ Stability (it won't tip over, fall down or slide easily).

✓ Safe door(s).

✓ Made of strong caging material, with a nontoxic finish.

✓ Bar spacing that is safe for the size of your bird. Ideal spacing is _____ .

✓ Horizontal bars among the vertical ones, or vice versa.

✓ Removable tray for easy cleaning.

✓ Wire floor above the tray.

✓ Several slots, so food and water dishes can be removed and replaced from outside the cage.

Squawk!

Don't assume the cage a bird is displayed in is the right size for the bird. In many pet stores, birds get their exercise by taking turns on play gyms, and are only caged for feeding and resting. Under those circumstances, they don't need large cages.

Big Enough

What's big enough varies with your bird's size, shape and exercise needs. Here are guidelines for the most popular species. In every case, I'm giving you the *minimum* your bird can get by with. Get a larger cage if you can afford it and you have enough room. When it comes to birdcages, bigger is almost always better.

Just as you seldom find a house where every room is the exact size and shape you want, you may not be able to find a birdcage with precisely the dimensions suggested here. That's no problem. With your shopping list as a guide, you'll be able to find a cage that's close enough to the correct size to keep your bird healthy, happy and safe.

Finches and Canaries

Small and quick, finches and canaries are happiest when they have enough space to fly from perch to perch. Since they don't take off like helicopters or hover like humming-birds, their home should be long, rather than tall. A rectangular cage that's 28 to 32 inches long, 18 inches wide and 20 inches high is suitable for a pair of finches. A single canary can get by in a rectangular cage that's 16 inches long, 12 inches wide and 15 inches high.

Budgies

Budgies are climbers and acrobats, and use every square inch of their cage getting their daily exercise. According to many budgie experts, there's a simple formula for finding the right size cage for a single bird. The best shape is a rectangle, and the three measurements—length, width and height—should add up to at least 60 inches. So if the length is 24 inches, the width might be 16, and the height 20 to create a comfortable cage.

Budgie owners who put their pet on a play gym for an hour or more a day can get by with a smaller cage. The minimum is 15 inches long, 15 inches wide and 18 inches high.

> ### Polly Sez
>
> A *play gym* or *cage-top gym* is an uncaged exercise area for parrots. It may contain a ladder, swing, perches of various diameters, and toys. Play gyms come in several styles and sizes, and accommodate parrots of all sizes, from budgies to macaws.

Cockatiels, Lovebirds, Gray-Cheeked and Other Small Parakeets

Provided she has a play gym and plenty of opportunities to use it, a single bird of one of these species can get by in a cage 18 inches long by 18 inches wide. A lovebird and most small parakeets will be okay in a square cage 18 inches high, but the cockatiel's long tail requires a cage at least 24 inches high.

If you don't have time to put Polly on a play gym daily, buy a rectangular cage that's at least 24 inches long, with enough width so she can flap her wings without beating them against the bars.

Amazon, African Grey and Pionus Parrots

Without spacious quarters for exercise, amazons become obese and african greys may become bored to the point of plucking out their feathers. These birds need cage dimensions in the range of 24 inches long, 18 inches wide and 30 inches high, provided they have free time outside their cages often, either on a play gym or keeping you company around the house. Pionus parrots can make do with cages not quite so high, but if regular exercise might be a problem, get a larger cage.

Conures, Lories and Lorikeets

Curious and playful, these species need enough space to climb, play, preen and perform acrobatic feats. Since conure and lori sizes vary among varieties, so does minimum housing requirements. The majority are under 13 inches long and can get by with a cage 20 inches long, 18 inches wide and 24 inches tall, as long as they spend an hour or more outside their cage daily. Otherwise, look for a cage in the 24-inch-long range. A few conures are quite large. For example, if you picked the patagonian, look for a cage 24 inches long, 24 inches wide and 36 inches tall.

Squawk!

Many modern cages have impressive-sounding specifications when it comes to space, but get most of their square feet from height rather than length. Unfortunately, height doesn't stimulate some birds into exercising the way length does. The best cage shape for most birds is a long rectangle, provided it has enough height to accommodate your bird's tail.

Cockatoos

Cockatoos are energetic, playful climbers who do best when they have enough space to let off some steam. A spacious cage at least 24 inches long, 24 inches wide and 36 inches high encourages them to exercise. If you have an exceptionally large cockatoo, such as the moluccan or the greater sulphur-crested, or if you don't think you'll be able to give Polly enough time out of her cage, buy her a bigger home.

Macaws

With their high activity levels, wide wing spans and glorious tails, there's no skimping on the size of a large macaw's cage. Scarlet, blue-and-gold, and green-winged macaws need accommodations at least five feet long, three feet wide and five feet tall to stretch out their wings and keep from damaging their tails. The even larger hyacinth macaw would make good use of additional space, while the military macaw can make do with a slightly smaller cage. Mini-macaws, such as the hahns and the noble, can get by with cage dimensions of 24 inches long, 18 inches wide and 30 inches high. Macaws also need time outside their cages to play on a gym or visit with you. If you won't be able to give your bird a few hours of supervised freedom daily, buy the largest cage you can afford.

Mynahs

Mynahs are active birds in the wild, but tend to shorten their life spans by becoming obese when caged. To prevent this, get the biggest cage you can afford. The minimum for a mynah is 24 inches long, 18 inches wide and 30 inches high.

Toucans

Toucans need plenty of room to run, and like to jump from perch to perch. A cage five feet long, three feet wide and four feet tall works well for a single bird.

Bird Brainers

Measure the doorways of your home before buying a big cage, or you may choose a welded model and then find out it doesn't fit. If you select a cage that needs to be assembled, put it together in the room where it will be used, so doorways won't be a problem.

Rare Birds

If your bird isn't on this list, it's probably a pretty rare pet. No problem. Just use good judgment when choosing the cage. To make sure your bird can stretch, flap her wings and preen, buy a cage with at least two measurements (length, width and height are the three measurements) that are at least one-and-a-half times her wing span. In other words, if your pet's wing span is 12 inches, buy a cage where at least two measurements are 18 inches.

If your pet has a long tail, make sure the tail will be free of the floor when Polly is on her perches. A tiny bird that has to fly to be healthy (such as a finch) needs a cage with sufficient length. And if you have more than one bird, get a larger cage than you would buy for a single resident.

Simple Shapes

The best shape for a birdcage is a rectangle or a square. It's tempting to put your pet in the prettiest cage you can find, but your bird would rather have something simple. Avoid cute cages shaped like little pagodas, or anything with peaked roofs, sharply slanted sides, extra alcoves or lots of ornamentation. A fancy cage may enhance your home, but it's bad for your bird. Nooks, crannies, angles and ornaments all invite injury and rob cages of usable space.

Also pass up those pretty round or cylindrical cages. They may be tall, but from your bird's perspective they are cramped and frustrating. Domed and rounded roofs are fine on top of rectangular cages, provided the spaces between the bars of the cage don't converge (see "Safe Spaces" later in this chapter).

Squawk!

Don't put a big bird and a small bird in the same cage. It isn't natural and the little bird might not survive a dispute.

Steady On

Some cages are designed to sit on tabletops, while others hang from stands. Larger cages may have a built-in stand with casters or wheels on the bottom. Still others are floor models—giant cages designed to hold cockatoos and macaws. While all well-made cages and stands will feel stable on a level table or floor, some are more difficult to knock over than others.

If a small bird is your only pet and there are no children in your home, a cage dangling from an upright stand will work just fine. But if you have youngsters and your toddler tries to shinny up the rod—down will come baby, birdie and all. So if kids, or even dogs, make yours an active household, your small bird's cage will have more stability if it sits atop a table or a stand with four legs.

Cages for large birds usually have wheels or casters. In active households, these should either lock or be removable, so your bird doesn't get an unwelcome ride every time a kid bumps the cage.

Bird Brainers

Your bird can commute from room to room and be with you when you eat, watch TV or spend time at the computer (say hi, Rooster) by sitting on an easily moved play gym or T-stand.

Safe Doors

A good door opens easily for you but is impossible for your bird to open. When fully opened, it provides your pet with an exit designed to make coming or going a smooth and nonthreatening transition. Above all, a good door is safe.

Safe doors include the types that open to the side, and those that open forward, drawbridge style. The drawbridge is an especially good door for those who like to let their bird come out of the cage on her own. By opening outward, it acts like a birdie balcony.

Most cages meant for medium to large birds have doors that swing open to the side. When opened, birds exit them easily, usually by climbing from door top to cage top. Side doors are usually heavy enough not to swing freely when climbed on, although occasionally one moves too easily for your bird's good. If you think yours might swing shut with Polly's weight, use a snap or a twist-tie to keep it still when the bird steps on it. Then Polly can climb on the door with no chance of it closing on her toes.

Whichever kind of door you choose, make sure the opening is big enough for you to get your hand in and your bird out (either in your hand or perched on your finger) without bumping her head. Any pain or trauma associated with leaving or returning to the cage could make Polly shy away the next time you invite her on an outing. The entrance should also be spacious enough so you can easily wipe down the cage's wire bottom and sides, hang toys and put your bird's bath water inside.

Stay Away from the Guillotine

Does the word "guillotine" conjure up images of safety? Yet, guillotine-type doors are found on many cages designed for small birds. Avoid them the way Marie Antoinette would have if she could have. One slip and they could break your bird's toes, or worse. If you already have a cage with guillotine doors, use a metal clip to hold the door wide open when you use it, leaving you with both hands free and a safe bird. Keep the clip handy by attaching it to the cage when you aren't using it.

This guillotine door is held open by a clip so it can't land on the bird.

No Escape

How a door latches is especially important when housing big birds. Many of them are escape artists, and what they may lack in magic, they make up for in persistence. Make sure your bird's cage closes securely. Many bird owners resort to padlocks to keep Polly from taking a powder. If you get one, keep the key or combination handy in case of emergency.

A bird as small as a cockatiel shouldn't need a lock, but does need a more secure latch than birds of comparable size. While any bird might get into the habit of playing with a latch, cockatiels and cockatoos are the most talented lock-pickers in the bird world.

Made of the Right Stuff

The right stuff for cages that are suitable for small birds is some form of metal that has been galvanized, chromed or lacquered to keep it from rusting. These cages most often come in shades of silver, gold, white or black, although you may be able to locate one in rose, turquoise or whatever color matches your decor. When choosing a metal cage, make sure the finish is smooth. If Polly finds a chipped or rough spot, she might pick at it until the finish peels. Aside from making the cage rust, eating the finish could make her sick.

The wrong stuff for any hookbill, even one as small as a budgie, is wood or bamboo. It's less sanitary than metal and more difficult to clean, but that won't be a problem for long. The reason so many bird toys are made of wood is that birds love to gnaw on it. Put Polly in a wooden or bamboo cage and she will think she's living inside a giant toy. Soon she will savor every section until the cage is completely destroyed.

Fine for Finches

Finches also relish cages that are partially made of wood, but they like them for their security, not their taste. Finches don't damage the wood, and they seem to feel espe-

cially safe in an old-fashioned box style cage with a wooden back, roof and sides. Cages of this type have wire mesh only across the front. Some pet shops sell ready-to-use fronts that you can attach to a homemade box.

If you want to display your finches in a prettier setting, check out the vitrine cages, advertised in most bird magazines. They have a Plexiglas or glass front, a wire mesh roof and sides and should have shutters to regulate ventilation and a few doors. Decorate the cage with bird-safe live plants and your finches will have a private palace that adds to the beauty of your home.

What About Acrylic?

A relatively new item in many large pet stores is acrylic cages. On the plus side, these cages catch and contain fallen feathers, scattered seeds, droppings and other debris, and keep them from landing on your clean floor. On the minus side, since acrylic cages don't have wire sides, birds can't get their exercise by climbing them. They also tend to heat up faster than wire cages, so if you get one, keep it away from direct sunlight. When buying an acrylic cage, make sure it has plenty of air holes for good ventilation.

The Mettle of Metal

Medium to large birds need cages made of metal so strong that their powerful beaks can't bend it, so check the gauge to make sure it's tough enough to withstand Polly's best efforts. One popular metal for large cages is stainless steel. On the plus side, stainless cages are strong, good-looking, easy to clean and usually include all ten qualities of terrific cages. On the minus side, stainless steel is pricey and may be welded in the wrong places. If your parrot is amazon size or larger, check the placement of the welds. Big beaks relish big challenges, and your bird may work on those welds like a prisoner with a new bride waiting on the outside. Birds have worked at welds until they break, so before buying a cage make sure the welds are located where Polly won't be tempted to use them for toys.

Cold-rolled steel is another excellent metal for birdcages. It's extremely strong and is usually powder-coated for easy cleaning. Several companies make cold-rolled steel cages that include all ten qualities of terrific cages. They are attractive and usually come in black, white or grayish green. Some of them have optional cage-top gyms, complete with food dishes and a tray. The tray under the gym serves two purposes: It keeps droppings from falling into the cage, and it makes for easy cleaning. These cages are moderately expensive, but worth it.

Wrought iron is another popular cage material, especially for medium to large birds. Most often made in Mexico, wrought-iron cages are usually painted flat black, although you may find an occasional white one. Modern wrought-iron cages

Squawk!

Big beaks bend wires. Always buy the strongest cage you can find.

Squawk!

Never use metal polish to shine up your bird's cage. It can poison Polly.

Squawk!

Before buying a metal cage, check on the coating. Occasionally a cage is coated with a zinc compound, and parrots could get zinc poisoning from swallowing it. Avoid any cage offered at a garage sale, unless the owner can assure you of its origins. The solder on older cages, and some from third-world countries, could contain lead, which can poison Polly.

are painted with lead-free paint. Years ago, that wasn't always the case, so don't buy the charming 20-year-old model you may see in the secondhand shop. On the plus side, wrought-iron cages are economical, giving your bird the most space for the money. On the minus side, they are harder to clean than cages made of more expensive materials, and they seldom include all ten qualities of terrific cages. Of course, you can attach extra feeders or put a better latch on the door yourself and still have a good buy. Another minus is that sometimes the paint rubs off, temporarily soiling Polly. Many owners alleviate that problem by having their wrought-iron cages sandblasted and powder-coated, which also makes them easier to clean.

Safe Spaces

Check the spacing between the bars of each cage you consider. Spaces should be narrow enough to keep Polly from poking her head out between the bars, but not so narrow that her toes are pinched when she climbs. The recommendations in the following table will work.

Recommended Cage-Bar Spacing

Species	Bar spacing (inches)
Finches, canaries, budgies, lovebirds	$3/8$ to $7/16$
Cockatiels, pocket parakeets, small conures	$1/2$, $3/4$ or $5/8$
Large conures, most amazons, african greys, lories, pionus parrots, large parakeets such as ring-necks, small cockatoos	$3/4$ to 1
Macaws, large cockatoos, large amazons, eclectus parrots	$3/4$ to $1 1/2$

After finding a cage with the right bar spacing, make sure the spaces are identical everywhere. In cages with peaked or domed tops, sometimes the spacing between the bars narrows near the highest point. This is a dangerous design because it can trap toes, wings or hooked beaks.

Horizontal and Vertical Bars

The bars on birdcages may be vertical or horizontal. Either one is fine, provided it is mixed with some of the other. Most birds love to climb and it's great exercise, but it's hard to climb when all the bars run the same way. Encourage your bird to climb by making sure her cage has a few horizontal bars among the vertical ones, or vice versa.

Removable Tray

A removable tray that slides out of the bottom of your birdcage will make changing soiled papers a snap. Most modern cages have this feature. Changing the papers is easiest when you don't have to cut the paper into special designs, so keep that in mind when choosing a cage. You will probably use yesterday's newspaper, paper towels, or used computer paper to line the tray.

Wire Floor Above the Tray

A bird in the wild doesn't walk on its own droppings, so good cages are designed with a wire floor, called a grate or grille, above the tray. The grate lets used food, as well as droppings, fall through, keeping your bird from munching a contaminated meal or shredding her dirty cage papers.

Besides helping birds of all sizes stay clean and healthy, the grate is an important safety feature for small birds. Minus a grate, there would be enough space at the bottom of the cage for a little bird to escape when the tray is removed for cleaning.

Several Slots for Dishes

Your bird needs more dishes than just one for food and one for water. Ideally, Polly's cage should have four feeder ports, allowing dishes to be removed and replaced from outside the cage. Finding a cage with four slots may be a problem, as most moderately priced cages have only two.

If you really like a cage that has just two, it's easy enough to add extra dishes, as any salesperson will surely tell you. Just be aware that without built-in ports, the additional dishes will attach to the inside of the cage or sit on the cage floor, and you'll have to open the door and reach inside to tend them. While that probably won't be a problem for you, pity the poor bird sitter when you're on vacation. Many a pleasant Polly transforms into a provoked Polly when her owners pull out of the driveway, making the sitter fear for his or her fingers. So if two cages appear equal, but one has two feeder ports and the other has three or four, you'll know which one to buy.

What if you can't find a cage with more than two slots? Will Polly be poorly fed while you're off snorkeling or skiing? Bon voyage and don't worry. I'll explain some alternative feeding methods when we get to Chapter 10 that will work for your bird sitter.

We've already talked about how avian Houdinis learn to open cage doors and even pick simple locks. But great escape artists don't just concentrate on doors. Birds have also lifted the latch on their food dish, dropped the dish to the cage floor and squeezed out through the slot. So if you have a big bird, make sure the feeder ports close securely.

Bird Brainers

Cage trays are often made of plastic and are the weakest part of a heavy-gauge metal cage. Before making a major purchase, be sure you will be able to buy a replacement tray if yours ever breaks.

*The well-designed
cage.*

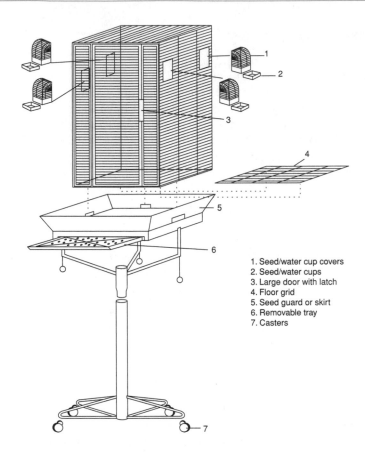

1. Seed/water cup covers
2. Seed/water cups
3. Large door with latch
4. Floor grid
5. Seed guard or skirt
6. Removable tray
7. Casters

Accessories that Keep Your Floor Clean(er)

A cordless vacuum cleaner for quick cleanups is every parrot owner's pal, no matter how their pet's cage is designed, but cages with matching seed skirts or guards catch and contain more mess than those without. Slanting upward and outward from the cage bottom, the skirts catch most of the stuff Polly flings from her cage and work well for birds of all sizes.

For small birds only, cage skirts or aprons made of cloth can be purchased separately in a variety of colors. Machine washable, with elastic at both ends, they simply slip on and off the bottom third or fourth of your canary or budgie's cage. Since they cling tightly to the cage rather than slanting outward, how well they work depends upon the placement of your bird's dishes. They are most effective when the dishes are below the top of the skirt.

Bird Brainers

Protect the carpet below your bird's cage by cutting heavy-duty clear vinyl or plastic to cover the area. It makes for quick cleanups, too. A generous amount works best, as birds can scatter stuff a couple of feet in all directions.

On the bright side, if you're handy with a sewing machine, you can make your own cage skirts to match your decor. On the minus side, elasticized skirts are a tempting toy to some small hookbills. Budgies and their slightly larger relatives may relish ripping them to shreds, but canaries and finches usually ignore them.

Hooded Dishes

Hooded food dishes help confine empty seed hulls, chopped carrots and the like to inside the dish. However, some birds, especially some cockatiels, refuse to use them. If you switch from open to hooded dishes, make sure your bird continues to eat and drink. You may have to slowly familiarize your pet with the new dishes by putting her open dishes back into the cage a few times a day so she gets some food and water. In a few days, your bird may become comfortable with her new dining dishes. If not, try putting millet or another favorite treat into the hooded monster and see if that makes it look more feeder-friendly. If your bird won't even take treats out of a hooded dish after a week of familiarization, give up. Don't turn anything this trivial into a battle of wills. Your pet should feel safe and secure while eating and drinking.

Many hooded dishes come in two parts and the hood section simply slips off. If you don't know how your bird will react to hooded dishes, buy that type. At least you'll still have nice new regular dishes if you have to remove the hood.

Nice, but Not Necessary

Some cage models may be offered with the option of a chest of drawers designed to fit below the cage, instead of a stand. The selling point is that the drawers are a convenient place to store bird supplies. This is only partly true. While it's a good place to keep cage papers, alternate toys and other nonperishables, don't plan on using it to store bird food. As you'll learn later, birds need lots more than seeds to thrive, and even seeds are best stored in the refrigerator.

Polly Sez

The term *hookbill* refers to any member of the parrot family.

Squawk!

Some cages come with hooded dishes, and your new bird might not be used to them. Watch carefully to make sure she eats and drinks. Going without water or food for several hours is unhealthy at best, and could be downright dangerous when added to the stress of moving into a new home.

Bird Brainers

Be sure to buy a birdcage. A T-stand or play gym, no matter how much fun, is still just a nice place to visit. Your bird needs the security of her own enclosed space for resting and sleeping.

Some cages created for hookbills come with a play gym permanently attached to the top. Does your parrot need a play gym? In a word, yes. But play gyms can be purchased separately and attached to the cage top, and portable, freestanding models are also available that can be placed anywhere you please. A permanently attached play gym has no advantage over a portable model, unless it comes with a tray to protect the cage below. If you attach a gym without a tray to the cage top, remember to remove the food and water dishes from inside the cage before your bird uses the gym. Otherwise, poor Polly might be stuck with poop soup.

Outdoor Aviaries

An outdoor aviary is an option, not a necessity. On the upside, it gives your bird a more natural environment, complete with fresh air, plenty of space, Mother Nature's schedule of light and darkness, and clean rainwater. It's also ideal if you're interested in breeding birds or collecting multiple species.

On the downside, outdoor living can present you and your pet with a whole new set of problems. Before considering this option, decide if your aviary will be able to meet the following requirements:

➤ Legally legit

➤ Cooperative climate

➤ Safe and secure

➤ Social stimulation

➤ Noise won't bother the neighbors

Legally Legit

Many municipalities have zoning laws and building codes that could complicate your plans. Before setting up an outdoor aviary, find out if your locale has laws about housing exotic birds outdoors, and if your structure will require a building permit.

Cooperative Climate

Southern California and the southern two-thirds of Florida have the best climates in North America for housing birds outdoors. If you live there, you should be able to keep your bird outside all year. Several states have long summers, where birds could comfortably live outdoors for between three and five months.

How will you know if your bird and your climate are compatible? Go back to Chapter 3 and look up your bird's area of origin. Now go to the encyclopedia (you knew that set would come in handy someday!) or the library, and look up that region's climate. Is it similar to yours, at least for several months? Bingo! Your bird could spend some of the year in an outdoor aviary.

Safe and Secure

People, predators and pests are all potentially harmful to your bird. Place your aviary where casual observers won't see it, as the theft and resale of expensive birds is a common crime in sunny climates. The structure should stand inside a securely (not just decoratively) fenced yard with a gate that locks, and the aviary itself should also lock. A burglar alarm and proximity light are also good safeguards.

Wild predators, including foxes, skunks, raccoons and snakes, seldom miss an easy bird meal. Domestic dogs and tenacious tabbies are just as threatening, so be sure the cage bars in your outdoor aviary are strong enough to withstand not only your bird's beak, but also a stray dog's teeth.

Some predators will worry the bottom of the aviary, relentlessly digging, pawing, gnawing and clawing until the wood gives way. Galvanized sheet metal that is buried several inches deep and surrounds the bottom 18 inches of the aviary should send them salivating elsewhere. The easiest way to build this barrier is to use flashing—precut galvanized sheet metal, sold in rolls.

Pests, including rodents, fleas and mosquitoes, will impose on your bird's' hospitality unless you screen them out. A fine but strong wire mesh around the outside of the aviary will do the job.

Squawk!

Use only natural, untreated wood when building any structure for birds. Wood that has been stained, pressure-treated or treated with preservatives is poisonous when chewed.

Squawk!

If your bird doesn't have trimmed wings because she flies around in an indoor aviary a few hours a day, take her back and forth in a small carrying cage, not perched on your finger. Even a well-trained pet will fly away when startled by a sudden noise or abrupt movement. It can happen as quickly as a thunderclap or tripping on the porch steps.

Social Stimulation

Is your bird a beloved house pet, used to being part of the family routine? Then she would feel rejected if she were permanently moved outdoors. Instead, give her an hour or two a day in the aviary, or put her outside before you go to work and bring her back in the house when you get home.

On the other hand, a pair of birds or a parrot that was never tamed might thrive in an outdoor setting.

Could Noise Cause a Problem?

If you live in a suburban setting, your neighbors may not enjoy bird sounds as much as you do. In fact, someone nearby may even work nights and sleep during the day.

Bird Brainers

A single parrot will usually be a lot quieter than a pair of the same species. Also, multiple birds of different species are usually quieter than birds of the same species. If you want more than one bird in your aviary, but noise is a consideration, buy birds of similar size but different species.

Under certain circumstances, a squawking bird may make your neighbors angry enough to call the police or animal control.

If you live on several acres, keep as many macaws, cockatoos and conures as you please. But if you have neighbors close by, consider quieter pets.

The Best-Laid Plans

An outdoor aviary can be both beautiful and natural, providing your bird with room to fly, branches of various widths for perching, a few toys and perhaps a swing for playing. It should have several dishes, positioned where they won't be rained on or dirtied by bird droppings. Your bird will also need an area where she can avoid rain, wind and excessive sunshine.

Most aviary owners enjoy designing their own outdoor bird haven, but prefabricated kits are also available. Pick up a copy of *Bird Talk* magazine and you'll find companies offering catalogs that contain everything from aviary kits to cage-making tools.

Galvanized Wire Woes

Because it inhibits rust, galvanized wire is often used in outdoor aviaries. During the process of coating the wire, bits of zinc sometimes stick to it. Since birds bite on wire and zinc is toxic, you'll have to get rid of the loose pieces before putting Polly inside. Wash the bars with a wire brush and rinse them with white vinegar. Then Polly can move into her galvanized aviary (or cage).

Avian Adventures

I used to feed sick and injured birds as a wildlife rehabilitation volunteer, which reminds me of another safety suggestion for your outdoor aviary. Make sure it has double doors. The first door should open into a small, screened-in entryway and close firmly before you open the second door—the one that lets you into the actual aviary. I remember three instances where we would have lost birds that needed to be on medication for a few more days before being released. Luckily, they were stopped by our "safety door."

The Least You Need to Know

➤ Your bird's wing span, tail length, exercise requirements and safety are the top considerations when buying a cage.

➤ Buy a cage created for a bird's comfort and safety, not one designed to appeal to people.

➤ Bigger is almost always better when buying a cage.

➤ Rectangles and squares are the best shapes for birdcages.

➤ Cage doors should be large and latch securely. Avoid the ones that slide up and down like a guillotine.

➤ The cage wire should be strong enough so your bird's beak can't bend it.

➤ If your new cage has hooded food dishes, make sure your bird is eating and drinking. Some birds won't use hooded dishes.

➤ If you live in a warm climate, an outdoor aviary may be an option.

Bringing Your Bird Home

It's almost bird day! There's excitement in the air. Soon you're going to bring your new bird home. I'm sure you can hardly wait, but let's do a little organizing first. This chapter will help you decide when to buy your bird, and tell you how to carry him home and where to put his cage. It will also tell you what your new pet needs right away, and how to keep him safe from toxic stuff and predatory pets.

Are you wondering how to handle your pet when he's the new bird on the block? How to guide your children into a good relationship with the feathered member of the family? How people come up with those terrific bird names? Good! That's all here too.

The Right Time

The best time to bring home your new bird is when nothing new is happening at your house. Wait until the repair people are finished, the relatives go home, the big party is a memory and the holidays are at least a month away. That will give Pauly quiet time to get to know his new family and acclimate to his surroundings.

For the first few weeks, try to keep household activity near Pauly to a minimum. It's too soon to vacuum near his cage, invite friends over to meet him, or let Junior serenade him on the trombone. Gradually, activity in the bird area of your home should return to normal. Once he feels secure, Pauly may sing and dance when Junior practices, show off for guests, and want to be part of every party.

The Right Place

Your bird will be happiest if he's part of the flock (that's family to you), so put his cage where people gather. The living room or family room may be ideal, provided that people actually use them. Younger bird owners might want their pet as a roommate.

Bird Brainers

Birds tend to be insecure in a cage that's exposed on all sides. A corner provides excellent security, but most birds do just fine as long as one side of their cage is against a wall.

The arrangement usually works well, as long as an adult makes sure the bird gets regular care. When my daughter Peggy was in high school, she kept a budgie and a cat in her room and they all came through just fine.

Drafts and abrupt changes of temperature are both bad for birds, so don't put Pauly's cage by an exterior door or in front of an air-conditioning or heating vent, fireplace, radiator, or any window that isn't insulated and well sealed. Although a little sunshine is good for birds, keep the cage out of direct sunlight unless shade is always available. In the wild, birds usually seek shade under a leafy umbrella. They seldom sunbathe because they overheat easily.

Handling Household Toxins

If possible, don't house your bird in the kitchen or bathroom. Cooking and showering make for abrupt changes of temperature. Also, fumes from some of the strong cleaners used in these rooms are potentially lethal to birds. So are the fumes from scorched nonstick cookware and other appliances coated with a nonstick surface, such as some irons and coffee machines.

Squawk!

Hot air rises, so check the temperature at cage level. If the cage is close to the floor, your bird's climate may be chillier than you think.

Once upon a time, I spent a couple of years in a studio apartment in Manhattan with three feathered roommates, so I know the ideal isn't always possible. Now that you know the dangers, you can keep your bird safe, even if he has to live in the kitchen. Since even the most careful cooks make mistakes, start by getting rid of your nonstick cookware. Is that a pout? Think of it as a tiny trade-off for a bird's animated antics. After all, pots and pans have no personality.

It's best if you can avoid using pesticides altogether, but if pests are a problem, or if you are cleaning with something potentially toxic, take your bird out of the area before you begin, and don't bring him back until the room has been well ventilated. If you take your bird out of the area in a carrying case and leave the cage behind, remove the food and water dishes, and cover the cage before spraying. Keep the spray away from your bird's other belongings, such as the play gym or T-stand, too. (When using a professional pest control service, tell them you have a bird.)

Other cage placement considerations include keeping it out of Rover, Tabby and your toddler's reach. More about them later.

Bird-Proofing Near the Cage

Look around the cage area. No wires or plants should be close enough so Pauly can peck on them, either from inside his cage or when he's climbing the sides or perching on the cage top. Although not every houseplant is toxic to birds, so many of the most popular ones are deadly (for example, philodendron and poinsettia) that it's best to make sure your bird can't reach any leaves at all. Later, you'll have to bird-proof the area where you put Pauly's play gym or T-stand too, but for right now let's make sure the area right around Pauly's home is harmless. (For a list of safe houseplants, see Chapter 7).

Bird Stuff You Need Right Now

After all the planning and decision making, you've picked out a bird and bought a cage. The red carpet (okay, the cage paper) has been rolled out for your beaked buddy, and there's going to be a lot more laughs in your life. But don't put the credit card away yet. Your new friend needs a few things.

Just look at the colorful display of bird toys, treats, food and cage accessories in the pet store. It's tempting to buy triple what you need. How in the world will you know what's necessary and what isn't? By using a list. Here's a list of your new bird's needs. Later I'll explain each item, so you can get the perfect one for Pauly.

Shopping List for Your New Bird
- ✓ Cage
- ✓ Dishes
- ✓ Perches
- ✓ Food
- ✓ Cage cover
- ✓ Birdbath or spray bottle for misting
- ✓ Two or three toys (hookbills)
- ✓ Nests for sleeping (finches)

Cage

You've either been there and read that, or you're surfing through chapters. Go back and read Chapter 5. It's about cages.

Dishes

Your bird needs four dishes. (Trust me on this; I'll tell you why in Chapter 10.) If your cage has only two feeder ports, additional dishes can be hung from the bars or placed on the cage floor.

Don't skimp by buying containers that may not hold up to your bird's bodacious beak. That's false economy. Food and water dishes that even a macaw can't mangle are available, along with clamps for attaching them to the cage. They are made of stainless steel, acrylic, super-strength plastic or other nonporous materials. Heavy-duty stoneware and porcelain crocks work well on the cage floor. Some of them are wider at the bottom, making them almost impossible to tip. That's a fine feature because birds often perch on the edge of their dishes while eating.

Bird Brainers

Finches or canaries may do better with an automatic waterer instead of a regular water dish. Why? Because tiny birds sometimes bathe in their water dish, and while that makes their feathers clean, it makes their drinking water dirty.

Squawk!

When buying ceramic dishes for your bird, make sure they were made in the USA. Ceramics should be well-glazed (read: glossy), and some foreign glazes still contain toxic stuff, including lead.

Perches

Good perches are important, because birds spend most of their lives standing on their feet. Imagine how your feet would feel if you had to stand barefoot on the same hard substance all day, every day. Birds get foot problems, too, but most of them can be prevented with proper perches (and good hygiene).

Most cages come with a perch or two, and some even have a swing, but they aren't always the right diameter for your bird. A perch is the right diameter when your bird's toes don't go all the way around it. If the front and back toenails touch or almost meet, the perch is too thin and your bird will have trouble standing up straight. Ideally, the tips of his toenails should touch the perch about two-thirds of the way around it. That helps him balance and gives his nails some wear, so they don't become overgrown. If you aren't sure what size to buy, err on the side of slightly too thick rather than too thin. The table on the next page gives suggested perch sizes for the most popular species.

Suggested Perch Sizes

Bird	Decent diameters for perches
Budgie	$^1/_2$ to $^5/_8$ inch
Cockatiel	$^3/_4$ inch
Finch or canary	$^3/_8$ to $^1/_2$ inch
Conure	$^3/_4$ to 1 inch
African grey or amazon parrot	1 inch
Large cockatoo or medium macaw	$1^1/_2$ inches
Large macaw	2 inches

It's best if your bird has perches of at least two different diameters, made of different materials. One of them should be wood, since that's what your bird would perch on most often in the wild. Wooden dowels are the most common bird perches, and they do the job, even if they are downright boring. Manzanita may be more interesting. An extremely hard wood, it's often available with several different diameters on the same perch. Natural wood with the bark still on is another option. Besides being good for your bird's feet, it will heighten his chewing pleasure.

Perches made of concrete, terra-cotta or a concrete blend are popular. Birds groom their beaks on the slightly abrasive surface, and these perches also keep some (but not all) birds' toenails blunted. One perch of this type can be a good thing (my birds each have one and use it a lot), but don't get carried away and change all your bird's perches to concrete. No bird should have to stand on hard, rough stuff all the time.

PVC (the white plumbing material that has become popular for everything from outdoor furniture to fishing rod holders) is also used for perches and play gyms. Unlike wood, which your feathered termite will eventually mangle, it isn't bothered by beaks and is extremely easy to clean. But beware, because it can be slippery. Buy a PVC perch only if it has been scored or sanded to give your bird traction.

Squawk!

Your pet shop probably carries sandpaper perch covers in various sizes. They are a lot cheaper than concrete or terra-cotta perches, and you'll get exactly what you paid for—not much. They won't do your bird's toenails any good and they may rub his feet raw, leaving them painful and susceptible to infections.

Bird Brainers

Canaries, finches, mynahs and toucans won't damage their perches, but most hookbills, even tiny budgies, love to whittle wood.

Rope perches are kind to the feet and birds enjoy picking at them, but I'm wary of rope since my budgie Pinto caught two toes in a rope toy. According to some experts, that isn't likely to happen to a bird with properly trimmed toenails, but Pinto's nails had been clipped only three days before his little trauma. Luckily, I was home when he started screeching, and I rescued him immediately. Pinto no longer has rope in his cage, but Sugar received a rope toy for the holidays that doubles as a perch. We're watching carefully to make sure she doesn't have any problems. If your bird has a rope perch or toy, keep his toenails trimmed (you should do that anyway, and I'll tell you how), and get rid of the perch when it becomes tattered.

Food

Pellets? Seeds? Vitamins? Treats? Veggies? Fruits? Table food? Are you confused yet? Don't be. Feeding your bird a good diet isn't difficult, but it is important enough to need its own chapter. So instead of simply selecting a bag of seeds, turn to Chapter 10. It will tell you how to meet your bird's nutritional needs.

Cage Cover

Placing a cover over your bird's cage before you go to bed serves two purposes. It says "bedtime" to your bird and keeps him from getting a draft during the night. Cage covers are available in different sizes and colors, but you don't have to buy one unless you want to. An old sheet or any lightweight, light-colored piece of material will do just fine. Don't drape Pauly's cage in dark material. It's best if he has a tiny bit of light all night, like a child's nightlight. Too dark a cover will leave your bird's bedroom as dark as Dracula's coffin.

Bird Brainers

Some people put a Frisbee in their bird's cage upside down and fill it with half an inch of warm water. It makes a fine bird bath, if Pauly doesn't chew it up instead. Keep an eye on your bird when he's bathing.

Bird Bath or Spray Bottle

Chapter 12 will give you the how's and why's of bird bathing, but for now all you need to know is that Pauly needs frequent baths, and will probably wade right in himself, given the opportunity. Bird baths are available at most pet shops, and some attach to a feeder port or the cage door.

Showers are just as effective, and all you need is a spray bottle set to shoot a fine mist. For economy, start with the spray bottle and you can get the bath later. Buy one just for your bird, label it ("bird bathing only") and put it in a special place. That way you won't make the mistake of using it for plant food or anything else that's dangerous to birds.

Two or Three Toys for Hookbills

Toys will stimulate Pauly's mind, and exercise his beak and body. When choosing a toy, safety is the number-one consideration—a safe toy is one that is tough enough for old buzzard beak. When buying bird toys, choose items meant for your bird's size and species. Too large a toy is a turnoff for a little bird, while too small a toy is dangerous because it can be shattered by a big beak. To find out why birds need toys, what types of toys are available and how to create your own, turn to Chapter 7.

Sleeping Nest for Finches

Finches need shelter to feel secure. Nests make of wicker or wood are available at most pet shops, and will keep your birds comfy during the night.

Here's a cozy nest for a finch.

Heading Home in the Birdmobile

You've done it! Congratulations! Now you have a bird, a cage, food and accessories to haul home. Here's how:

First, ask the salesperson or breeder if they provide a carrying box for your bird. Most pet shops have little cardboard containers with ventilation holes and a handle, suitable for carrying a small bird on a brief journey. Don't try it on a long trip, though. Once your bird acclimates to the tiny carrier, he may begin biting and tearing his way out.

Big birds and birds going on long trips need sturdier carriers. No, you shouldn't use your new cage. It isn't a safe carrier. A traveling cage should be small enough to discourage a bird from fluttering about (and possibly hurting himself) on the trip home. It should also be bare, except for one perch (if possible) just an inch or so off the bottom. You'll need a separate carrier for each bird, as even best friends might hurt each other in such close quarters. For birds the size of amazon parrots, the smallest dog crate available does just fine (that's how Rooster made all his moves).

Many pet shops sell inexpensive carriers that are made for taking birds on car trips. Owning one could come in handy later, when you want to take your bird to the veterinarian or on an outing. If you have a long trip ahead and don't want to buy a carrying case, you may be able to borrow a bird carrier or a small dog crate from a friend. If so, wash it out well and line the bottom with paper towels before putting your bird inside.

Bird Brainers

Find out as much as you can about your new pet before bringing him home. Learn what he's used to eating, what his favorite treats are, where he likes to be petted, where he hates being touched and anything else that will make the transition easy for him.

A small dog crate like this one makes a good carrier.

On the Road

Whatever kind of carrier you use, secure it with a seat belt or tie-downs so it won't slide or roll over during the trip, and make sure the air-conditioning or heating vent isn't giving it a direct hit. If the drive is under two hours, no food is necessary. For longer rides, sprinkle a few seeds or pellets (whichever your bird is used to) on the floor of the carrier. Moist bread, or a bit of fruit such as chopped apple, are good ways to give a bird liquid while on the road.

From Carrier to Cage

As soon as you and your bird arrive home, make sure the doors and windows leading outside are closed. Then, fill the cage dishes with the food your bird is used to eating and room temperature (never frigid) water.

If your bird is in a small cardboard carrier that fits through the cage door, simply place the container, bird and all, on the floor of the cage. Then open the carrier, slide your hand out of the cage and close the cage door. Your bird may be out of the carrier before you even get the door shut, but if not, it won't take long. After an hour or two, reach in and remove the carrier, making as little fuss as possible. If you have a canary, finch or any other bird with untrimmed wings, be especially careful when opening the cage door.

Squawk!

Don't travel with your bird on the floor of your vehicle. That's where heat from the engine and toxic fumes are the most concentrated. Also, avoid smoking when your bird is confined to an area as small as a car. Naturally, the trunk is a no-no.

Bird Brainers

If you live close to the pet shop, leave your bird there while you take the cage and accessories home and set them up. Having a furnished home to move into right away will be less stressful for your bird than waiting while you put it all together.

Option One

If the carrier is too large to fit through the cage door, you have a couple of options, depending on how friendly your bird feels at the moment. Did Pauly climb right up and perch on your finger before you bought him? Then he might do it again. If you're sure his wings are trimmed, open the carrier and offer your finger by moving it at a moderate speed toward his lower chest, about an inch above his feet. Make your move confidently and without hesitation. When your finger reaches the point where Pauly will have to step slightly out and up to get on it, say "up" in a pleasant voice.

If he steps aboard, contain your glee (yes, you should be delighted), and gently place Pauly on a perch in his new cage. Careful—don't hit his head, bump his sides or trap his tail when putting him through the door. Aim him through the center of the opening, just a little on the low side.

A little low and through the middle puts Sugar inside.

Another good reason for keeping Pauly away from the top or sides of the door when putting him inside is that he may grab a cage wire in his beak, step off your hand, climb up on the cage and view his new home from above. If that happens, don't make a big deal of it. After all, his wings are clipped so he isn't going anywhere. Instead, let him have a bird's-eye view for several minutes with the cage door open (he'll see the food), and he may decide to go in on his own. If not, repeat the "up" sequence and try putting him through the door again.

Whatever you do, don't fling him toward the cage quickly. Stuffing him in isn't the answer. All it will do is frighten him into resisting. Bribery is better. While he's on your hand looking toward the door, wiggle a treat through the bars with your other hand. If that doesn't entice him in, use your hands to herd him in gently, or wait him out. He'll probably go in on his own when he's hungry.

Did Pauly growl, back away or try to bite when you opened his carrier and offered your finger? Then don't push it. He's just been through the trauma of moving, doesn't know you yet and is feeling incredibly insecure. Just close the carrier as if nothing happened and use option two.

Option Two

If you have an untrimmed bird in a big carrier, or a parrot who isn't ready to climb on your finger, open the cage door first. Then hold the carrier so that its door will be flush with the open cage door, and open the carrier. Now your bird has an enclosed hallway leading into his new home. Most birds are glad to leave the crowded carrier for a comfy cage with food, water and real perches, and will do so within a few minutes. Others may be terrified and want to stay in the protected enclosure a little longer. As trying as this may be to your arm muscles and your patience, let your bird decide when to make his move.

Squawk!

Resist the urge to tap on the bottom of the carrier or shake it a little to get your bird moving. Your patience now will pay off later in a better relationship with Pauly.

The First 48 Hours

The combination of a new cage, a strange place and unfamiliar faces may make Pauly think he was captured by aliens. The quickest way to make him comfortable is to go about it slowly. In other words, be there, be supportive, but don't be in his face.

Try to bring Pauly home when you have a vacation or a long weekend, so he won't feel alone and abandoned. After all, he's used to living near lots of birds and people. While he may not be ready to accept your touch just yet, Pauly needs your comforting presence.

He's gorgeous, isn't he? And that makes inviting your friends over to admire him just too tempting. Resist the urge, for Pauly's sake. In a few weeks he'll settle in and seek attention. Then you can have a welcome Pauly party.

Low-Key Love

Sudden noises will scare Pauly. So will approaching his cage too quickly. Try to keep your household as quiet as possible for the first 48 hours after his arrival. That doesn't mean you can't play music or watch television, just that the speakers shouldn't blast him off his perch. Avoid making sharp sounds, such as banging the pots and pans when you put them away, and don't bring the vacuum cleaner monster by just yet.

If you have preteens or teenagers, discuss the bird with them before he arrives. When they understand how easily Pauly could become frightened, they may listen to their music through earphones and refrain from slamming doors for a few days. Keep smaller children from playing rough-and-tumble games near the cage, but encourage them to talk or read to their new pet.

If Pauly is already hand tame and welcomes your attention, go ahead and play with him. Otherwise, keep your distance for the first couple of days. Give him food and fresh water, but don't even change his cage papers. Instead, get him used to you by sitting down near his cage to read, write or watch television. In fact, any quiet activity you can do near him without spooking him is fine.

If you're the talkative type, that's even better. Let Pauly hear the soft sound of your voice often. Tell him what a pretty bird he is. Tell him stories. If you've already named him, use his name over and over. Say "hello" when you walk in the room and "good-bye" when you leave. If it isn't your nature to be talkative, set up situations where you'll have to talk near him, if not to him. For example, if you have a cordless phone, carry on your conversations from whatever room Pauly's in.

After a couple of quiet days, your household should gradually resume its normal noises. But especially scary stuff, like vacuuming beneath the cage, should be put off for at least a week. While louder and livelier activities should be introduced a little at a time, Pauly shouldn't be treated like fine china forever. Eventually, he will have to take it in stride when Junior practices the trombone and Julie prepares for cheerleading tryouts.

Millet Magic

If you're worried because your little bird seems too scared to eat well, hang a spray (that's a sprig) of millet in his cage. Finches, canaries, budgies, cockatiels and other small birds (and some big ones) are as delighted as a kid with a candy bar when they get a spray of millet.

A nice long spray and a clip for hanging it should be available at the pet shop. Clips are reusable and cost a dollar or so; single sprays of millet cost about forty cents.

Position the spray near a perch, so your bird can reach it easily. Then stand back. Your bird may need a little time to examine the new thing dangling from his wall, but most birds munch millet within minutes.

Squawk!

If your cat ever puts a fang on your bird, take your bird to the veterinarian immediately, even if the only damage is a tiny scratch. A bacteria transmitted by cat bites is deadly to birds, and can kill them in 24 hours if they aren't treated with the proper antibiotics.

Perils from Predatory Pets

Cats and dogs are born predators, and pet birds are prey animals in the wild, so Rover and Tabby can't help but be excited by Pauly's arrival. They aren't being bad. It's just part of being a dog or cat. Can you keep Pauly safe with other pets around? Sure. According to a survey by the American Pet Products Manufacturer's Association, 60 percent of bird owners also have a dog and 41 percent have a cat. Here's what you need to know so they all can live happily ever after.

Pinto and Bluebell were happy to demonstrate how much they like millet.

Tabby's Threats

Cats are most attracted to little birds because they flit around more than large birds. Be sure cages for finches, canaries, budgies, cockatiels, lovebirds and all other species are so secure that they won't topple, even if Tabby takes a flying leap off the counter top and lands on them. The Tabster may have been a couch cat for years, but a new bird could stimulate latent instincts.

Since cats are persistent, agile and incredibly patient, try to make protecting Pauly second nature. We put Sneaky Snake (our cat) in the bedroom and close the door when we let our budgies or cockatiel out of their cages. In fact, the first thing we ask each other before one of us heads for the birdcage is, "Where's Snake?"

It's different with Rooster (our amazon parrot). He can play on his cage-top gym or perch on the T-stand, no matter where Snake is, because Snake's slightly scared of him. I'd never put Rooster on the floor with Snake and leave the room, but he's safe on a stand, as long as someone is nearby.

> **Avian Adventures**
>
> People who get a kitten after they already have a pet bird often end up with a delightful duo. Cats raised with birds usually can be trusted around "their" birds, although they still consider other birds to be prey. But that's only half of it. Parrots think cats are pretty cool and often entertain themselves by calling the cat. My hispanolan amazon, Cuka, called "her cats" every night ("Here kitty, kitty, kitty"), and wasn't content until they curled up on top of her cage.

Rover's Reactions

After their initial excitement wears off and they receive a few firm "No!" commands, most dogs gradually lose interest in small birds, as long as the birds are in their cages. But even the most gentle dog will be dangerous around a loose bird. Keep your small bird caged when your dog is in the room. Rover may approach Pauly with the best intentions, use a paw to manipulate the budgie's direction so they can meet muzzle to beak, and accidentally crush the little bird in the process. It only takes one paw, one time, to stamp out Pauly. Quell your curiosity about how they will react to each other. What you don't know won't hurt your bird.

Dogs are more dangerous to big birds than cats are, especially when the bird is walking around on the floor. Twitching tails and wet noses look like toys to some birds, and birds always taste their toys. Rover may be the calmest dog in the county, but imagine how he'd react if an amazon parrot pinched his nose while he was snoring on the rug. Keep Pauly on his perch when Rover is around. Most important, *you* be around whenever more than one pet is loose in the same room.

The Child–Bird Combo

"Difficult but worth it," might be your motto when helping children and birds learn to live together. Everyone's safety is the most important consideration. Children can hurt birds, and vice versa. Kids and birds can also scare each other without even trying. As prey animals, birds fear fast movements and shrill sounds, while youngsters move quickly and have high-pitched voices. On the other hand, children fear loud noises too, and piercing squawks may make them cringe.

If you have babies or toddlers, and a small bird, your best bet is to place your bird's cage high enough so your child can't reach it. Then, children who are too young to know better won't poke curious fingers between the bars and possibly get a painful bite. Putting the cage out of reach will also keep your toddler from opening the door and freeing Pauly. A childproof latch on the cage door is a good idea if your kid is into climbing.

If Pauly is a medium to large parrot, don't hang his cage high. Instead, use a baby gate to keep Junior out of the bird room when you aren't around to supervise. In Part 4 I'll tell you how height affects birds' dispositions. For now, all you need to know is that housing a parrot too high can be bad news for his personality. Height has no adverse effect on finches or canaries, and may not make much difference to budgies or cockatiels, but it sure can turn bigger birds into wannabe tyrants.

From about the age of four (depending on the child's self-control and emotional maturity), children who show interest in Pauly can help you care for him. Examples of ways that kids can help (provided you have patience and won't freak out over some spilled seed) are bringing you the bird's dirty dishes, putting the daily seed and pellet rations into the food dishes, changing the water and even misting the bird—all under your encouraging supervision, of course. When children are very young, helping you care for a pet should be fun—a privilege, not a responsibility. Do it yourself when you're in a hurry. Chubby little fingers sometimes spill stuff.

Bird Brainers

Children enjoy communicating with birds. In fact, behaviorists believe people talk more to their birds than they do to their dogs or cats.

Children who are ready to help care for a pet are also ready to learn some simple rules. Here are a few to get you started. You may have to change some to fit your situation:

➤ Don't poke your fingers into Pauly's cage.

➤ Don't tease Pauly (you might have to explain what teasing is).

➤ Don't open the cage door.

➤ Don't put anything into the birdcage without permission from Mom or Dad.

➤ Don't let your friends play with Pauly. (Explain that they haven't been taught how to behave around a bird and may scare him.)

➤ And most important of all, if Pauly is bigger than a budgie, never put your face near Pauly.

By the time they are fourth graders, some kids develop a real understanding of animals. In fact, older children often interact with birds better than grown-ups do because they take the time to learn the bird's body language. If Pauly is hand tame and Junior has patience and wants to work with him, show Junior how to use the "up" command (see Chapter 13). Then put Pauly on the floor, have your young bird trainer sit on the floor too, and watch how well they work together. Don't do the drill sergeant thing, but gentle advice ("Let's see what happens if you put your finger a little lower") could work wonders.

Maybe you're getting a bird because your child has been begging for one. Even so, don't expect Julie to take full responsibility (no matter what she promised). Your child will learn the most valuable lessons about pet care when it's a family affair and she has an excellent example (yes, that's you) to follow. Get a pet only if you are willing to oversee and help with its care without making threatening remarks ("If you don't clean the cage right now, I'm giving that darn bird away!"). Birds aren't disposable objects, like broken toys or outgrown skates. A pet deserves affection, care and a permanent home, and threatening to give it anything less sends your child a sorry message.

Older children and birds can develop close bonds.

What type of bird should you get your child? The following table shows a few best bets.

Good Birds for Children

Children 9 through 12
Budgie
Cockatiel
Brotogeris (a.k.a. pocket parrot)
Lovebird
Quaker parakeet (a.k.a. monk parakeet)

Teenagers can also handle
Pionus parrot
Jardine's parrot

Chances are Pauly will be watching when Junior and Julie kiss you good-bye and go off to college. When helping your child select a bird, remember that it may be yours one day. Even if your kids amaze you by taking care of it on their own, try to give the bird some attention so the transition won't be too difficult when the kids are gone.

The Naming Game

Many bird owners pick names that refer to their bird's appearance (Kelly, Sunny), favorite food (Peanut, Mango), or personality (Happy, Chipper). Others name their bird for its area of origin (Congo, Paco). Birds are named after politicians, actors, musicians, and beloved aunts and uncles. If the perfect name doesn't come to mind as soon as you see your bird, live with him for a few days and his reactions will help you name him. Maybe he'll make a special noise every time you enter the room, or dance when you play a certain song.

Bird Brainers

While your first choice for a child's bird might be the budgie, there is a downside to this tiny charmer. Budgies have shorter life spans than the other birds on the list, and are fragile because of their small size. You may want a sturdier pet for your youngster.

Many excellent names aren't gender specific, and that's a good thing, because you may not know if your bird is male or female. Even if you make a mistake and realize it later, it's usually fixable. Our goose, originally named Sammy, became Samantha when she laid an egg.

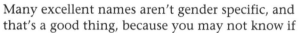

Avian Adventures

I named one of my birds even before I paid for him. My mexican red-head strutted toward me across the pet shop floor and bowed his head for petting when I knelt to meet him. His attitude was cocky and his red head reminded me of a rooster's comb. "Hi," I said. "You look like a little rooster." And Rooster he stayed.

When You Already Have a Bird or Two

Do you already have a pet bird? I'll bet you can hardly wait to see how he will react to your new bird. But waiting is a must. Unfortunately, you'll have to be patient. Real patient. Okay, a whole month patient. That's how long you should keep your birds separated to protect your "old" pet from any diseases the newcomer may carry. Since most bird diseases have an incubation period of seven to fourteen days, potential problems should show up within a month, even if the new bird caught a virus just before you bought him.

Many viruses are airborne and can travel through your home anyway, but it's still safest to put your new bird in a different room, as far from your other bird(s) as you can. Feed and clean up after your regulars daily before taking care of the newcomer. Also, be sure to wash your hands well after interacting with your new pet, and keep everyone's dishes separate and clean.

Will it be easy? Nope. But not for the reasons you think. Sure, you'll have to wash so often your hands will have water wrinkles, but the worst part could be the noise. Birds that can hear, but not see each other, may call back and forth incessantly until the month is up and they share the same room. While that could be lovely if you're isolating canaries, earplugs may be the ticket if you're trying to manage macaws.

Bird Brainers

Whether you have large or small birds, two need a more spacious home than one. A new home is best. It's neutral territory to both birds, which leads to bonding rather than brawling.

Bird Brainers

Sometimes you can shortcut the getting-to-know-you period. If your birds moon over each other while living in cages side by side, try them out on a play gym together after a week or two.

Getting to Know You

If your new bird looks and acts as healthy as the day you got him after 30 days is up, it's okay to make him a roommate (but not a cage mate) of your other bird. Put Pauly's cage beside Polly's, but not so close that one of them could pinch (or worse) the other one's toes during a disagreement.

What if you want them to live together, preen each other, maybe even make baby birds? Let them live side-by-side-but-not-real-close for a month—then, if they are small birds and seem to be getting along, go ahead and put them together. Big birds are capable of doing serious damage to each other, so before putting them together, move on to one of the following steps:

1. Move their cages close together, open their doors and let them meet each other on top of their cages, if and when they choose.

2. If they are both hand tame, test their attitudes toward each other on neutral territory by putting both of them on the floor or the same play gym. In either case, watch their reactions carefully and be ready to separate them immediately if they show signs of aggression. You can always try again after they know each other better. Cage big birds together only after they obviously seek each other's attention and no longer behave aggressively toward each other. And keep your ears tuned for arguments during the first few days.

The Least You Need to Know

➤ Bring your bird home when nothing exciting is happening at your place.

➤ Put your bird's cage in a draft-free area where the family congregates—but not the kitchen, unless you have no other choice.

➤ Keep your bird away from toxic fumes and beware of non-stick coatings. They emit dangerous fumes when they overheat.

➤ Buy dishes, perches and toys that are suitable for the size of your bird.

➤ Bring your bird home in a carrier designed for safely transporting pets.

➤ Give your bird low-key attention for the first 48 hours.

➤ Keep your bird off the floor if you have other pets.

➤ Birds make good pets for older children, but bird care should be a family affair.

Chapter 7

Home, Safe, Stimulating Home

In This Chapter

➤ Designing Polly's pad

➤ The joys of toys

➤ Helping Polly play

➤ Encouraging exercise

➤ Home, safe home

Sure Polly's in a cage, but she's a pet, not a prisoner. This chapter will tell you how to turn a bunch of space surrounded by bars into a happy home. It will also help you select toys and exercise equipment to stimulate your bird's body and brain, and tell you what types of toys to avoid.

Interior Design

Wouldn't you hate it if you had to climb over your TV set to get to the refrigerator? Or slide sideways between the couch and the wall to get to the bathroom? That's how Polly will feel if you overcrowd her cage, or place her perches, toys and dishes where they are hard to get to or interfere with each other.

Whether or not a bird sits on a perch or plays with a toy often has to do with the item's location. Starting with perches, be sure that Polly's are placed at different heights, and that no matter which direction she sits on them, her droppings won't land in her food or water dishes. One perch should be secured as high as Polly can

Bird Brainers

Many parrots are clumsy, and baby parrots are the most awkward of all. If Polly is a baby, have mercy on her awkwardness. Place her food and water dishes, and a couple of her perches, rather low in the cage until she learns to climb well. After a month or so, she'll be able to attain greater heights.

Squawk!

Don't hurry to the nearest clump of trees to cut branches unless you are absolutely, positively certain the trees haven't been sprayed. Take wood only from the healthiest-looking trees, and make sure you secure them well in Polly's cage.

comfortably stand in the cage without stooping or bumping her head. That's because birds naturally seek a high spot when resting or settling in for the night.

In Chapter 6, I talked about the variety of perches available in pet shops, but barely touched on some of the best perches of all— the ones you gather yourself (given the time, inclination and opportunity). Natural wood has to be replaced often because birds will chew it, but it's hard to beat for several reasons. It's free, it doubles as a toy, it satisfies Polly's urge to chew and it helps keep her beak in good shape. Hardwood perches of ash, beech or oak usually last the longest. You'll have to replace softer wood such as poplar, pine, basswood, willow and branches from fruit trees more frequently, but it will be worth it to watch Polly sink her beak into them.

Clutter-Free Cages

When designing Polly's cage, avoid clutter. Cramming too much stuff into her cage could overwhelm her and keep her from enjoying any of it. It could also crowd her so much that she won't have room to stretch, preen or play.

So what should you do with the five fabulous toys you bought (you know who you are), even though I suggested only two or three? Put three of them in a drawer for later. Parrots eventually destroy or become bored with their toys, and it's always nice to have a new one ready as a replacement.

Swings

One popular cage accessory that every bird should have a chance to try is the swing. If Polly's cage didn't come with a swing, or if the diameter of the swing is wrong for her feet, you'll find many choices at the pet store. Choose one that's big enough so Polly doesn't have to hunch over to use it.

When attaching it to the cage, make sure it won't take Polly for a ride over her dishes, or bang against perches or the sides of the cage. Don't be disappointed if Polly doesn't hop on it right away. Some birds seem to love swinging, but others may ignore their swing or use it as just another perch. If Polly won't go near her swing after a week or two (it often takes birds a long time to try something new), try moving it to a different location in the cage.

Why Toys Are a Must

What if you were completely healthy but couldn't work, travel, watch television, read, exercise, play golf, go fishing, dancing, swimming or do whatever you do for R&R anymore? Imagine you couldn't shop or cook either, and all your meals were slipped through a slot in the door by the person who picks up after you. In fact, all you could do is sit in the same room staring at the same walls. For variety, you might change chairs, but that would be your only option.

Maybe you're so stressed out that you'd like to try it for awhile, but deep down you know it would get old real fast. Forced into comfortable but completely boring confinement, you'd probably become even more stressed, because you'd have no outlet for your energy. Soon you'd develop nervous tics and bad habits—maybe even self-destructive ones like biting your fingernails, or twisting and pulling at your hair. Eventually, you'd feel like screaming. And maybe you would.

Bird Brainers

Parrots aren't the only birds that like swings. Your finches and canaries will also enjoy being swingers.

In the wild, parrots are kept busy finding food, choosing mates, raising young and evading predators; but pet parrots have everything done for them, and they live in comfortable confinement. When they are bored or ignored, they can't make themselves feel better by playing golf or going to the mall. It's no wonder some of them behave badly, scream incessantly, and develop self-destructive, nervous tics.

Avian Adventures

According to bird behaviorists and just plain parrot owners, an adult parrot is as emotionally developed as a two-year-old child, and as intelligent as a three-year-old child. What would a toddler with nothing to do be like? Few parents want to find out, which is why toys are a mighty big business.

Like humans, birds need things to keep their minds occupied and relieve stress. Stress? Yes, pet birds do suffer stress, and it can cause a multitude of behavior problems (as you'll see in Chapter 19). For now, all you need to know is that toys are a necessity, not an extra. Besides using them to stimulate their brains and exercise their bodies, birds also use toys to act out (and get over) their aggressive moods, alleviate anxiety, and relieve boredom. While toys alone won't solve every parrot problem, they sure do help.

Toys are designed to be used by birds in different ways. Following are the basic types that are fashioned for parrots. When choosing toys for your bird, make sure she has one from the exercise category and another of a different type.

Staging mock fights with a toy is natural and healthy, so choose items that are big and tough enough to stand up to your bird when she's feeling aggressive. For example, toys featuring colorful plastic beads are favorites with budgies, but are unsafe for birds big enough to shatter them.

Exercise Toys

Climbing helps keep caged birds in good shape, so the best exercise toys encourage climbing. An oldie, but still a reliable goodie, is a series of four or five interlocking rings with a bell at the bottom. When hung from the top of the cage, it will stimulate your bird to go up and down through the rings, providing excellent exercise.

Originally created in colorful plastic for budgies, the hanging ring toy has been enlarged and strengthened, so amazons, cockatoos and even macaws can benefit from weaving their way up, down and through. Bamboo versions work well enough for cockatiels, lovebirds and some of the smaller parrots. For bigger birds, buy either strong nylon or metal rings. Choose rings that are big enough for your bird to get her whole body through, and hang the toy far enough from the sides of the cage so Polly can flap her wings while doing gymnastics.

Other exercise toys that cultivate climbing include wooden ladders, knotted natural ropes, heavy-duty nylon chains and almost any series of colorful shapes. Suspend climbing toys from the cage top and well away from the sides of the cage.

Squawk!

Lots of toys have rings on them. Make sure they are either way too small for your bird to put her head through, or big enough so her whole body can go through. Otherwise, she could get a ring stuck around her neck.

Polly Sez

Preening is how a bird keeps her feathers clean and orderly. It's what a bird is doing when she runs her beak down her feathers.

Preening Toys

Available in all sizes and shapes, preening toys stimulate Polly to preen them, much as she would another parrot in the wild. Sugar's favorite is a bouquet of peacock feathers held together by a metal connector and attached to the side of her cage. We have to buy her a new one about every four months because she preens them bald.

Our budgies have a smaller preening toy made of sisal. Pinto played with it often for the first five years of his life, and it had to be replaced a couple of times. Ever since Bluebell joined him, it's been practically abandoned, though. Now he loves preening his lady.

Given the right equipment, parrots make their own fun.

Puzzle Toys

Puzzle toys are designed to make birds figure out how to get the built-in reward they can see but can't reach. For example, Rooster has a yellow wooden box with almonds inside that hangs from a chain. The box is solid on the top and bottom, but its sides are bars made from dowels. These are spaced so he can see the almonds, even manipulate them a little, but can't get them out. Rooster knows he'll have to chew through the bars to get to the almonds, and has started the demolition process. I've heard of parrots who managed to manipulate the almonds in such a way that they pulled one or two out through the bars without mangling the wood, but that isn't going to happen at my house. Meanwhile, Rooster is happily occupied, so the toy is working well.

Another type of puzzle toy is a divided dish of tough molded plastic designed to hold three of a parrot's favorite treats. Its cap is a lid with three holes, so

Squawk!

Sometimes big birds become so attached to their preening toy that they treat it like a mate and aggressively defend it against anyone who comes near the cage. If your bird was always friendly, but starts growling or biting after he gets a preening toy, take away the toy—forever.

Polly can see the goodies inside. Her task is to lift the lid, which moves up and down on a chain, or knock it askew so she can get to the treats. Rooster got one of these contraptions for the holidays and hasn't figured it out yet (but it's only the beginning of January now). So far, he likes beating up on it because the plastic bumping the chain makes neat noises. One of these days he'll hit it just right and find a peanut or an almond.

Chew Toys

Chew toys are usually made of wood, rawhide, nylon, acrylic, strong plastic or a combination of several of these materials. Sometimes hard nuts, such as walnuts or brazil nuts, are also included. A variety of shapes and colors are usually strung together so that the bird can move them up and down a chain, rattle them, bite them or beat them up.

One of Rooster's chew toys is made of a piece of hard wood with the bark still on (today), and several large, colorful, molded plastic beads. He also has one made of leather that's shaped like a shoe, with a small lava rock dangling from the end of it. Pinto and Bluebell share a tiny chew toy made of wooden rings and colored beads with a bell at the bottom.

Natural wood perches double as chew toys.

Grasping Toys

Most medium to large parrots, and a few small ones, like toys they can grasp in one foot and pulverize with their beak. Since these toys are small and don't hang from the top or sides of the cage, they don't count as clutter. Polly can have a couple of regular toys and a grasping toy, too.

The most popular grasping toys are made of soft wood and are safely dyed a variety of brilliant shades. They are inexpensive, come in a variety of shapes, including rectangles, triangles, lollipops and barbells, and can be purchased several to the bag. That's a good thing because Rooster destroys one every other day. I thought he went through a lot of them, until I saw a cockatoo turn his into toothpicks in three minutes.

Some birds enjoy grasping metal toys, and spoons seem to lead the list. Try giving one to your bird. Occasionally, a large parrot will learn to use her spoon as an eating utensil. More commonly, parrots amuse themselves by dropping the spoon to the cage floor, just as their human walks by. Maybe they think they've trained their person to jump on command.

Bird Brainers

Small chunks of natural wood with the bark still on make great grasping toys. Before getting out your pruning shears, make sure the tree hasn't been sprayed with pesticides.

Bird Brainers

One unshelled walnut or brazil nut makes a good grasping toy.

Bird-Activated Toys

One of the newer high-tech toys is a music box for birds. Foot- or beak-activated, it comes in two sizes (big and bigger), and is meant for parrots that are conure size and larger. Rooster's plays *Take Me Out to the Ball Game*. He's had it for 10 days now, and so far, I activate it for him and he cocks his head and listens. That's good enough for now. It takes birds a long time to learn how to work something that's totally different from anything they've tried before.

Do I Take My Own Advice?

Did you count how many toys I described as belonging to Rooster, and catch me ignoring my own advice about not crowding the cage? I plead guilty to being unable to pass up an intriguing new toy, but not guilty on the crowding charge. Rooster has three toys in his cage, and one is a grasping toy. Two other toys are attached to his cage-top gym and two hang from the T-stand. The rest are in a drawer awaiting the next rotation, along with a bunch of cockatiel and budgie gizmos. I rotate at least one toy every month in each birdcage and on the play gyms. It gives my birds something different to see and do.

Fun for Finches, Canaries and Other Passerines

While toys aren't as important to finches and canaries as they are to parrots, Caruso will probably groom a preening toy and may enjoy pecking at a colorful hanging toy with a bell attached. Or he might like to play with items he can push around. Try putting a whole (in the shell) walnut, pecan or peanut in the cage, or even a Ping-Pong ball.

Tiny songsters also enjoy natural wood, but as perches rather than chunks for chewing. Make sure the branches haven't been sprayed, and attach them to the cage with the bark and even some leaves on. Just remember that canaries and finches have to fly to be healthy, so don't crowd the cage. Make sure Caruso has smooth sailing from perch to perch.

Polly Sez

Passerines is the scientific name for small to medium perching songbirds. They have grasping feet, with one toe pointing to the back and three pointing front. Finches and canaries are passerines, as are more than half the birds in the world.

Bird Brainers

Don't trash an old toy that bores your bird but is still in good shape. Instead, wash it well and put it away. In six months, Polly may welcome it back.

Buyer Beware

There's no institute or regulating body that tests bird toys for safety and suitability. Your bird depends on you to do that. Examine each toy carefully before you buy it, and avoid the following:

➤ Cheap, brittle plastic toys. They can be shattered by a budgie and could do serious damage to your bird's mouth.

➤ Mirrored toys. While generally safe for small birds, they don't belong in the same cage with big beaks.

➤ Rope toys. Buy them only if you are diligent about trimming your bird's nails. Otherwise, they can trap toes.

➤ Weighted toys. Lead is often the weight used in weighted toys, so unless the label says otherwise, avoid them. Your bird could break the toy and play with the poisonous weight.

➤ Chain toys with loose links. Birds love chain toys, but beware of bargains. Safe chains have closed links, so they can't catch a curious toe or busy beak.

➤ Ring toys the wrong size for your bird. Never buy a toy with a ring that your bird may be able to put her head but not her body through.

➤ Toys with bells. Birds like bells, but for safety's sake, make sure the clapper isn't made of lead. It should be attached so your bird won't be able to work it loose and cut her mouth on the sharp edges. Small cowbells are often favorites. Birds also enjoy traditional jingle bells, but it's best if they play with them only with supervision. There have been cases where tongues, beaks or toes were caught in the cracks.

➤ Toys that may not be strong enough to stand up to your bird. No matter how attractive the toy, don't buy it if there is any question in your mind about whether your bird can break it.

Your canary will enjoy a natural perch.

Create a Toy

Let's face it: A lot of the toys we buy our birds are more for our amusement than theirs. We like to watch their reactions to the newest innovations, but our birds don't know the difference between new-age toys and homemade playthings. They just want to entertain themselves, and often find simple toys as intriguing as expensive ones. As soon as you learn what type of playthings Polly likes best, you'll be able to create homemade toys for her.

How's this for simple? Many hookbills of all sizes think that several pieces of uncooked pasta make a party. Sugar (my cockatiel) is playing with the three-colored, twirly type right now. Of course, raw pasta is a one-day (sometimes one-hour) toy. Pulverizing it is the fun part.

If you use unscented toilet paper and paper towels, give Polly the empty tubes when you use up the rolls. She'll have fun ripping them up. Or make a puzzle toy out of a toilet paper tube. Just fold and pinch one end shut, put an almond or a peanut inside (unsalted in the shell) and pinch the other end shut. Then give it to Polly. If she doesn't catch on, poke a couple of holes in the tube so she can see the nut inside.

Right now, Rooster is on his T-stand (you know, the one with the colorful toys dangling from it). But he's not playing with them. Instead, he's peeling the bark from a stick of pine and throwing it at me. One piece just went down the back of my shirt. Natural pine—untreated, unsprayed and free from any tree disease—makes a wonderful grasping toy. If the needles are still on, it's even better. It only takes a few minutes to gather enough so Polly can have a piece every day or so for months. If pine isn't available, your bird will welcome willow.

Oops! This macaw could hurt his mouth by breaking a budgie toy.

Many birds like to chew leather. Get untreated and untanned or vegetable tanned rawhide at the craft store. Cut it into strips, tie a strip to the cage and Polly has a plaything. For variety, string Cheerios or macaroni on it.

You've got the idea, now go for it. You can create a toy that combines a few of your bird's favorite things.

Introducing a New Toy

Birds accept new items slowly. Polly may not appreciate something new invading her home, even if the something is a toy you bought or built just for her. Instead of putting a new plaything in her cage immediately, lay it down beside her cage or hang it near the cage for a few days before making it part of Polly's decor. Anyplace where Polly can see but not touch it may pique her interest, and make her accept it sooner, rather than later.

Bird Brainers

Most parrots savor shoelaces. Some say it's because the little plastic tubes on the ends remind them of pinfeathers. If you have a plain white shoelace, new or used, wash it, rinse it well, and tie it to the side of the cage after it dries.

Why Won't Polly Play?

Gee whiz! You've bought the neatest looking toy you could find, maybe even created one especially for Polly. Then you introduced it slowly, by the book. That was 10 days ago and she's still stepping around it as if it were a tree snake. What went wrong?

Nothing went wrong. Polly's just being a parrot. Parrots survive in the wild by being more conservative than Rush Limbaugh. They shy away from strange objects and unfamiliar food. Why? Because they are born with a fear of becoming a bigger bird's (or a snake's) breakfast, and they are instinctively careful about what they eat. After all, even the prettiest wild berries might be poisonous. Now you know Polly's secret. Under all her bluff, she has a careful, conservative nature, and is most comfortable with routine. Think of it as a positive trait that she inherited from generations of wild ancestors with sense enough to be survivors.

Will Polly ever play with her new toys? Sure. But it may take several weeks. Whatever you do, don't give up and stop putting toys in Polly's cage. She needs the stimulation of new things for her physical and mental health, even if she hasn't learned how to play with them yet.

Squawk!

When making a toy with knotted leather thongs or when tying leather directly to your bird's cage, be sure the knots can't work themselves loose and form a noose that could trap your bird's head.

Helping Polly Play

If your bird was introduced to a new toy slowly, but still hasn't touched it within 10 days, some of these ideas may help:

➤ Put the new toy in a different part of the cage. Location may be everything.

➤ Sometimes you can speed up acceptance by tearing paper towels into strips and tying them loosely around the new toy. Few birds can resist something so easy to shred, and Polly may start playing with the toy in the process.

➤ Take the new toy out of the cage and play with it yourself while your bird watches. Then leave the toy beside, but not in the cage. Play with it a couple of times a day for a few days. Then put the toy back in the cage in a different location.

➤ If the toy is made of molded plastic, nylon or another non-porous material, put a dab of peanut butter or another favorite soft treat on it. Wash it off well at the end of the day.

➤ Remove the toy if your bird refuses to play with it, and put a different one in its place. Even though you chose it carefully, Polly might have thought the game was lame. Of course, parrots reserve the right to change their minds. Give her the toy again in a few months and see what happens.

After looking at a toy for a few days, Polly may want to play with it.

Play Gyms for Psittacines (That's Parrots)

Play gyms, cage-top gyms and parrot playgrounds are your bird's membership to the athletic club. They provide exercise equipment so Polly can keep in shape, occupy herself and vent enough steam to be a well-behaved bird. One good gym is all you need because you can make occasional alterations to add interest.

Since climbing is one of the best exercises for birds, good play gyms include either a ladder, several branches from a real hardwood tree or dowels placed so they encourage climbing. They may also have a swing, food and water dishes with built-in holders, a variety of additional playthings, or eyelets so you can choose and attach your own toys.

Polly Sez

Psittacines is the scientific name for parrots, and only parrots.

An incredible selection of play gyms is available. When choosing one, first eliminate every gym that's too small for your bird. Check out the perch diameter, the amount of space between dowels, branches, or rungs of the ladder (your bird should have to reach a little), and whether Polly's tail will clear the bottom when she sits on the swing or the perches. The highest perch should be spacious enough so she can flap her wings without hitting anything. Also, be sure the top of the swing is tall enough so she can sit up straight.

Play gyms come in all shapes and sizes. This one was created for a cockatiel.

Next, decide whether you want a freestanding floor-model gym (preferably on casters for bigger birds), a hanging gym that attaches to your ceiling like a planter, a tabletop model (nice for smaller birds) or onc that attaches to the top of the bird cage. Some cages come with gyms on top. The best ones have a tray under them so droppings won't fall into the birdcage and foul the food, water and perches.

Most modern gyms, no matter what the design, include a tray to catch the droppings. A few still don't, and Rooster has one of those dinosaurs in a cage-top model. He got it before some of the super new ones arrived on the market, and likes it so much that we haven't trashed it yet. How do we know how much he likes it? Because he turns the dowels beside the swing into wood chips at least once a week, and needs a replacement climbing dowel about once a month. To keep Rooster from fouling his food and water, I remove his dishes when he plays on the gym.

Does Polly need a play gym to be healthy? Yes and no. Yes, she needs the climbing exercise and the opportunity to play outside her cage. No, it doesn't always take a play gym to keep a parrot healthy. If Polly waddles after you from room to room and climbs up the recliner to watch the evening news on your arm, she doesn't need a special area for exercise. But if you have small children, or if Rover or Tabby's claim to the carpet keeps Polly on high ground, she needs an exercise area of her own.

Avian Adventures

If you (or your spouse) are handy with tools, you can build a unique play gym that matches Polly's persona. First, look at the different types of play gyms available in pet shops and through ads in bird magazines (see Appendix A for a list of magazines), and decide on the basic style you want. Then make one with Polly's preferences in mind. Dowels of various diameters are available in lumberyards, hardware stores and craft shops. Buy extra. The more Polly enjoys her gym, the more often you'll have to repair it.

Sound Security

If no one will be home for long hours, keep music playing for Polly. Birds are stressed by the sound of silence. In the wild, silence signals the approach of a predator, but background noise, like birds chirping and monkeys chattering, mean all is well. Since you probably don't have several birds or a noisy monkey, simulate the sounds of safety with a radio, a television or a continuous-play tape player. Besides feeling protected, Polly may learn some slogans or songs.

Bird Brainers

Don't buy a play gym for canaries or finches. A spacious cage will give them enough exercise. Also, they shouldn't play outside their cages because their wings aren't trimmed.

Bird Brainers

Tapes that entertain and train birds while their owners are away are available in some pet shops and through ads in bird magazines. More about them in Chapter 15.

Safe House Plants

Because so many bird owners have children and other pets, most parrots live in a controlled environment, where their out-of-the-cage exercise takes place on a play gym or in a special part of the house. But if your household consists only of adults and Polly, you may want to let her pigeon-toe through the whole place when you're at home.

In Chapter 6, I suggested keeping plants away from your bird's cage and other equipment, since so many houseplants are toxic. That's easy, but it isn't enough if Polly has lots of freedom. Even if all your poisonous plants are hanging out of her reach, one fallen leaf could kill her. Some plants, like lily of the valley, are so deadly that just drinking water out of the vase that held them can be fatal.

As conservative as birds are about unfamiliar food, pet birds still have a tendency to taste things they shouldn't. Since birds are attracted to plants, the safest way to make sure wandering Polly isn't poisoned is to keep only nonpoisonous plants in your home, patio and porch. Here's a partial list of safe plants that are commonly found in homes and patios. If one of your plants isn't listed, chances are it's toxic to birds. If you don't know what type of plants you have, or wonder if a particular plant is safe or poisonous, ask at your local nursery.

House and Patio Plants that Are Safe Around Birds

African violet	Monkey plant
Aloe	Nasturtium
Asparagus fern	Norfolk island pine
Baby's tears	Parlour palm
Bamboo palm	Peperomia
Begonia	Petunia
Boston fern	Prayer plant
Bougainvillea	Purple-passion vine (a.k.a. velvet plant)
Christmas cactus	Rubber fig
Creeping fig	Sago palm
Date palm	Snake plant (a.k.a. mother-in-law's-tongue)
Fan palm	Spider plant (a.k.a. ribbon plant)
Fiddleleaf fig	Swedish ivy
Kangaroo vine	Umbrella tree (a.k.a. schefflera)
Kentia palm	Wandering jew
Lady palm	Weeping fig
Maidenhair fern	Zebra plant

Fresh Air and Sunshine

On pretty spring and summer days (or any time of year in the deep South), you might want to give Polly some fresh air on the porch or patio. While it's easier to put her outside on her play gym or T-stand than it is to move her whole cage, don't do it unless the area is completely enclosed or you will be with her the whole time (take your telephone with you). In an open area without a cage around her, Polly would be an easy catch for a loose cat or dog, or a hungry hawk or raccoon.

When putting Polly outside, make sure she's out of direct sunlight. An area may be shady when you set the cage out but baking in the sun an hour later.

If you won't be with Polly while she's outside, make sure you can hear her from the house and keep an ear out for any calls that might mean danger. Even big birds in strong cages can be hurt by a huge dog or a mean person. Also, beware of burglars. Parrots have a high resale value, and a bird that regularly spends time outside alone may be targeted by a thief. For more about outdoor safety, see Chapter 8.

The Least You Need to Know

➤ Design Polly's cage so she has room to spread her wings and move from perch to perch. Her perches should be at different heights. Place them so her droppings won't land in her dishes.

➤ Every bird needs a couple of toys for her physical and mental health. One of them should encourage climbing.

➤ Play gyms give birds a change of scenery and an opportunity to exercise. They can be purchased ready-made, or you can build one yourself.

➤ Many houseplants are poisonous to birds. If you aren't sure about yours, ask at the plant nursery.

➤ Fresh air is good for birds on a nice day, but Polly can't handle direct sunlight.

➤ Beware of predatory animals and humans when putting Polly on the porch or patio.

Chapter 8

Out and About

In This Chapter

➤ Preventing not so great escapes

➤ Playing it safe outdoors

➤ Getting your lost bird back

➤ How to hit the road

I'll never forget an incident that happened several years ago, when I lived in the Florida Keys. Ray, a big, strapping fellow in his mid-20s, worked at the local dive shop on Grassy Key. Ray was memorable because wherever he went, his cheerful cockatiel rode along on his shoulder. The friendly bird knew a few words, whistled several tunes and was always willing to be petted. Everybody knew the pair because the contrast between Ray, a large man, and little Fred was so charming.

One day I bumped into Ray at the post office, and almost didn't recognize him because his bird wasn't on his shoulder. "Where's Fred?" I asked, and then wished I could have swallowed my words when Ray's face reddened and puckered. "Gone," he whispered, his voice barely a croak.

Days later he told me what happened. As they were leaving the dive shop, something startled Fred and he tried to fly. His wings were clipped, but had grown out just enough so the wind caught him and carried him out to sea. Ray raced into the water and swam after him, but lost sight of his little friend within seconds and never saw him again.

What a tragedy! But Fred's death won't be a complete waste if his story reminds you to keep your bird safe outdoors. In this chapter, I'll tell you how.

Watch those Wings

It's tempting to take a tame bird outside, especially if the bird enjoys a change of scenery and likes to play on the (chemical-free) lawn. But keeping Pauly safe outside your home takes some doing. The problem is, Pauly will probably be hard to catch (or find) if he takes off, and he isn't equipped to contend with Mother Nature. Born in captivity (usually), your pet bird never had to forage for food, avoid raptors (that's hawks and eagles, not dinosaurs from *Jurassic Park*) or even find his way from one place to another. So after the impulse that made him fly off fades away, Pauly won't know how to get home.

Bird Brainers

Wings are considered trimmed when the first five to eight primary feathers on each wing are clipped. But five doesn't begin to keep a cockatiel down. It takes eight clipped feathers on each side to keep your crested companion earthbound.

"Aha," you may be thinking. "Pauly's wings are trimmed, so he can't go far enough to get lost. If he tries to take off, he'll just flap his way to a soft landing a few feet from me."

You're right, of course. That's exactly what should happen. But things don't always happen the way they should. Just last night, Sugar (our cockatiel) left Tom's arm, soared over the sofa and landed on top of a chair at the other end of the room. Boy, were we surprised! After all, we just trimmed her wings… last week wasn't it? Well, no… maybe it was a little longer than that. When we looked at Sugar's wings, we knew it was a lot longer than that, because she had two new flight feathers on one side and three on the other. And while that's not enough flight feathers to fly well, it's more than enough to get a small bird into big trouble in the great outdoors.

So the first thing you should do before venturing outside with Pauly is to open his wings and examine them. Don't rely on remembering when you trimmed them. Time flies, and soon trimmed birds do, too.

Have Pauly's wings grown out since you brought him home? Chapter 18 will tell you how to trim them at home. What? You'd have to wrestle with Pauly just to look at his wings and you're afraid he might win! Shut the door. He's not ready to play outdoors. But someday he will be. Check out Chapters 13 and 14. Meanwhile, take him to a professional for a trim. The inexpensive service is available at many pet shops.

Keeping Your Bird Safe Outside

If Pauly is hand tame and you want to give him some fresh air and freedom, *don't skip any of these steps*:

➤ Make sure his wings are trimmed.

➤ Live with a less-than-perfect lawn. Never let Pauly play on grass that was treated with herbicides, pesticides, fertilizer or any other chemicals.

➤ Keep Pauly out of trees, unless the tree is shorter than you and hasn't been treated with anything. Birds tend to climb, and even trimmed birds are mighty hard to catch once they reach the top of a tall tree.

➤ Don't leave Pauly alone when he's loose outside. Either take a cordless phone with you or let the answering machine do its job.

When I say "don't leave Pauly alone," I mean not even for a second. We live where a creek meets a river, and a hundred or more (yes, we've counted) wild ducks hang out here. Sometimes hawks or eagles pick up their dinner from our yard, and trust me, it happens in a heartbeat. Living in suburbia doesn't make Pauly safe from raptors, either. Years ago, when I lived in a neighborhood in Miami, Florida, my dog and I were an instant too late to stop an owl from making off with our half-grown pet duck. Besides raptors, dogs, cats, raccoons, skunks, children too young to know better, children old enough to know better and thieves could all target Pauly.

Squawk!

Here's a scary statistic. According to a survey conducted by the American Pet Product Manufacturers Association, seven percent of cockatiel owners and four percent of parakeet owners adopted their pets after finding them in their yard. Makes you wonder how many escapees weren't so lucky.

Avian Adventures

Some pet birds do survive in the wild. Maybe you've read about the tame parrot escapees thriving in flocks in Florida and southern California. It's true. My husband and I saw one flock of quaker parakeets while we were fishing in the Florida Everglades, and another flock just outside the gate at Busch Gardens near Tampa. Scientists who study birds tell us that in warm climates where food grows on trees year-round, some lost parrots do learn to live in the wild. What we don't know, but can only guess, is how many more pet birds don't even make it through their first day of flying free.

Oh No! Who Opened the Window?

Although I believe pet parrots of all sizes should have their wings trimmed, I know that some people really enjoy seeing their bird fly around the house. My own mother is one of them. When we lived in the same town, I used to trim her cockatiel's wings regularly. Before I moved across the country, I showed her how to do it and made sure the closest pet shop performed the service, in case she didn't want to.

That's my mother with Buttercup.

Buttercup was only trimmed twice after that—both times during my visits. The last few times I visited, trimming Buttercup was not a priority. In fact, it kept being put off until I realized my mother didn't want me to trim her pet. Instead, they had an early morning ritual where Buttercup soared in circles around the living room and returned to her cage on command. It all happened before I got up (after all, I was on vacation), so I caught them in the caper by accident. Both of them were obviously having fun. So much for good intentions.

Bird Brainers

Put the toilet seats down, and make sure there is nothing cooking in the kitchen and no dishes soaking in the sink when your bird is out and about.

Not everybody (especially not my mama) listens to even the best-intentioned advice. So if you did it your way and own a fully flighted bird, or if you did it my way but too much time has elapsed since the last time you gave your bird a trim—you should know what to do if Pauly wings it out the window.

A Tape in Time

Here's an entertaining project you should do even if you never plan to take Pauly outside. Do it now—before you forget—even if you're sure you'll never lose track of time and let his wings grow out. Just turn on your tape recorder and let Pauly be a singing, squawking, whistling or talking star. Tape his voice, urge him on a little so you get all his best sounds, and label the tape. Even if you never play it back to him, it will come in handy in an emergency (as you'll soon see). But playing it for him every so often, even if it's only once a month or so, is even better.

Bird Brainers

If you plan to let your bird fly free in the house, make sure all the windows and doors are closed, the ceiling fan is off and there are no poisonous plants or chemicals exposed. Keep window screens in good condition, without holes or tears.

Now What?

Take these steps if your bird takes off:

➤ Keep calm (yeah, sure). Okay, don't give in to hysteria. You have to be sensible enough to watch him. Try to see where he lands. If that's impossible, at least know which direction he went.

➤ If Pauly lands in a nearby tree (most escapees do) and is hand tame, approach the tree slowly and try to lure him down with his favorite things. Play your tape recording of his voice. Whistle, show him a peanut, sing a song—whatever your bird usually responds to.

➤ If you have another bird, bring him outside in his cage if the weather is warm. First, make sure the cage doors, feeder ports, and the tray are secure, so you don't have double trouble. Sometimes one bird will be able to call another to come home.

➤ Take Pauly's empty cage outside and put it where he'll have a bird's-eye view of the proceedings. Open the door as wide as it goes, and secure it so it won't close before he climbs in. Then put a spray of millet, a well-used toy and your bird's favorite treats inside—some in the dishes and some on the floor. Don't overdo it. You want the cage to look inviting, not strange. Put the tape recorder on the ground nearby and play your bird's recording. Then walk away (several yards) and watch patiently.

Bird Brainers

Should you use a ladder if your bird is in a tree? It depends on your bird and the height of the tree. A frightened bird may just keep climbing until he is higher than the ladder.

➤ Keep your eyes on Pauly in case he takes off for another tree, but use the time productively. If you have a cordless phone, call your neighbors while you're watching Pauly. Tell them what happened and describe Pauly. Leave your number and ask them to call immediately if they see him. Also call local veterinary offices, the humane society and any animal shelters in your area. Alert them about the escape, describe Pauly and leave your number. Sometimes radio and television stations make public service announcements about lost pets. It's worth a try, so call them too.

➤ If you have a spouse or older children at home, or a helpful friend, enlist their support. Pauly's favorite person can watch him while the other people make phone calls or knock on the neighbors' doors. Whatever you do, don't get into a blaming game with your family over who opened the window. Pauly won't come down if there's anger below.

➤ Even if you can still see Pauly, call the local newspapers and shopper papers and put classified ads in their lost and found sections. You can always cancel the ads if Pauly climbs down, but you'll want them in the papers as soon as possible if he flies out of sight.

➤ Prepare posters (this is a good project for your panicky children) and post them around the neighborhood. Include a description of Pauly and your phone number, and offer a reward.

LOST

blue and gray parakeet
(budgie)

Name: Petey
Last Seen: 200 block, Elm St.

Reward for information.

Please call 231-1234
or bring him to 252 Elm St.

➤ If your bird is still in the tree after dark, get up early. Birds are active at dawn, and Pauly may move.

➤ Keep trying, even if you can't find Pauly in the morning. Check back with the animal shelters every few days. Replace unreadable posters. Keep the ads in the papers. Check the lost and found section of newspapers from nearby communities. When you feel like giving up, don't. Instead, reread the Introduction to this book. I'll keep my fingers crossed for you.

Going Places by Car

While dogs are the companion of choice for people who like to take their pets along on outings, sometimes birds become travelers too. A veterinary checkup is one reason to take your bird for a ride. Moving is another. My birds moved with me from Florida to New York, and from New York to Montana, and weren't bothered a bit. Whether you're taking Pauly on a short drive or a cross-country trek, the following steps should keep him happy and healthy. Here's your checklist for safe travel:

Squawk!

Don't take your bird with you to the train or bus station. Both have a no-pets policy.

➤ Use your bird's cage for long trips, if it fits in your vehicle. It's part of home, and Pauly will probably prefer traveling in it.

➤ Remove anything from the cage that moves enough so it could hit your bird on sharp turns or quick stops—swings and exercise toys, for example.

➤ Remove the high perches from your bird's cage or carrier. When traveling, use only one perch and attach it very low.

➤ If Pauly's regular cage is too big for your vehicle, get him a traveling cage. A variety of travel accommodations are advertised in *Bird Talk* magazine (see Appendix A), and are available in some pet shops and by mail order. Choose a carrier big enough so Pauly can stand up straight, turn around and stretch his wings (at least one wing at a time).

➤ Pauly should ride on a seat, never on the floor. Heat from the engine often makes the floor the hottest part of the car, and toxic fumes are most concentrated there.

➤ Secure the cage or carrier with a seat belt, bungee cords or rope so it doesn't tip or roll over.

➤ When positioning Pauly's cage or carrier, be aware of where the vehicle's vents will blow. Birds need plenty of ventilation, but drafts are dangerous.

*Here are a few
kinds of carriers
for traveling.*

➤ Don't smoke in the car when traveling with Pauly. His respiratory system is too sensitive to handle smoke in close quarters.

➤ Instead of water, offer moist bread and juicy fresh fruit, such as slices of apple or peach, or a few grapes. Pauly will get enough liquid from them, and water won't spill all over his cage on stops and turns. Give him fruits he's already used to eating.

➤ Bring water from home and use it to fill the water dish when you stop driving for the day. Water varies a great deal between cities, and strange water can make pets (and sometimes people) sick.

➤ Bring along Pauly's regular food. The pet shops you encounter on the road may not carry the same brand you use at home, and changes of diet should never be abrupt.

➤ Always carry a spray bottle of water. If you break down someplace where Pauly could become overheated, a good misting should keep him comfortable.

➤ Bring along a cover for the cage or carrier. If you get in a situation where Pauly could become chilled, covering the cage will help ward off drafts.

➤ Don't let Pauly cook in the car. While you're out enjoying 75-degree weather, Pauly could die in the 100-degree heat inside your vehicle. The temperature inside your vehicle, even when it's parked in the shade, is usually 25 (or more) degrees hotter than the temperature outside, and every year hundreds of pets die from being left in closed cars for just a few minutes. It's best not to leave your bird alone in a vehicle at all, but if you must, make sure it's in the shade. Don't put the windows down so low that Pauly could be stolen, freed or teased, but do put them down far enough on both sides so he gets plenty of ventilation.

➤ When going on overnight trips, make reservations in advance at hotels or motels that accept caged birds.

Squawk!

Please, please clean up after your pet when staying at a hotel or motel. If all of us remove all traces of feathers, discarded food and droppings, bird owners will still be welcome in the future.

Crossing State Lines

If your trip takes you across state lines, it gets a little more complicated. Every state has its own laws about what kinds of animals may be brought in, so contact the Fish and Wildlife Department of each state you will visit, and find out if it's okay to bring your pet. Mention what kind of bird you have (african grey, for example, not just parrot).

Some states permit some parrots but not others, and quaker parakeets (a.k.a. monk parakeets) have the dubious distinction of being banned in the most places. That's because flocks of these sturdy survivors thrive in several areas. Originally escaped pets, they have bred and multiplied in warm climates, and stand accused of damaging crops.

When you plan a trip across state lines, here's a checklist to follow:

➤ A few days before your trip, take your bird to the veterinarian for a checkup and a health certificate. Chances are no one will ask to see the certificate, but it's better to be safe than sorry.

➤ If you're going to take your bird on a long trip, take him on a couple of short trial runs first. That way you'll know if he has a tendency to get carsick. If he does, the next section is for you.

Bird Brainers

Birds make great companions in motor homes. Place the cage away from drafts and air vents, just like you would at home, and make sure it's firmly secured for travel. Carry bottled water for your bird and plenty of food, unless your bird's favorite brands are easily obtained almost anywhere.

Polly Sez

A *health certificate* is a form signed by a veterinarian certifying that your pet is healthy and doesn't carry any communicable diseases.

Taking a bird along on an airplane requires advance planning. First, call the airline and ask about their policy for shipping pets. Some will allow your bird in the cabin, provided the carrier fits under your seat. Others permit pets only in the baggage compartment. Find out what size and style carrier is required, what information must be included on the health certificate and the cost of the trip. Also ask about temperature restrictions. Many airlines won't accept pets if the outside temperature is too hot or too cold at either the departure point or the destination. Since the requirements and restrictions vary among airlines and change frequently, discuss them with an agent several weeks ahead every time you travel.

Queasy Critters

Just try saying that three times fast! I never knew birds got carsick until Rooster upchucked a blob of banana while crossing the George Washington Bridge. After that, I did some research. Yes, birds can get carsick and often do. No, they shouldn't take medication to prevent it.

For a trial run to see how well your bird takes to the road, put Pauly in the same cage or carrier he will travel in and strap it in so it doesn't tip. Then take care of a few chores. Go to the post office. Pick up something at a drive-up window or just enjoy a short drive in the country. Between 15 and 30 minutes is plenty for the first time—unless your bird gets sick sooner.

If Pauly loses his lunch, the drive may have stretched the limits of his motion tolerance. Make a note of how long he rode before he got sick and how recently before the ride he ate. Next time, take his food dish away an hour before you hit the highway. Build up his tolerance by taking several trips just under his limit. Then gradually extend his time in the car.

Bird Brainers

Just to be on the safe side, when making air travel plans write down the date and the name of the agent you spoke with.

Experiment. Some birds ride best when they have a little food every so often, instead of an all-you-can-eat buffet. For example, Rooster never had a problem after the banana incident. Since then, whenever we travel, instead of letting him gobble up one of his favorite foods, I limit him to his everyday seed and pellet combo with a grape or two for moisture. When he doesn't stuff himself, he doesn't get carsick.

Sometimes fear contributes to a bird's motion sickness. If Pauly seems afraid of the traffic whizzing by on the highway, try driving at night the first few times. Some birds ride best with a cover over their cage. While that's a sensible solution for brief trips, desensitizing your bird through frequent short drives—first at night, and then during the day—will make him a happier camper. Play the radio, sing along and talk to Pauly while you're on the road. As soon as he realizes riding is fun, his stomach may settle.

The Least You Need to Know

➤ Trimming your bird's wings frequently will keep him from accidentally flying away. Check your pet's wings often. Flight feathers grow back before you know it.

➤ If you take your bird outside, stay with him. Keep him out of trees and away from anything (lawns included) that may have been treated with chemicals.

➤ If your bird gets loose, watch which direction he went. If you see him in a nearby tree, try to entice him down by putting his cage nearby with some goodies in it. Inform your neighbors, your veterinarian and the local animal shelters. Hang posters in the neighborhood. Put ads in the newspaper. Don't give up.

➤ You can fly with your birds. Just make sure you know the airline's rules well before your trip.

➤ Keep your bird safe during car trips in a secure carrier that is positioned with the bird's comfort in mind.

Part 3
Keeping Your Bird Sane and Sound

Pick up any magazine (for humans) and I bet you'll see at least one feature on how to keep fit. While every article will have a slightly different angle (it has to, or no editor will buy it), you already know what the advice probably boils down to. You'll be told to eat moderate amounts of a variety of low-fat foods, with the emphasis on fruits and veggies, and to get enough exercise.

Another frequent magazine feature offers advice on how to live better and accomplish more by organizing your time. It may tell you to make lists, so you spend time doing something instead of deciding what to do. Then the author will probably offer short-cuts that help you achieve more in less time.

The same advice that keeps people physically and mentally fit works for birds. And a little organization, mixed with a couple of shortcuts, will help you finish your bird chores in no time, leaving you more time to have fun with your pet. This section has it all. It's an avian fitness manual with a bonus: It also gives you a crash course on how a bird's body works.

Chapter 9

Good Cagekeeping

In This Chapter

➤ Why birds are clean critters

➤ Washing your bird's home and furnishings

➤ Easy cleanups

In their natural habitat, birds are among the cleanest creatures on earth. Flying free or perched high in a tree, their droppings fall to the ground, where a bird never has to step on them or dine near them. Wild parrots don't sit beside a partially eaten persimmon and watch it rot. Fruit, seeds and nuts are theirs for the picking, and they pick only the freshest and juiciest. Then they eat a few bites and drop the rest, reseeding their environment and feeding the furry creatures on the forest floor.

Pet birds are placed in a different situation. They can't eat and run, and their droppings are as close as the bottom of the cage. Genetically programmed to eat like birds, they scatter seed and throw food around. Some people say they are dirty, but they aren't. Unfortunately, some bird owners are.

Polly's immune system isn't equipped to fight the germs generated by rotting food and accumulated droppings. And since she wasn't born with the ability to wash dishes or clean her own cage, those simple chores are yours. Please do them regularly. Her life depends on it.

Keeping the Cage Clean

Good hygiene isn't hard or time-consuming. It's just a matter of getting into a few good habits and using common sense. The table that follows will help you organize your chores, and I'll tell you how to do each item easily and effectively. Common sense will tell you the rest. For example, if Polly devours a chunk of watermelon and smears the residue all over her cage, it's a lot easier to wash it off while it's still wet than to wait until cage-cleaning day. By then, you might as well be peeling glue.

Cage-Cleaning Chores

Everyday Duties

Wash, rinse, and dry the food and water dishes.

Fill the dishes with fresh food and water, and put them back in the cage.

Change the cage papers.

The Weekly Wash

Clean the cage.

Scrape and wash the perches.

Wash the toys.

Disinfect the dishes.

Twice-a-Month Missions

Disinfect the cage, perches and toys.

Do the Dishes

Once a day, wash all of your bird's dishes in the dishwasher or in hot water and dish soap. Then rinse and dry them thoroughly. Drying bird dishes in the sun is ideal, as sunshine kills lots of germs. Many bird owners have two sets of dishes. That way, their bird can use one set while the other set is drying.

Did you know that disinfectant doesn't work its way through dirt to kill the germs below? The truth is, it only works on clean surfaces. On the day you disinfect the dishes, wash them first. Then soak them for half an hour in a solution of 30 parts water to one part chlorine bleach. That will disinfect them. Rinse and dry them well before giving them back to Polly. Don't make the disinfecting solution stronger than required. More is not better.

Polly Sez

The word *germ* refers to any microscopic organism, especially one that can cause disease. It is usually used for the toxic three: bacteria, fungi and viruses. *Disinfectant* is deadly to germs. It destroys all three.

Cage Paper Capers

Yesterday's news is often today's cage paper. It's economical and does the job just fine. Save yourself some time by accumulating a few newspapers and tracing the outline of the bottom of your cage tray on the top sheet. It will take you less than five minutes to cut out a month's supply of form-fitted cage sheets, and changing your bird's cage papers will be a snap for the next 30 days. Other options are used computer paper and paper towels. Cage paper that's precut to fit various size trays may be available at the pet store.

Bird Brainers

When you change the cage papers, look at your bird's droppings. A change in the appearance of her poop could be an early warning that Polly is sick.

Scrubbing the Cage

When it's time to clean her house, put Polly on a play gym or T-stand, or in her carrier. Remove all the furnishings from the cage, including perches, toys, cuttlebones and whatever else she shares space with. Then slide the tray out of the cage and, if possible, remove the grill above the tray. Get dirt out of the difficult corners with a vacuum cleaner, or flick it out with an old paintbrush.

Bird Brainers

Many bird owners say the easiest way to wash the cage is to take it into the shower with them. You might want to give it a try.

Using hot water and mild soap (hand soap or dish soap are fine), scrub the cage, tray, and grill with a nonabrasive pad or a brush. Give them a good, hard scrub, and if you couldn't remove the grill, lift it up so you can wash both sides. Then rinse everything well.

When you're satisfied that Polly's place is spotless, you have two choices. Either dry the cage thoroughly with a towel, or take it outside and let the sun finish the job.

Squawk!

When mixing disinfectant solution, wear gloves, protect your eyes (glasses or sunglasses will do), and put the water in the bucket before adding the bleach. Keep Polly far away from the proceedings. Birds and strong fumes don't mix.

Disinfecting Day

On the days you disinfect the cage, start by cleaning it as usual. When you finish, put on rubber gloves and apply your disinfecting solution of one part chlorine bleach to 30 parts water, using a sponge. Let the cage sit for half an hour; then rinse it thoroughly, dry it with a clean towel and put Polly in her hygienic home.

Pristine Perches

Although perches need a thorough cleaning once a week, whether they look dirty or not, common sense tells you to clean them sooner if remnants of Polly's dinner or droppings are stuck to them. Remove perches from the cage to clean them. Soak them in hot water and mild dish soap for several minutes, then scrub them with an abrasive brush. The wire bristle perch scrapers that are sold at pet stores do a good job on wooden perches. Finish by rinsing the perches well and drying them (in the sun, if possible). Damp perches aren't good for Polly's feet, so make sure they are completely dry before placing them in the cage.

Wooden perches are porous, so I prefer disinfecting mine by sponging them with vinegar, a natural disinfec-tant, diluted one-to-one with water. After they sit for half an hour, I rinse them and let them dry in the sun—weather permitting. Otherwise, I towel them dry, then let them air out for about 15 minutes before returning them to the cages. My birds' concrete and other non-porous perches are disinfected with chlorine bleach, just like the cage.

Some bird owners never use anything but vinegar and the sun for disinfecting, and their birds do fine. Others use chlorine bleach disinfecting solution (or other safe disinfectants) on all their bird's perches and toys, and their birds do fine too. Your avian veterinarian will be able to suggest other disinfectants. Whatever you use, read the directions first. Dilutions vary with each product.

Tidy Toys

No new tricks here. Wash Polly's playthings in hot water and dish soap once a week, unless they become soiled sooner. Rinse them thoroughly and, if possible, dry them in the sun.

When disinfecting my birds' toys, I use vinegar solution on wooden and rope toys, and chlorine bleach solution on plastic, acrylic and other nonporous items.

Polly's Other Possessions

Some play gyms or T-stands are murder to take apart, so soaking them may be beyond the realm of reason. The easiest way to give them a good scrubbing is to take them in the shower with you. Other possibilities include using dish soap, a good scrub brush and the garden hose during warm weather. Disinfect with a sponge and the safe disinfectant of your choice. If Polly's play gym includes dishes, give them the same treatment as the ones in her cage.

Keeping Cleanups Simple

Keep cleanups easy by thinking ahead. If you're tempted to give your parrot a fresh strawberry, but have to leave the house within minutes, save the sticky treat for later. You know she'll bury her beak in it, then wipe off the evidence on her cage bars and perch. When strawberry scraps sit for hours, you'll have to soak them or pry them off. But if you get to the goo before it dries, a damp rag takes it off instantly.

Squawk!

Don't rush rinsing. Remove every trace of soap, chlorine, vinegar or any other disinfectant from your bird's cage, perches and toys.

Hurrah for Cordless Vacs

Do tiny seed hulls fly out of the cage every time Caruso flaps his wings and fans his food dish? Does Polly toss pellet crumbs and nut shells onto your clean floor? Keep a cordless vacuum cleaner near the cage. It picks up the pieces as quick as you can see company coming down the driveway.

The Least You Need to Know

➤ Birds are naturally clean creatures and get sick when forced to live in a dirty cage.

➤ Wash your bird's dishes and change her cage papers daily. Use a safe disinfectant on your bird's dishes once a week.

➤ Clean your bird's cage, perches and other possessions weekly. Disinfect them with a safe disinfectant twice a month.

➤ Never rush rinsing. Birds use their beaks to climb and play, and soap and disinfectant residue don't belong inside your bird.

➤ Make cleaning simple by wiping off messes when they happen, not after they harden.

Chapter 10

What's Yummy in Your Bird's Tummy?

In This Chapter

➤ Balancing your bird's diet

➤ What's so great about sprouts?

➤ Making food fun

➤ Feeding the finicky bird

➤ Supper for softbills

Back in Chapter 5, I said your bird needs four dishes. Sounds like he's dining out, doesn't it? Let's see, that's one for the salad, one for the soup, one for the main course and one for dessert, right? Not exactly, but it's closer than you might imagine. It's actually one for the main course, one for salad and fruit, one for whatever you're eating and one for water. Surprised? It will all make sense soon. In this chapter I'll discuss avian nutrition, and help you choose the best diet and the healthiest fun foods for your bird.

Balancing Your Bird's Diet

Variety may be just the spice of life for people, but it's a vital part of life for birds. In fact, if good avian nutrition could be summed up in one word, that word would be "variety." Besides being best for the body, a varied diet stimulates avian minds and helps prevent boredom. "Uh oh," you may be thinking. "Is feeding my bird going to take up lots of time?" No way! Few of us fuss over our own meals, so I'm going to keep it simple. Let's get past the confusing part first.

Do you shop in one of those enormous pet stores—the type that sprang up in metropolitan areas during the last decade, and look like the Kmarts and Wal-Marts of the pet world? Their bird food section alone takes up an entire aisle and contains pelleted foods with labels proclaiming "complete nutrition," packaged seed mixes and serve-yourself bins full of exotic seeds, treats and feeds. If the multitude of choices confuse you, you're in good company. Many long-term bird owners are in the same quandary, and avian nutrition is a hot subject of debate.

Aren't Seeds Sufficient?

The words "bird food" and "seeds" were practically synonymous for many years, and thousands of pet birds subsisted on seed-only diets because their owners didn't know any better. Today we know that seeds alone aren't enough to provide a bird with all the nutrition he needs. As books and magazines spread the word that seed-only diets were bad for birds, many aviculturists carried the news to extremes. They stopped feeding seeds entirely.

Many articles still give seeds a bad rap and encourage bird owners to use the relatively new pelleted foods. But in the wild, some of our pet birds are predominantly seed-eaters. Budgies, cockatiels and a variety of colorful grass parakeets—all natives of Australia's grasslands—eat more seeds than anything else when flying free. So do the finches of Australia, Africa and Asia, and our super songsters, the canaries. On the other hand, rain forest species such as amazon parrots and macaws may eat a few seeds in the wild, but seed is a small part of their diet. So, seeds are a natural food for some birds, and a more or less learned taste for others.

The problem is, almost all birds love seeds and aren't particularly partial to pellets, unless they were raised on them. So what should a bird owner do? Must Pauly and Caruso be deprived of one of their favorite foods in order to be healthy? Not at all. Here's the truth about seeds and how to use them.

The Plus Side of Seeds

Although they are not complete nutrition, seeds do have some advantages:

➤ Birds love them.

➤ Seeds are almost a natural food.

➤ Seeds are easily available.

➤ Seeds are inexpensive.

➤ Seeds are easy to feed.

The Seedy Side of Seeds

Yes, there are disadvantages, too:

➤ Birds love them too much. Some become seed junkies. They behave as if they were addicted to seeds and refuse other foods.

➤ Seeds are almost, but not quite, a natural food. Why? Because wild birds seldom select mature seeds as a first choice. They prefer immature, developing seeds. These growing or green seeds are nutritionally superior to the mature seeds found in commercial mixes.

➤ Seeds are nutritionally incomplete.

➤ Seeds are too fattening for some species.

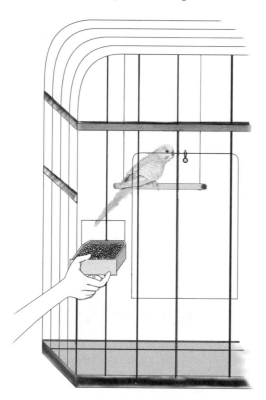

Budgies prefer seeds as a main course, but also need nutrients from fresh produce.

What Is a Seed, Anyway?

A fresh seed is a shell full of nutrients. It contains everything needed to start a new life—for a specific plant, not a bird. All seeds aren't equal, either. Some are higher in fats; others in carbohydrates. All of them contain protein, but some have more than

Squawk!

Check your bird's seed dish twice a day. If the top layer is empty hulls, either shake the dish gently to bring the edible seeds to the top, or hold it over the garbage can and blow away the empties. Many birds don't dig for their seed, and will go hungry even though there is plenty of good seed below.

others. For example, millet, a favorite food of many small birds, contains 14 percent protein, 60 percent carbohydrates and four percent fat. Compare that to sunflower seeds, the undisputed favorite of many medium to large birds. Sunflower seeds are 15 percent protein, 18 percent carbohydrates and 28 percent fat.

Yet even with the vast differences you'll see in the table below, seeds are all the same in several ways. Every seed that's typically fed to birds contains less than one percent calcium and phosphorus, and is also deficient in several other vitamins and minerals. Here is a list of the seeds that appear most often in commercial mixes, along with their carbohydrate, fat and protein content. No, the numbers don't add up to 100 percent. Seeds also contain other stuff, like moisture and fiber:

Seeds You'll Find in Most Mixes

Seed	Carbohydrate	Fat	Protein
Canary grass	56%	4%	14%
Flax	20%	37%	25%
Hulled oats—groats	65%	4%	12%
Millet	60%	4%	14%
Milo	70%	4%	12%
Niger	13%	44%	20%
Safflower	17%	28%	15%
Sunflower	18%	28%	15%

Sunflower/Safflower? Isn't that a Misprint?

Those of you who have had birds for years may be wondering why the table says sunflower and safflower seed have the same fat content. After all, seed mixes boasting "no sunflower seeds" have been marketed for years; they are recommended for over-weight parrots and contain a high percentage of safflower seeds. The truth is, safflower seeds make a good substitute for sunflower seeds because they are practically the same from a nutritional standpoint. The theory is that safflower seeds are smaller than sunflower seeds and aren't as much fun to eat, so overweight birds will probably eat less of them and consume fewer calories overall.

Quality Counts

Besides the differences shown in the table, the same kind of seeds may have different nutritional values. Say what? Isn't a millet seed always a millet seed? No, not if it's dead or dying. And not if it was grown in poor soil. Mineral deficiencies in the soil show up in the plant, as the gardeners among you already know.

So how can you include some good, nutritious seeds in your bird's diet? Just follow these simple suggestions:

➤ Buy seed mixes designed for your bird. For example, finch, canary, budgie or parakeet, cockatiel, small hookbill or large hookbill.

➤ Check the ingredients and choose a mix with several different types of seeds. Variety is a plus.

➤ Beware of bargains. Buy major brands from stores with a fast turnover.

➤ Buy bagged rather than boxed seeds. That way, you'll see what you're paying for. Most seed mixes house a bug or two, especially during warm weather, but you shouldn't buy a mix that's teeming with moths, weevils or beetles.

➤ Check the date. If the seed is dated, buy the freshest bag you can find. Never buy a bag that's more than six months old.

➤ Buy only enough seed for two or three weeks.

➤ Freeze the seed for at least 24 hours. That will kill any insects.

➤ Store the seed in the refrigerator.

➤ Give your bird other nutritious foods daily. *No matter how fresh and varied your seed mix, it won't provide your bird with complete nutrition.* Seeds lack lots of things birds need, including some amino acids (from protein), and several vitamins and minerals.

Bird Brainers

Test for freshness by soaking a few seeds in water or planting them an eighth of an inch deep in damp sterile potting soil. The ones in water should show signs of sprouting after two days. Seeds in potting soil will take a little longer, but you'll get lovely young plants that you can cut and feed to your bird. More on sprouting later.

Now that you know seeds are good for small birds, and okay in moderation (like lemon meringue pie) for larger parrots, here are some other foods that will help keep your feathered friend fit. Let's begin with a recent trend, widely touted as a panacea—bird nuggets, or pelleted foods.

Are Pellets Perfect?

Pellets are dry bird food. Composed of several healthy ingredients, including vitamins and minerals, they were created to provide balanced nutrition while being easy to use. Although all dry bird food is generally referred to as pellets, there are two types.

Extruded foods, sometimes called nuggets, are bound under temperatures high enough to pasteurize them, while pelleted formulas are bound by compression under moderate temperatures.

While commercially prepared dry dog food has been on the market for about 40 years, pelleted bird food is the new kibble on the block. The earliest brands showed up on the shelves about ten years ago, after five years of field testing on thousands of birds. What does that mean? It means no one knows yet if pellets are perfect, no matter how "complete" they claim to be in their advertising. Pelleted bird food hasn't been around long enough to have an effect on avian life spans. In fact, we're years away from knowing whether it will give birds longer, healthier lives or cause problems after years of use.

So are pellets a rip-off? Probably not. I believe they are a big improvement over the seed-only diets that people used to feed their birds. But pellets alone? Not for my birds.

First of all, I wouldn't know which pellet to pick. On my desk are two major brands. One of them is labeled "complete daily diet," while the other one says it "includes the nutrition your bird needs...." What's interesting is that even though they are both made for parrots and other similar size psittacines, they are quite different. According to the guaranteed analysis on the back of the packages, one of them contains a minimum of 15 percent protein, while the other is 23 percent protein. One has a minimum of 6 percent fat, the other 4.5 percent fat. The first ingredient in both brands is corn, but after that their ingredients differ considerably. One is heavy on wheat, the other on soybean meal, and so on.

Which one is best for Rooster, my mexican red parrot? I'm clueless. That's one of the reasons I give him some of each, plus a variety of other things, including seeds. But there are other reasons why Rooster doesn't find just pellets in his food dish. They aren't one of his favorite foods. They also aren't one of his natural foods. Mexico has some mighty weird trees (the boogum comes to mind), but no one has ever discovered a pellet tree growing in Rooster's native land. And, most important of all, no one really knows the specific requirements of every species of pet bird.

Pelleted food has been developed for almost all pet birds, and includes canary and finch food, and softbill formulas for mynahs, toucans and lories. Pellets come in sizes and shapes to suit every member of the psittacine family, and some brands have separate formulas for the various stages of your bird's life: weaning, adult maintenance, senior, and even stress formulas. While pelleted food probably isn't perfect, it's better than any commercial mix produced for birds in the past. Pellets are constantly being tested and improved, and I believe the companies that make them truly believe in their products. After all, they want your bird to live long and be healthy so you'll keep buying their brand of bird food.

Should you make pellets part of your bird's diet? Absolutely. Here's how I did it.

Convincing Birds to Eat Pellets

It can be difficult (and that's an understatement) to convince a grown bird, even one who eagerly consumes a varied diet, to try pellets. Some birds simply don't believe the little nuggets are food. Pellet manufacturers know this, and suggest gradually converting birds to pellets, as described in the following table.

Converting Your Bird to Pellets

Days 1–3	Combine one-quarter pellets and three-quarters regular diet
Days 4–8	Combine half pellets and half regular diet
Days 9–14	Combine three-quarters pellets with one-quarter regular diet
Day 15	Begin feeding pellets only

This schedule worked with our cockatiel (who now eats pellets and seeds), and it may work with your bird. But it didn't work with our amazon parrot or our budgies. In fact, had I followed the schedule blindly, without monitoring actual intake, those three might have starved because they didn't touch their pellets at all.

When trying to convert Pauly, check his food dish and his droppings daily. What goes in one end comes out the other, so if the paper is cleaner than usual, your bird isn't eating enough. When you reach the three-quarters pellet and one-quarter seed part of the schedule, make sure some pellets are being consumed. Try to catch Pauly in the act of eating them (not just making them go crunch and then dropping them). If you don't see him eat them and the cage papers are too clean, abandon the program. Don't let him suffer a sudden weight loss. Birds have high metabolisms and going hungry endangers their health. Besides, there are other ways to entice Pauly into eating pellets.

Pellets at My Place

Rooster eats pellets as part of his diet now, but it took a little ingenuity. First, I considered his likes and dislikes. What Rooster likes best is whatever we're eating, but spaghetti is probably his favorite food. He also has an amusing habit. When we give him cereal out of the box, he dunks it in his water dish before eating it. Even though he loves cracking almonds and gnawing wood, he prefers his cereal soft.

That gave me an idea. I cooked spaghetti, soaked pellets in the sauce until they softened, and

Bird Brainers

Horrors! You're changing the cage papers and see that your bird's droppings are red, purple or brown. Don't panic; it's the pellets. If you just started adding colored pellets to your bird's diet, expect the stools to have a new hue.

Squawk!

Don't try to switch food by making your bird go "cold turkey." You may think he'll eat pellets if he gets hungry enough, but it isn't always true. If your bird doesn't recognize pellets as food, going hungry won't change that. What hunger will do is weaken his resistance to disease and put his life in danger.

149

presented them to Rooster during dinner. He gobbled them up. For the next few weeks I softened pellets in water just before dinner and mixed them with his serving of people food. He ate turkey with pellets and gravy, chili with beans and pellets, and so on.

At the same time, one of his food dishes always had some dry pellets mixed with the seeds. After a few weeks of eating pellets flavored with the family dinner, Rooster started dipping the dry pellets in his water dish and eating them when they softened. He still doesn't count them among his favorite things, but he has accepted them.

Bird Brainers

Hand-fed baby birds are already used to eating formula, and readily consume pellets, especially if they are soaked for a couple of minutes and are fed softened. Make the transition from formula to pellets gradually. Birds should never be suddenly switched from one diet to another.

The budgies are still holding out. Every day I give them a mixture of seeds and pellets, and every night I throw away empty seed hulls and the pellets. Pinto and Bluebell both love cereal and eat a variety of raw vegetables and fruit, but refuse to try pellets. In fact, if I mix their pellets with people food, they ignore the tidbit entirely.

Why keep trying? Because that's what you have to do when you want to improve your bird's diet. Birds aren't being stubborn or uncooperative when they refuse a new food. They're just being birds—cautious creatures who survived in the wild for thousands of years by being careful around new things. Will my budgies ever eat pellets? Probably. Some birds have to see them mixed with their seeds for a year or more before trying them, and Bluebell isn't even that old yet.

Pellet Pros and Cons

On the plus side, name-brand pellets (don't shop for bargains) are:

➤ As close to complete nutrition as modern science can formulate for pet birds

➤ Easy to feed

➤ Easy to digest

➤ Easy to clean up

➤ Resistant to spoilage

➤ Available in different sizes and formulas to feed different species

➤ Available in maintenance diets or special formulas for breeding birds

➤ Probably the healthiest bird food on the market

On the minus side, even name-brand pellets are:

➤ Bland (trust me, I tasted several brands)

➤ Boring (birds enjoy cracking seeds and nuts, and it gives them something to do)

➤ Not a bird's natural diet

➤ Hard to convince seed eaters to try

➤ Made of formulas that may contain preservatives, artificial colors, artificial flavors or other substances you would prefer your bird not to eat. Recipes vary between brands. For example, some use vegetable juice for color, while others use food coloring. Read the label before you buy.

➤ Not the only food your bird needs. Even if pellets were nutritionally perfect, your bird would still need the physical and mental stimulation of crunchy vegetables, fresh fruits, and an occasional food he had to work for, like millet or an unshelled almond.

Bird Brainers

African greys need more fat in their diet than do amazon parrots of the same size. For pet greys, sunflower seeds supply enough fat. Even if your african grey always eats his pellets, offer him some sunflower seeds every day. They make a good dessert or training treat.

Calcium from Cuttlebone

Cuttlebone comes from the cuttlefish, a critter closely related to the squid. It's inexpensive and provides a source of calcium and other minerals, as your bird needs them. Cuttlebone often comes with a clip for attaching it to your bird's cage. If you buy one without a clip, just punch a couple of holes in it and attach it to the bars with wire. Place it close to a perch with the soft side toward your bird.

Pauly can use cuttlebone just as it comes from the pet store, but for songbirds like Caruso, the cuttlebone needs to be treated or it will be too salty. Just soak it in water for 24 hours, change the water, and soak it for another 24 hours. Let it dry thoroughly, and it's ready to take care of your finch's or canary's calcium requirements.

Provide calcium by attaching a cuttlebone near a perch.

A Gritty Question

Until recently, almost every pet bird had a separate, small dish in his cage that contained grit. But lately, grit has become controversial. Today, many bird owners don't know if they should offer it to their bird or not.

What does grit do? Since birds have no teeth to grind their food before they swallow it, a little grit in their gizzards (the muscular part of their stomachs) helps them grind the shells off their seeds so they can digest the nutrients. Many wild birds forage for grit, and its generalized use in the poultry industry makes sense because chickens and turkeys swallow their seeds whole. But parrots don't. All those empty hulls on the surface of Pauly's food dish are your insurance that he cracks every seed before eating it.

Polly Sez

Grit is an inexpensive mixture of sand, tiny pieces of gravel and possibly some oyster shell. It's sold in pet shops and the pet section of many supermarkets.

Most bird experts agree on two points when it comes to using grit:

➤ Canaries and finches need small amounts of grit.

➤ Medium and large parrots do not need grit at all.

The controversy centers on whether or not budgies, cockatiels and lovebird-sized parrots need grit or not. Until researchers find out more, the best bet is to give these small parrots limited amounts of fine grit. Offer it occasionally, but not free choice. There have been cases where pet birds swallowed so much grit that their digestive tract became impacted. Why did they take so much? No one knows. Maybe they were bored.

Should You Use Supplements?

Vitamin and mineral supplements have a place in bird nutrition, but usually aren't needed by pet birds that are fed (and actually eat) a varied diet. Bird pellets already contain optimum nutrition, and shouldn't be supplemented by anything but vegetables, fruits, grains, legumes, seeds and a portion of the family dinner. On the other hand, vitamin and mineral supplements may be helpful if your seed junkie is still stubbornly refusing to eat his veggies or try his pellets.

Squawk!

When giving vitamin and mineral supplements, follow the manufacturer's directions or your avian veterinarian's advice. More is not better. In fact, more might be dangerous.

Vitamin and mineral supplements come in liquid and powder forms. The liquid goes in your bird's water, where it may alter the taste and dissuade your bird from drinking enough. It's also an invitation to bacteria. Powder is better.

If your bird eats any fresh fruits or veggies, sprinkle vitamin-mineral power on them, or mix it into his

portion of people food. If seeds are his only suste-
nance, remove his dish for a couple of hours, then
mist some seeds lightly and sprinkle them with
powder. With luck, he'll eat them immediately, and
some of the dampened supplement will end up in
his mouth when he cracks the hulls. Remove the
moist seeds after an hour, wash and dry the dish,
and give him fresh, dry seeds.

If your bird is sick or recovering from an illness or
operation, or if you breed birds, supplementation
may be a good idea. Ask your avian veterinarian for
a recommendation.

Bird Brainers

Many brands of seed mixes are
vitamin- and mineral-enriched, but
the supplements are often added to
the seed hull. That would be fine if
parrots had wet tongues like we do,
because some of the supplement
would stick to them when they
hulled the seeds. But alas, parrots
have dry tongues and get very little
benefit from vitamin-enriched hulls.

Food from the Refrigerator

One of the essentials missing from seeds (and even
beans and grains) is vitamin A. But it's easy to feed
because it's as close as your refrigerator or cupboard. Carrots, broccoli, spinach, sweet
potatoes and yams are all high in vitamin A. In fact, your bird can get his daily dose of
vitamin A, plus myriad other beneficial vitamins and minerals, from any dark green or
orange veggies.

Introduce veggies a little at a time. Start with just a few tiny pieces of carrot or broccoli,
and add variety as Pauly accepts each new item. For tiny birds, keep the pieces small
(some like them grated in the food processor). Bigger birds should also be introduced
to small pieces at first. Once they accept vegetables as food, many medium to large
hookbills learn to like larger chunks of produce—something they can hold and eat,
the way we munch carrot sticks.

Most birds are glad to find some fruit in their diet. Introduce it gradually, and no
matter how much Pauly likes it, don't give him too generous a portion. Overeating
fruit causes loose stools.

Avian Health Food—Just Rinse and Serve

Vegetables	Fruits
Asparagus	Apples (cored)
Beans (all kinds, including green, yellow, white, red, pinto, etc.)	Apricots (pitted)
	Bananas
Beets and beet greens	Blueberries
Broccoli	Cantaloupe
Brussels sprouts	Cherries (pitted)
Cabbage	Figs

continues

continued

Vegetables	Fruits
Carrots	Grapes
Cauliflower	Guava
Celery	Honeydew
Cilantro	Kiwi
Collard greens	Mango
Corn	Oranges (rarely)
Cucumber	Papaya
Dandelion greens (from untreated lawns)	Peaches (pitted)
Endive	Pears (cored)
Mustard greens	Persimmons
Okra	Pineapple
Parsley	Plums
Peas	Raisins
Potatoes	Tangerines (in small amounts)
Pumpkin	
Radishes	Watermelon
Spinach (in small amounts)	
Sprouts	
Summer squash	
Sweet potatoes	
Tomatoes	
Turnips and turnip greens	
Winter squash	
Yams	
Zucchini	

Will Canned or Frozen Veggies Do?

Canned vegetables won't do. They have too much salt to be good for birds. But frozen mixed vegetables are fine in a pinch. Although not ideal, they're a whole lot healthier than no veggies at all. I stock my freezer with them before going on vacation because they are easiest for the pet sitter. Prep time for two tablespoons of frozen vegetables is one minute in my microwave on the high defrost setting, but microwaves vary. Stir the veggies when they come out of the microwave and let them sit at least a minute before presenting them to Pauly. Then there won't be any hot spots.

People Food, Not Table Scraps

Sharing your meals (provided you don't consider chips and beer to be dinner) will round out your bird's diet. Almost everything you eat is good for birds, if they eat it in moderation. Birds enjoy and benefit from pasta, legumes (beans, lentils and such), well-done meat, poultry and fish, potatoes, cooked vegetables, rice, eggs, and more.

Avoid smoked or processed meat because of the high salt content, and give only small amounts of cheese and other dairy products because birds aren't able to digest them well. In other words, share a sliver of pizza with Pauly, but eat the pepperoni yourself.

There are two dangers when feeding Pauly from the family pot. One is giving him food too hot to handle. Believe it or not, birds can't tell temperature and will literally burn their insides out by gobbling food while it's still steaming. The other potential problem comes from feeding Pauly with a spoon that was already in a human mouth. Our bacteria is different from bird bacteria, and they can get very sick from ours. Both of these dangers are easily avoided. Get in the habit of using a separate spoon and saucer when feeding Pauly from the family pot. Just scoop his portion into the saucer and let it cool to room temperature before giving it to him.

Never use Pauly as a feathered garbage disposal. If you won't eat something, don't give it to him. When sharing fruit, give him a slice, never the core. Pesticides converge at the core, so seeds from apples, peaches, plums and other fruits belong in the garbage, not the birdcage. When feeding fresh vegetables, give Pauly his share from the sections you are using—not a carrot scraping, a wilted lettuce leaf or a rotting banana.

While almost all of the foods we eat are fine for birds, there are a few exceptions. Avoid giving your bird these foods:

➤ Avocados

➤ Alcohol (not even a taste)

➤ Chocolate

Bird Brainers

Most birds love nuts. Chop an unsalted almond, peanut, walnut, pecan or other unsalted nut, and give it to your tiny bird as an occasional treat. Medium to large hookbills prefer whole nuts and enjoy shelling their own.

Squawk!

A piece of lettuce or a celery stick may be quick and easy, but light green, watery veggies aren't high in the vitamins and minerals your bird needs. They make great fun food though, so let your bird enjoy them in limited amounts, along with his dark green and orange health foods.

Squawk!

Rinse fruits and veggies well before giving them to your bird. Even a tiny trace of pesticide is dangerous.

➤ Junk food that's full of fat, salt or sugar. (If you want to share a snack, try popcorn. Use an air popper and give Pauly his portion before adding the butter and salt.)

➤ Mushrooms

➤ Rhubarb

➤ Wilted or spoiled produce, and fruit cores, pits and seeds

Bird Brainers

Amount matters. When serving your bird anything new, give him a tiny taste. That's more enticing than a large portion of something strange. If your bird likes it, you can always offer him seconds.

Sprouts Are Special

If I had to pick just one food to improve a seed junkie's diet, that super food would be sprouts. Sprouted seeds and beans are incredibly more nutritious than dry seeds, and contain a beneficial buffet of vitamins, minerals and essential amino acids. Best yet, even stubborn seed-eaters sometimes give them a try.

Buy seeds for sprouting in a health food store or your pet shop, if they carry them. They must be certified safe for eating (organic is ideal). The table below has a list of the most popular seeds for sprouting. Once your bird accepts one or two, the more variety, the better.

Seeds for sprouting	
Azuki	Nigerseed
Alfalfa	Peas
Buckwheat	Pinto beans
Canary grass	Radish
Chickpeas	Rapeseed
Kidney beans	Sesame
Lentils	Sunflower
Millet	Wheat
Mung beans	

Special sprout mix for small birds
Canary grass
Millet
Nigerseed
Rapeseed

1,2,3, Sprout!

Sprouting seeds is simple. You can do it with or without special equipment. If you want equipment, your local health food store probably carries a small container with a tray and dividers, created especially for sprouting. You can also sprout seed by using a small pot with a lid and a sieve. Just sprinkle a few seeds in the pot, add some lukewarm water and let them sit for 12 hours. Then drain them into the sieve and rinse them well (shake them) under running lukewarm water. Put them back in the pot, cover the pot, and let them sit another 12 hours.

Repeat the drain and rinse cycle, and cover them for 12 more hours. Open the lid and there they are—bursting with nutrition and ready to feed your bird (after one final rinse). If you made too many, garnish your salad or sandwich. Sprouts have no shelf life and become dangerous really quickly when they mold.

Although sprouts are super because your bird gets the combined benefits of the seed and the sprout, you can provide excellent green food (and variety) by planting your bird's seed mix quite shallow in sterile potting soil. Keep the mini-garden damp but not wet, and in a few days you'll be able to cut fresh greens for your bird.

If you don't have the time or inclination to grow sprouts, you can get them at most supermarkets, although not in as many varieties as you can grow from seed. Select only the freshest, and buy small amounts because they don't keep well.

Squawk!

Don't sprout the leftovers after you plant your garden, because those seeds are treated and aren't meant to be food.

Squawk!

If corn for sprouting is sold at your health food store, use it with care. It molds even faster than most other sprouts and its mold is particularly toxic. Why bother with it at all? Because birds are crazy about sprouted corn, and it may be just the ticket to convince a seed junkie to try sprouts.

Introducing Sprouts

To start your bird on sprouts, add small amounts to his diet daily. Begin by chopping up the sprouts, and add them to his seed or pellet dish. That should cue him that they are food. After he tries them (it may take days, and they must be fed fresh daily), put bigger pieces in his veggie dish. Eventually, he'll learn to love them whole (yes, little birds will, too). Just watching my birds savor their sprouts makes me feel good because I know how healthy those little seedlings are. The first time your bird eats his sprouts, I know you'll smile too.

Foraging for Fun

Your bird's wild cousins have to find their own food, and the daily search is a social activity that exercises their brains and bodies. Meanwhile, our pet birds have cooks, maids and butlers (that's you and me) who keep their food dishes full. We all know what happens to people who have no active hobbies, no inclination to learn anything new and hire help to cater to their every whim, don't we? They become flabby and dull (and here you thought they took their hired help and their Lear jet and went off to the Caribbean!). Well, birds that have nothing to do also end up with soft bodies and stale minds. Can food exercise and entertain your bird? If it's challenging enough, it can.

Bird Brainers

Millet isn't just for hookbills. Finches and canaries love it, too.

Working to Eat

Make Pauly work for some of his food by offering it in natural ways that will stimulate him physically and mentally. It's also amazingly easy and takes almost no time at all. If Pauly is a big bird, give him a chunk of corn on the cob. He'll use it as a grasping toy and eat it right off the ear. Other items he'll have to work for are chunks of carrot, unshelled nuts and a chicken drumstick (cooked, of course). Cut off most of the meat first, but leave a little meat and all the gristle for your parrot. Don't be surprised if you hear a crunch. Lots of big birds bite right through the bone and munch the marrow.

Pet stores sell inexpensive clamps designed to fit on cages so that food or toys can be hung from the top and sides. Get at least two and hang them where your bird will have to climb to get at the goodie. For small birds, begin by hanging a spray of millet. Most little birds (and some big guys, too) find millet irresistible.

Bird Brainers

Carotene can make your canary prettier by brightening his feathers. It's found in carrots, yellow squash and dark green vegetables. When you grate them for Caruso, you're giving him not only a health food but a beauty treatment as well.

Birds of all sizes will work for their veggies after they learn to like them. Dangle a whole string bean or wax bean from a clamp, and watch your bird do a job on it. My budgies attack their green beans instantly. They gnaw their way down from top to bottom, surgically removing and eating the young beans inside the shell. Other veggies you can hang from clamps are celery tops, bell pepper strips, broccoli or cauliflower florets, peas in the pod, parsley and anything else listed in the table on p. 153. Clamps are also a boon to your bird sitter. He or she will be able to clip vegetable chunks to them, even if Pauly won't let a stranger put a hand in his cage.

Another hard-to-eat treat for medium to large hookbills is the bird kabob. All you need is a strip of untreated rawhide and a few healthy treats. Poke a hole through an inch-long wheel of corn on the cob, a slice of sweet potato, and a radish (anything in the fruit and vegetable table that won't fall apart easily will do). String the items on the rawhide, knot it at the bottom so the treats can't slide off, and tie it to the top of the cage so it dangles near a perch. Pauly will have to capture it and make it hold still before he can eat it.

A tasty bird kabob combines nutrition and exercise for your bird.

Packaged Treats

Commercial treats of every shape and description are available for birds. Puzzle toy treats encourage birds to forage for their food by placing almonds in wooden cages or poking them into chunks of wood. Natural pinecones packed with seed also make a tantalizing toy. You can buy them or make them yourself by packing any healthy food into the nooks and crannies of a natural pinecone and hanging it from Pauly's cage.

Seed, nut, fruit and veggie and honey sticks are all popular packaged treats. They come in a variety of sizes to fit every bird, from finches to macaws. Think before hanging one from the cage bars, because where you place it usually determines how hard your bird will have to work to eat it. The best bet is

Squawk!

Pet amazon parrots tend to become obese. In their native habitat they don't eat much fat, so fatty foods play havoc with their health in captivity. Keep your amazon alive years longer by feeding it lots of veggies, whole grains, legumes, and some fruit and nuts, along with its pellets and seeds. Limit sunflower seeds and peanuts to training treats, and go easy on the safflower seeds.

to make it real easy the first time, then increasingly harder. Treat sticks tempt most birds, so read the ingredients. If your pet is stubborn about eating fruits and vegetables, a stick containing these essentials might change his mind.

Buying from Bins

Many larger pet shops sell seeds, pelleted foods, unshelled nuts, beans and other specialty food items in serve-yourself bins. It's a good way to create a unique mix with your bird's special needs in mind, or simply to pick up some training treats. Unless you're an expert on avian nutrition, however, I'd leave creating Pauly's main course to the major companies. Use the bins to find out which pelleted foods he prefers and to pick up a few of his favorite things. When shopping the bins, you can buy as small an amount as you want. That's less expensive than getting stuck with several pounds of something that Pauly refuses to try.

Fussing Over Finicky Eaters

In the wild, eating is the biggest social event of a parrot's day (unless it's mating season). Amid song and chatter, the whole flock feeds as one. Since the only flock a pet bird has is his human family, when Pauly sees you eat, he wants to eat too. Otherwise, he feels like a social outcast—the kid nobody wants on their team.

Squawk!

The worst time to try to get your bird on a better diet is when he's sick. Changing foods is stressful, and a sick bird is already stressed out.

Squawk!

Always make sure your canary has food in his dish. Caruso eats about a fourth of his weight every day. His metabolism is so high that he could die of starvation if he went without food for a day.

You can use Pauly's desire to eat with the family flock by introducing him to new foods during dinner. Bring Pauly's perch into the kitchen or dining room, and let him watch. Parrots are copycats (according to *Webster*, one definition of the word *parrot* is "to repeat or imitate"), and Pauly is more likely to try something new if he sees you eating it. Does that make you the official taster for his feathered highness? Only if you think of yourself that way. In Pauly's bird brain, you're the leader of the flock.

Besides letting Pauly watch you eat the healthy foods that you want him to try, here are some other suggestions for turning your seed junkie into an eager eater:

➤ Birds have few taste buds and a limited sense of smell when compared to humans, so eye appeal creates the initial attraction. Entice your finicky friend into trying new foods by making him an offer he can't refuse. Turn healthy food into fun food by presenting vegetables and fruits of varied colors, textures and shapes. For example, cut carrots as wheels one day, and serve them coarsely chopped the next. Mix them with cut green beans, peas or diced green pepper to make eye-catching combinations.

➤ Pauly may prefer his veggies cooked. Offer him a small portion (at room temperature) of whatever cooked vegetable is part of the family dinner.

➤ After Pauly eats in the morning, take away his main course (seeds, pellets or a mixture of the two), and don't feed him again until evening. Then present him with some veggies and fruit, or a portion of the family dinner. Leave the meal in his cage for an hour. Then remove it (whether he ate it or not) and give him his regular diet again.

➤ Grate carrots, green beans or broccoli and mix them with Pauly's precious seeds. He'll have to move hundreds of tiny veggie tidbits around just to separate them from his seeds, and will probably taste them in the process. Remove the dish after an hour and give him clean seeds.

Avian Adventures

Years ago, I had a cockatiel who refused to eat anything but seeds for five years. Every evening, I gave Omelet vegetables, fruit and food from the table, and every night I threw them away. An expert told me, "Never give up," so I dutifully fed her the right stuff, even when I didn't think she'd ever eat it. Just before she turned six, Omelet nibbled at a celery top. A few months later, she picked at a piece of carrot. By the time she was seven, she eagerly ate four or five different vegetables, and a couple of cereals. That was as good as it ever got, but it was a whole lot better for her than seeds alone.

Sustenance for Softbills

The softbills we're concerned with are lories (and lorikeets), mynahs and toucans. When it comes to appearance, feathers are about the only thing these species have in common. Yet there are more similarities than differences in their diets.

Lories and Lorikeets

Wild lories and lorikeets feast on nectar, fruit, pollen, flowers and sometimes an insect for protein. It's easy enough to re-create a similar diet for your pet, because prepared nectar formulas made especially for these birds are available in most pet shops. Add some sliced or chopped fresh fruit in season and a few diced veggies (raw or cooked), and your lory will have a healthy diet. If you're out of fruit or in a hurry, canned fruit with no sugar added will do.

Polly Sez

Lories, mynah birds and toucans are members of the bird family called *softbills*. The name refers to their diet and has nothing to do with their beaks, which are quite hard. In the wild they forage for fruit, nectar, a few vegetables and insects.

Bird Brainers

Does your bird need live insects in his diet? The question is still controversial, but most authorities think not. Although toucans get most of their protein from beetles and other insects in the wild, many experts believe pellets provide all the protein your pet needs.

What goes in as liquid comes out as liquid, so the downside of owning a lory is loose, sticky stools. There is an alternative, and you should know about it, even though I don't recommend it.

For the past several years, dry diets have been marketed for lories, and many lory owners now feed their pets soaked pellets. These diets make the birds' stools dryer and easier to deal with. The problem is, no one knows the long-term effects of feeding a born nectar eater a dry diet. So far, it seems to be working, but we're years from knowing if the new formulas are a safe substitute for a more natural, wetter diet. If you choose the new, rather than the traditional method of feeding your lory, give him some nectar or fruit every day anyway. As my mother says about chicken soup, "It couldn't hurt."

Meals for Mynah Birds

Pellets that are made especially for mynahs and soaked in fruit juice (not citrus) or water are the best main course for your bird. Unlike a lory, a mynah needs lots of protein, and pellets will supply it. In addition, give your mynah any of the fresh fruits listed in the table on page 153. Since he'll probably gulp the pieces whole, chop them up for him.

Add variety to his diet with chopped or shredded raw veggies, chopped hard-boiled eggs, any kind of cooked beans, cooked chicken or turkey, a dab of peanut butter, and sometimes a bit of shredded cheese. A mynah also appreciates an occasional treat of mealworms or crickets. No, you don't have to hunt for these critters. They're available in most pet shops.

What's Good for Toucans?

Your toucan will do well on mynah bird pellets soaked in fruit juice or water. In addition, he should have a variety of fresh fruits (cantaloupe, papaya and grapes seem to be special favorites). Add variety to his food dish with an occasional dollop of peanut butter or some cooked beans. He may also like soaked dog kibble, but don't buy a brand until you're sure it's low in iron. Toucans tend to store too much iron, which eventually damages their livers. When in doubt, check with the manufacturer. Toucan food should have less than 150 parts per million (it's listed as 150 ppm on the label) of iron.

Toucan taboos include cat food, monkey chow and any dog kibble that has over 150 ppm of iron. Citrus fruits, including pineapple and tomato, contain more acid than a toucan can handle. Other taboo foods are raw vegetables, seeds and nuts.

The Least You Need to Know

➤ Different birds have different nutritional needs.

➤ Birds do best when they eat a wide variety of healthy foods, including fresh veggies and fruit. Wash them well.

➤ Formulated foods, commonly called pellets, contain all the nutrition birds are known to need. Introduce them slowly by adding them to your bird's regular meals.

➤ Never try to starve a bird into eating something new. Birds aren't stubborn about trying things. Rather, they are genetically programmed to be cautious. If they don't recognize something as food, they won't eat it, and they won't live long without nourishment.

➤ Never give your bird junk food, alcohol, food scraps or leftovers you wouldn't eat. Fruit cores and pits are especially dangerous because they contain pesticide residues.

➤ Attach a cuttlebone to your bird's cage. It provides calcium and other minerals.

➤ Canaries and finches need a little grit to help with digestion. Other small birds may be offered a few grains occasionally.

➤ Lories, toucans and mynah birds eat soft foods. They need a different diet than other pet birds.

Chapter 11

The Wonder of Wings and Other Feathered Things

> **In This Chapter**
>
> ➤ Facts about feathers
>
> ➤ How birds use their senses
>
> ➤ Big hearts beating, rapid breathing and buoyant bones
>
> ➤ The ins and outs of digestion

Besides flight, birds have other uses for their fabulous feathers. Feathers help them attract a mate, act as camouflage to hide them from predators and help control their high body temperature. But feathers aren't the only things that make birds unique. They also use their senses in distinctive ways and have amazingly efficient bodies. Here are some facts about feathers, how birds use their senses and how their bodies are built. I hope they will help you understand some of your bird's ways.

Where did feathers come from? They evolved from reptilian scales. The first egg-laying reptiles, extremely distant relatives of our birds, roamed the earth about 280 million years ago. About 130 million years after that (or 150 million years ago), along came Archaeopteryx, the first bird, complete with sharp teeth, a long, bony tail and claws on its wing tips. Archaeopteryx's body was protected by feathers, just as all its reptilian relatives were protected by scales.

Facets of a Feather

Feathers are composed of *keratin*—the same stuff that makes fur, fingernails, claws, beaks, spider webs and human hair. It's a protein molecule manufactured by skin cells.

Archaeopteryx give new meaning to the phrase "early bird."

But while hair is relatively simple stuff, some feathers are incredibly intricate. The most complicated are flight feathers. They have about a million parts, all precisely fitted to each other. Most of the parts are the same form, repeated over and over, so we only need to know a few terms to understand the facets of a feather.

Beginning at the bottom, the *quill* is the hollow base attached to the bird's skin. As it continues up the middle of the feather, it's called the *shaft* (scientific types call it the *rachis*). The soft sides of the feather are the *vanes*.

The next time Pauly loses a flight feather, check it out up close—or better yet, under a microscope. First, you'll notice the individual *barbs*—feathery branches growing out of each side of the shaft. The vanes of an average flight feather contain 600 pairs of barbs. But that's only a tiny fraction of a feather. Each barb is made up of even smaller branches called *barbules*, and people with the equipment to count them report about 500 pairs on each barb. Then there are the *barbicels*—tiny fibers attached to each barbule. Each barbicel has a little hook at the end. The hooks are called *hamuli,* and they interlock, keeping the million parts of the feather neatly in place. In fact, when Pauly preens (that's the bird word for grooming), you could say he's zipping up his feathers.

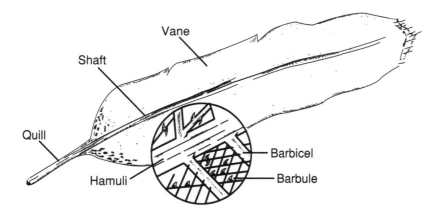

Here's how a flight feather is made.

Why Feathers Fly

Although feathers are… well… light as a feather, they can still lift big birds, such as two-pound macaws, keep them aloft and send them on their way at speeds up to 25 mph. That's because flight feathers are surprisingly sturdy, due mostly to the barbule and barbicel zip-lock security system.

The upper surface of a bird wing is raised, while the lower surface is hollowed out.
This means that as a bird's wings slice through the air, they force air to move above and beneath them at different rates of speed. Consequently, air races over the top of the wing faster than it moves across the bottom. The faster-moving air above the wing reduces the air pressure, and the pressure differential between the two surfaces supplies lift.

Bird Brainers

Finches and canaries fold their wings during flight, a trait they have in common with woodpeckers and starlings. This action makes their flight style seem erratic. Birds flying with steady wing beats appear smoother.

Speaking of Feathers

Our slang is full of feather talk. Here are some examples:

➤ A feather in his cap.

➤ You could have knocked me over with a feather.

➤ He's such a feather brain.

➤ She's a featherweight.

➤ Birds of a feather flock together.

➤ Do you think the boss knows she's featherbedding?

➤ They were really making the feathers fly.

➤ What a lovely outfit. She's sure in full feather.

The Meaning of Preening

Preening is the way a bird maintains his flight equipment so he can always take off instantly. Healthy birds spend time every day cleaning and smoothing ruffled feathers, and keeping their barbules tightly zipped. Sometimes preening is social. Mated birds, or even just good friends, practice mutual preening by grooming each other in places that birds can't reach by themselves. When you see a bird working on another bird's head and nape of the neck, it's similar to us scratching a friend's back.

Pauly also preens to be clean and pretty. In the wild, he wants to look good and attract the opposite sex. Some tame birds preen to get their owner's attention.

Most birds have a gland by the base of the tail that emits something akin to hair conditioner. Birds wipe this oily goop on their feathers to keep them pliable and make them water repellent.

Bird Brainers

Don't look for the preen gland on your amazon parrot. Amazons don't have one, and don't seem to miss it.

Those Fascinating Feathers

Feathers are considered part of a bird's skin, and grow from feather follicles, just like mammalian hair grows from hair follicles. But while mammal hair growth may have no pattern, feather follicles line up in even rows, like a military band marching around the bird's body. Between the lines of feathers are rows of thin, nearly transparent skin. We don't see it unless the bird has a medical problem, because healthy feathers overlap, completely covering the body.

Birds sport several kinds of feathers, which are generally categorized into three types. *Contour* feathers are the ones you see in all their glory. They cover the contours (okay, body) of the bird. The majority of the contour feathers are called *coverts*, but the *flight feathers*, the large strong feathers on the wings and tail, are also contour feathers. While most feathers are attached to a bird's muscles, some of the intricately constructed flight feathers are connected directly to bones, giving them additional strength. *Filoplumes* grow at the base of each contour feather. With a lean shaft and only a few small

Bird Brainers

Most birds' feathers account for six percent of their body weight, but the percentage tends to be somewhat higher in small birds. The little ones need extra feathers because they lose heat faster than large birds do.

barbs at the ends, they resemble hair. Filoplumes act like sensors. They tell a bird the exact position of every one of its contour feathers.

Flight feathers on the wings are divided into primary and secondary feathers. *Primary feathers* are the longest and grow closest to the end of the wing, providing most of the thrust. *Secondary feathers* grow closer to the body. They provide lift and help sustain the bird during flight. Most parrots have eleven primaries, and six or more secondaries. Flight feathers on the tail help with steering. Think: rudder.

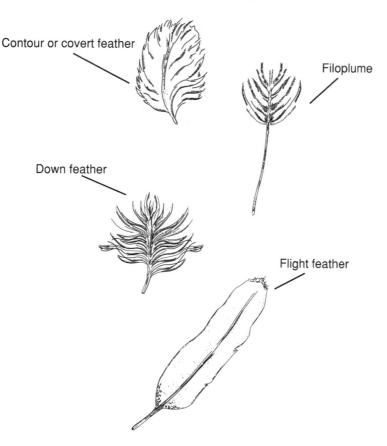

Contour or covert feather

Filoplume

Down feather

Flight feather

These are the four major types of feathers.

Down feathers grow beneath the contour feathers and are seldom visible. They are your bird's long johns. Furry and soft, they provide insulation and are comparable to the undercoat of many mammals. They have wispy shafts and are just a flimsy mass of barbs and barbules. Birds need their downy underwear to maintain their normal body temperature of between 106 and 110 degrees. When a bird fluffs up against the cold, his down feathers trap air and insulate his body.

169

Here are the parts of a parrot.

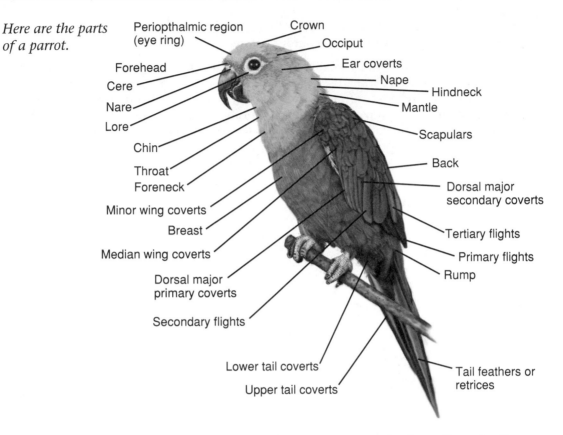

A few parrot species have a special type of down called *powder down*. These fragile feathers, found on the lower thigh, break constantly, creating a fine dust that helps to waterproof and condition the rest of the feathers.

Bristles are made up mostly of shaft, but have a few small barbs at the base. Think of bristle feathers as bird nose hair. They also grow around the eyes and mouth of many species, and are considered organs of touch, like a dog's whiskers.

Avian Adventures

How many feathers does a bird have? Scientists counted feathers on several species and say the bird bearing the most is the emperor penguin. It has more than 30,000 feathers, and needs every one of them to keep cozy in its native Antarctica. Wearing the fewest feathers, with just under 1,000, is the ruby-throated hummingbird. Even your little budgie has nearly 3,000.

Feathers: Dead or Alive?

Pauly's feathers are dead most of the time, in the sense of being without a blood supply—much like our hair. They are only alive while they are developing.

As soon as an old feather falls out, its replacement begins growing. The new feather looks like an angry pimple poking out of the skin at first, but then a little tube emerges. Composed of keratin, the tube contains the growing feather. At this point, the feather is called a *pin* or *blood feather*. It has its own vein and artery, is very much alive, and needs the tube to protect it. If it breaks during development, the bird might bleed to death.

When the new feather matures, its blood supply dries up. Then it's ready to unveil itself in all its glossy glory. The keratin sheath falls off or is picked off by the bird, and the feather, now "dead," is ready to use and won't endanger the bird if it breaks.

Avian Adventures

Because all feathers (except flight feathers) are connected to tiny muscles, birds can control every single one individually, and raise or lower it at will. You've seen your bird control his crest if you have a cockatiel or cockatoo. It isn't as obvious in other species, so next time you go to the pet shop spend a couple of minutes watching a crested bird. He will raise his crest feathers when he's interested in something, and lower them when he's bored or resting.

Color Chemistry

Feather color comes from a variety of pigments, plus the absorption and reflection of light. The complex combination results in the hues we actually see.

The pigments in Pauly's feathers include *carotenoids* and *melanins*. Carotenoids produce yellow, red and orange tones. Melanins, which produce brown freckles and black hues in human skin, make feathers brown, black or gray. Many parrot feathers also contain a rarer pigment called *turacoverdin*, which produces various shades of green.

What about the beautiful blues we see in so many birds? No matter what your eyes tell you, scientists say it doesn't exist. No pigment produces blue feathers. Instead, the barbules (remember them?) on the feathers contain tiny particles that reflect light, making the feather look blue to us. And purple? It's a combination of carotenoids and reflected light, as are many other brilliant bird colors.

Avian Adventures

From the late 1800s through the early 1900s, plumed hats were in style and fashionable women wouldn't leave home without one. Although feathers from herons, egrets, albatrosses and ostriches were the most popular, an ornithologist from the American Museum of Natural History, while taking a walk in New York City, counted feathers from over 40 species decorating hats. For a few years, feathers were more valuable than gold, with milliners paying plume hunters $80 an ounce. Hundreds of thousands of birds were slaughtered for their feathers year after year, until angry bird lovers took action. Naturalist George Bird Grinnell founded the Audubon Society in 1886, and its members eventually managed to get legislation passed that made it illegal to wear wild bird feathers. Although too late to save the Carolina parakeet, the law brought back many other species from the brink of extinction.

Special Senses

Besides feathers, a bird's senses set it apart from other animals. Like mammals, birds have senses of sight, smell, hearing, taste and touch. In some ways their senses are similar to ours, but in other ways they are unique. Since the similarities are obvious, let's concentrate on the differences.

Those Flashing Eyes

Pauly has big eyes when compared to any mammal. In fact, a bird's eyes usually account for 1/30 of its total weight, while a dog's eyes, for example, often add up to only 1/8,000 of its total weight. Birds see detail better than mammals and are able to detect color. They need that super vision to find food, avoid predators, select a mate and choose a camouflaged nesting site.

While Pauly's eyeballs are practically fixed in his skull, he makes up for it with wide-set eyes and amazing mobility in his neck and head. He can even see what's happening behind him by swiveling his head 180 degrees.

Distance, color and range come easy, but depth perception is more challenging. Pauly doesn't cock his head just to be cute. Most birds (raptors excepted) have two-dimensional vision, which gives them limited ability to judge distances. Your bird deciphers depth by tilting his head in different directions, so he sees an object from several angles. After seeing different views, his brain compiles a composite picture and tells him how far he is from the object.

Like a dog (and some other mammals), Pauly has three eyelids on each eye. The extra one is a transparent third eyelid called the *nictitating membrane*. It moves across the eye from the inner to the outer corner and back again, several times a minute. Think of it as a pair of work goggles, protecting Pauly from debris and wind as it "blinks" across his eye. He'd need it in the wild.

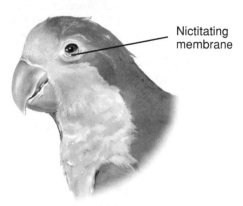

Nictitating membrane

The nictitating membrane protects birds in flight.

Where Is It? The Avian Ear

Pauly uses his ears for hearing and balance, just as we do, but while most mammals' ears are obvious appendages, his are well hidden. That's because a bird has to be streamlined for flight. For quick takeoffs, effortless flight and protection, bird ears are just little openings to the outside world, covered with tiny contour feathers. To find Pauly's ears, check out the area just behind and below his eyes. The feathers should look just a little different there. Part them and you'll see the small, slit-like opening that begins your bird's ear canal. That's the powerful avian ear.

Both birds and people can hear sounds ranging from a low of 100 cycles per second to a high of about 20,000 cycles per second, or from the lowest boom of a bass drum to a high whistle. Birds distinguish between sounds much faster than we do, but their ability to determine where sound is coming from is similar to ours.

Bird Brainers

The balancing function of the inner ear is every bit as important as hearing to a bird. Birds need perfect balance to soar and perch.

Does Pauly Have Bad Taste?

Scientists say the avian sense of taste is rather primitive. For example, while we have around 9,000 taste buds, parrots only have about 350. Logic tells us that with so few taste buds, parrots shouldn't be too particular about their diet.

So much for logic. Parrots have favorite foods, just like we do, and can be as finicky as three-year-olds when it comes to trying new flavors. No one knows how important color, texture, temperature and shape may be to palatability, but parrot owners know their pets eat what they like and ignore the rest (or fling it from their dish).

How Well Can Birds Smell?

No one knows how well birds can smell, but it's generally accepted that most of them have little sense of smell (there are exceptions, but none of them are potential pets). That's because odors stay close to the ground (think of a hound dog hunting), and birds spend most of their time in the air where scent dissipates quickly.

Again, there are discrepancies. Many pet parrots who share meals with their owners seem to get excited when they smell their favorite dinner cooking. Is it because they recognize the routine their owner goes through when cooking the meal, or do they differentiate aromas? Rooster loves spaghetti and marinara sauce, pungent with garlic. While waiting impatiently for his serving to cool, he dances and whistles. Does the smell tantalize him? I asked him, and all he said was, "Hello, pretty bird."

Beaks and Toes for Touching

Pauly uses his beak and feet to learn more about his environment. Think: toddler. Around two, children touch everything they see, and put things in their mouths as fast as they can get their hands on them. Well, parrots are always toddlers when it comes to testing the things around them.

Bird Brainers

Parrot beaks do double duty. They are strong for cracking seeds and nuts, and sharp enough for slicing into the succulent sweetness of ripe fruit. Does that make them nut-cracker sweets?

Larger parrots and some cockatiels use their feet much as we use our hands. They pick up and examine objects, and even hold food with one foot while munching it, similar to a person eating a Popsicle. Beaks also help birds climb and are useful for determining if a perch is safe. Before Rooster steps on anything, including my finger, he mouths it to make sure it's capable of holding him. Then he uses his beak for balance while climbing on. It doesn't hurt, but some of my friends cringe at the sight anyway.

Squawk!

If your bird is hurt and you aren't sure if a bone is fractured or not, take your pet to an avian veterinarian immediately. A broken bone can quickly lead to life-threatening respiratory infections, including pneumonia.

Dem Bones

Birds are built a lot lighter than we are. Imagine a canary as tall as you. If you weigh 120 pounds, the sizable songster would weigh 60 pounds—just half your weight. That's because you and other mammals have dense bones, but birds' bones are thinner—light enough for flight. To make birds even more buoyant, their non-weight-bearing bones are hollow and are filled mostly with air, while ours are packed with marrow.

Tiny cross pieces (like spokes on a wheel) give bird bones some strength, but they are brittle in comparison with mammal bones. The air pockets or sacs inside bird bones are connected to the lungs, and are actually part of the respiratory system. (Watch Pauly breathe. When he inhales, the air goes all the way down to his toes.)

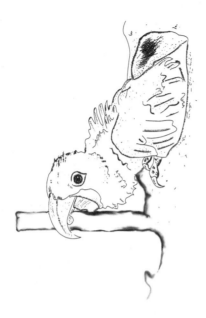

Parrots often check out a perch with their beak before climbing on.

Besides having airy bones, birds don't have heavy heads like mammals do. Their skulls are lighter, and their eating machine is a lightweight beak, weighing a mere fraction of our heavy teeth.

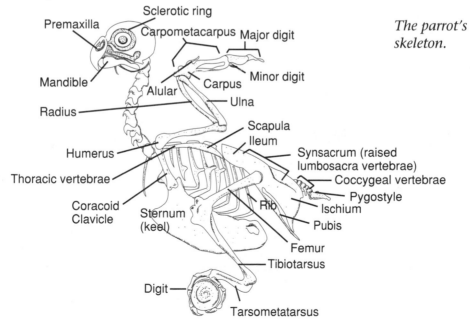

The parrot's skeleton.

How Birds Breathe

Besides having air sacs in some of their bones, birds also have nine air sacs in their bodies. But they don't have diaphragms. When you think of a bird breathing, don't picture his lungs expanding and contracting like ours do, taking air in and pushing carbon dioxide out. Instead, think of an accordion, because birds breathe like a bellows.

When Pauly takes a breath, the air enters his nares (nostrils) and goes into his throat. Next, it enters a slit in the roof of his mouth called the choana. There the air is warmed, moisturized and cleaned. After the air is "filtered" in the choana, it moves on through Pauly's trachea and syrinx membrane, and then enters his bronchi (in the lungs).

Pauly's whole body expands as his air sacs fill up. His body also contracts on the same breath as the force of the bellows pushes air from the air sacs into his lungs and out again. Because of the bellows system, birds have the constant supply of oxygen they need for the rigors of flight. Unlike us, they don't have to wait for their lungs to refill after every breath.

Did you ever notice how fast your bird breathes? That's because he needs two complete breaths (in and out twice) to exchange gases, while we (and other mammals) get the same benefit from one complete breath. Most of us take between 12 and 16 breaths per minute. Canaries take 60 to 100 breaths per minute, budgies take 65 to 85 and larger parrots average 25 to 40.

Big-Hearted Birds

Although Pauly's heart is similar to yours because it has four chambers, it's four or five times larger in relation to his size. Your heart is about the same size as your fist, but a bird your size would have a heart as big as a cabbage.

Pauly's heart also beats a lot faster than yours. While yours beats between 60 and 85 times a minute, a canary's heart beats between 500 and 1,000 times a minute when he's relaxed, and even faster when he flies. A budgie's heart rate is between 350 and 550 beats per minute, and large parrots average between 150 to 300 beats per minute.

Avian Adventures

Did you ever wonder why chickens and turkeys have white and dark meat? It has to do with the relationship between blood vessels and activity level. Active muscles need the most oxygen, and it takes a lot of blood vessels to carry the load. The more blood vessels, the darker the meat. Since domestic chickens and turkeys walk around but seldom fly, they have many more blood vessels in their legs than they do in their breasts and wings.

Fueling a Feathered Furnace

Birds' thermostats run on high all the time. While your body temperature is around 98.6°, your beaked buddy should top the thermometer at around 107°. Not only that, but you have three million or so sweat glands helping you stay cool, and your bird doesn't have any. Pauly keeps his cool because of his air sacs. Much of the air he breathes is used for maintaining body temperature.

It takes a lot of energy to run on high all the time, so birds have a fast fueling system. They eat often, consume large amounts for their size and have a short digestive tract.

Fueling begins when Pauly picks up a piece of food in his beak. Using his tongue to manipulate the item, he cracks the seed or nut, or shreds the plant. After that, nothing much happens in his mouth. Since Pauly lacks teeth and saliva, he can't moisten or chew his food, so he swallows it as is.

The unprocessed food travels to the esophagus and is partially moistened there. Its next stop is the crop, where it acquires additional moisture and starts breaking down. The crop sends the food on, a little at a time, to Pauly's stomach.

The first station it reaches in his stomach is called the *proventriculus,* and digestive juices are added there. Then the food moves on to his second stomach station, the *gizzard.* Think of the gizzard as

Bird Brainers

Small birds eat 20 percent or more of their body weight daily. In order to eat like a bird, a 140-pound person would have to devour 28 pounds of food a day.

Polly Sez

Think of a bird's *crop* as his grocery sack. It's located at the base of the neck, and because of it, birds can eat and run (okay, fly). Having a crop is a real plus for your bird's wild cousins. They can gulp down their dinner, stash it in their crop, fly to safety before a predator finds them, and digest their meal in peace.

Polly Sez

Imagine your bird walking on wet sand. What would his footprints look like? If your bird is a parrot, an X will mark the spot. That's because parrots have a *zygodactyl* foot, or two toes in front and two in back. The majority of birds, including canaries, finches, mynahs and toucans have an *anisodactyl* foot—three toes forward and one in back.

Pauly's teeth, because it grinds up his dinner into tiny digestible pieces and sends them on their way to the small intestine. There the food becomes nutrition and is absorbed into his bloodstream.

The part of his meal that Pauly can't use becomes waste. It travels through his large intestine and enters his cloaca, joining the liquid waste created by his kidneys (birds don't have bladders). The cloaca is a common chamber where all Pauly's waste ends up, whether it is urine, feces or reproductive matter. The waste in the cloaca is released through the vent. Since the vent is only one opening, a bird's droppings are a mixture of urine and feces. The cloaca has limited storage space, so birds release small amounts of droppings at frequent intervals.

Did that system sound complicated? Actually, it's amazingly efficient. Digestion is about seven times faster in birds than it is in humans. In fact, from beak to vent takes about three hours.

The Real Poop on Livers and Kidneys

A bird's liver performs functions similar to our own. It filters the blood, stores energy, and works in concert with other organs. The kidneys cleanse the blood of toxins, and regulate the balance of electrolytes and water. Bird urine is part liquid and part solid. Most of the white, sticky part of Pauly's droppings is actually uric acid, the waste product of protein metabolism.

The heart, lungs and digestive tract.

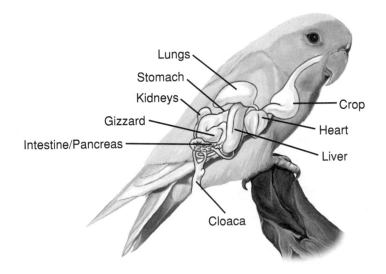

In birds (and reptiles), blood returning from the legs, the lower intestines and the reproductive system passes through the kidneys before getting back into general circulation. Why do you need to know that? Because an infection in the reproductive system or an intestinal infection could lead to a kidney infection. Also, birds should never receive an injection in the leg or lower abdomen. The drug would travel through the kidneys and probably be neutralized before it reached the part of the body that needs the medication.

The Least You Need to Know

➤ Feathers are alive and have their own blood supply during their growth stage. During that period, they are encased in a tubular sheath and are called pin or blood feathers. If a blood feather is broken or damaged, a bird can bleed profusely. When trimming wings, never clip a blood feather.

➤ Birds have ears, even though they are hard to find. They hear in about the same range as we do, but decipher sounds much faster.

➤ Parrots use their beaks and feet to examine their environment. Don't pull away if a tame bird tries to mouth your finger before climbing on. Many birds use their beaks to make sure a perch is safe before putting their weight on it.

➤ Bird bones are light for flight. Some even have air sacs and are part of the respiratory system. Always handle your bird carefully because thin bones are brittle.

➤ A broken bone in a bird is a true emergency. If you suspect a fracture, take your bird to the veterinarian immediately.

➤ Birds have a much faster heart rate and a higher temperature than we do.

➤ Bird droppings are a combination of urine and feces, since birds have only one opening for elimination.

➤ Birds shouldn't receive injections in the leg or lower abdomen because the medication would probably be neutralized before it did any good.

Chapter 12

Avian Aerobics

In This Chapter

➤ Why exercise is essential

➤ Flapping for fitness

➤ Helping pudgy parrots

➤ Bird exercises and other fitness games

Wild birds have busy bodies. Through jungles, rain forests or grasslands, they fly many miles foraging for food, then make the return trip to their roosts before dusk. Because life is a daily struggle for survival, wild birds also have busy minds. They choose mates, search for suitable nest sites, lay eggs, produce young, feed their hatchlings and protect them from predators. Yet even with that job description, they still find time to climb and play, groom each other, sing or squawk.

On the other hand, Polly has her food delivered and doesn't have to choose a mate or a nest site, and protect her young from bigger birds or hungry snakes. She isn't responsible for survival of the species, or even the next generation. Yet she was born with the same equipment as her wild cousins—an abundance of energy and an alert mind. That's why exercise is essential for Polly. To be a healthy, well-behaved bird, she needs an outlet for her high activity level.

Providing Polly with enough exercise is easy. Given the opportunity, she'll take care of it herself. This chapter is all about exercise. It will help you arrange activities Polly can take advantage of on her own, and tell you how to give her a quick workout whenever you want to.

Pent-Up Energy

Lacking an outlet for their high activity level, some pet birds amuse themselves through incessant screaming, destructive actions or an aggressive attitude. Others turn their nervous energy on themselves, and mutilate their feet or feathers. Some become cage potatoes. They eat out of boredom, become dull and obese and die many years before their time. In fact, lack of exercise is one of the most common causes of bad bird behavior, and is frequently to blame for poor health.

Bird Brainers

Parrots yawn often. Sometimes they're just tired, but experts believe they also yawn as a form of exercise. Yawning stretches the muscles controlling their beaks and helps them take in more oxygen.

It's a pity so many pet birds suffer needlessly from pent-up energy when exercising a bird is so simple that even the busiest person can handle it. If you own canaries or finches, exercising your bird is as easy as buying the right size cage so Caruso can fly from perch to perch (see Chapter 5). The rest of this chapter is for parrot owners, whether your pet is a budgie or a macaw.

The Fundamentals of Flapping

Does Polly often flap her wings several times in succession? If she does, she's doing herself a favor. Flapping is an excellent aerobic exercise. It improves her muscle tone and cardiovascular condition. Flapping also prevents several problems associated with poor circulation. Among these are foot and toe disorders, weak vision and flawed flight feathers.

Uh oh. Your Polly isn't into flapping. Since it's one of the most natural exercises birds do, let's find out why Polly won't put her wings in motion.

The two most common reasons why a pet bird might not flap are:

➤ There's no room to spread her wings without banging the sides of the cage.

➤ She's too obese to bother.

Not enough room is easy to correct. All it takes is a little money, a little creativity or a little time. If spending a little money sounds easiest, buy Polly a bigger cage. If her cage is already considerably wider than her wingspan, a few stimulating toys might induce her to exercise. Get a rope toy or a closed chain that she can cling to, and attach it to the top of her cage so it dangles freely. Swinging from a toy tempts many pet birds into flapping fun.

If creativity is more your speed, find just the right natural (untreated) tree limb—one with branches of various thicknesses coming out at different angles. Either cut it to fit inside Polly's cage or make your own play gym by attaching it to a base so it stands upright. Natural branches seem to stimulate birds and often inspire flapping, while nothing but horizontal perches lead to lethargy. If Polly doesn't climb her personal tree within a few days, make it worth her while by attaching treats, such as Cheerios, strawberries or grapes to the ends of the branches.

Making a little more time for your parrot is the best alternative, provided you do it regularly. To benefit from flapping, birds should do it at least five times a week. The easiest method, provided Polly cooperates, is simply opening her cage door and letting her climb to the top of her cage, or putting her on her play gym. The extra space and the feeling of freedom may be all it takes to get her flapping.

Let's Fly

Taking an active role is even better. Once Polly eagerly steps on your finger (see Chapter 13), you can become her personal fitness coach. First, make sure her wings are trimmed. Then take her to a room where she would land on soft carpeting or a bed if she fell or flew from your finger. Use the Egyptian hold (I'll describe it in Chapter 13), give a verbal cue like "let's fly," and lower your hand fast enough so she has to flap to keep her balance (but not so fast that you frighten her). Praise her and give her a tiny treat, then repeat the exercise. Use the verbal cue every time, so she doesn't think your hand may suddenly drop when the two of you are relaxing together.

After Polly flaps twice, look at her carefully before trying it again. If she's panting even a little bit, she's had enough for the first time. Increase the repetitions gradually until you can coach her in flapping exercises for a full minute. Two minutes is even better, but take your time reaching that goal. Overdoing is dangerous.

Bird Brainers

Some medium to large parrots like to swing from a knotted rope like a kid on a tire swing. Start swinging Polly by dangling the rope over a bed so she'll land softly if she lets go, and make sure there's sufficient space so she won't accidentally hit something. Swing gently at first.

Helping Pudgy Polly

If Polly is pudgy and has been sedentary for years, see your avian veterinarian before beginning any exercise program. Any exertion can be dangerous for severely out of shape birds. And overweight cage potatoes need more than gradual doses of exercise. They also need a diet planned by a professional.

Ask your veterinarian about flapping, bathing, swinging and the other exercises in this chapter. After examining your pet, he or she will tell you which ones are safe for Polly, how often she should do them and for how long at a time. You'll still be Polly's fitness coach and even her dietitian, but play it safe and let your veterinarian plan the programs.

Rooster flaps for fitness.

Protecting Polly

Before playing climb the chair, follow the leader or fetch with Polly, make sure every part of the house she will walk around in is safe. Here's a partial checklist. I have no way of knowing if a pet boa constrictor lives under your bed, so add or subtract to fit your situation:

Before putting Polly on the floor checklist

✓ Doors and windows closed

✓ Curtains drawn (if Polly's flight feathers aren't trimmed) so she won't crash into a window

✓ Toilet lid down

✓ No alcoholic beverages where Polly might taste them

✓ No hot drinks where Polly could tumble in them or drink them

✓ Fireplace screened so Polly can't enter the chimney

✓ Nothing cooking in the kitchen

✓ Nothing soaking in the sink

✓ Aquarium covered

✓ No poisonous plants

✓ No loose dogs or cats

✓ Family aware that Polly's loose, so no one opens an outside door by mistake

✓ Family knows where Polly is so no one sits or steps on her by mistake (this accident happens most often to budgies and cockatiels)

Birdercise

What do people do at Jazzercise class besides bends and stretches? We do aerobics to music—lively dance steps in time to rock, rap, country, reggae and salsa—in fact, anything goes as long as it has a good beat. Because of the beat, we put out a lot more effort while having much more fun.

Birds benefit from aerobic dance, just like people do. When I want to arouse Rooster into wild dancing, all I have to do is play the soundtrack from the movie *The Mighty Quinn*. Those reggae rhythms never fail to excite him. When "his" tape comes on, he begins bobbing up and down. Within seconds, he works himself up and starts turning circles, flapping and screaming. I've tested him by playing other songs before and after his favorite tape. While he listens to other tunes, and sometimes sways a little, he doesn't get down and boogie until his favorite music plays. And when his tape ends, so does his aerobic dance.

Are you wondering what I do while Rooster gets off on a Jamaican beat? Okay, I admit it—I'm his partner. While he twirls, flaps and screams on his

Bird Brainers

Does anyone in your family play a musical instrument? Encourage them to practice near Polly (provided the decibels aren't rocking the room). Most parrots love private concerts. I practice fiddle for mine, and they dance on their cage tops and don't even squawk about wrong notes.

play gym, I kind of follow his lead on the floor. Yes, we look funny. Yes, we have fun. Besides, it's good exercise and better bonding for both of us. Try it. You and your parrot can rock and rumba too. But first, you'll have to find out what type of music or special songs turn Polly on.

Music can create moods, and some parrots respond to it even more strongly than people do. To find out what strums Polly's strings, play several lively songs for her and sway a little or sing along so she sees you enjoy them. You'll know by her body language which ones she reacts to. When she starts to show excitement, let her know you feel the beat too. Go ahead. Flap those arms. Turn around. Give a little wiggle. Sing, shout. Yeehaw! You're doin' the Macaw Macarena!

Every party has a pooper, but it won't be Polly. Soon she'll recognize her special songs and dance to them, even if you don't. But she'll be happier if you do. And you'll be happier too.

Bathing for More than Beauty

Most birds love baths. When Rooster sees me coming with the spray bottle (filled with lukewarm water and adjusted for fine misting), he spreads his wings and dances. I've

Squawk!

Don't bathe birds at night. Polly should be completely dry before bedtime, and drying can take several hours.

tried spraying my birds from different angles, and I believe they like it best when I hold the bottle a few inches below and a little to the side of them, and aim upward at an angle. It makes the mist fall on them like delicate drizzle.

Why include bathing in a chapter about exercise? Because after you wet her down, Polly will have to preen (groom her feathers), and preening requires so many bends and stretches that it reminds me of Jazzercise class. Give Polly a minimum of three baths a week. A good misting is also a fun way to end a flapping session.

Beak Over Feet

Climbing exercises will improve Polly's muscle tone and coordination while helping her stay in shape. Cages with some horizontal bars among the vertical (or vice versa) encourage climbing, as do toy rings, chains, ladders and natural branches positioned nearly vertical. Climbing rings should be large enough for Polly to put her whole body through, and ladder rungs should be spaced for birds her size. Ladders are also useful as part of a play gym. Extra-long ones that will exercise Polly from her cage door to the floor and back again are also available.

You can also convince Polly to climb when playing with her outside her cage or play gym. Instead of watching television with her perched on your hand, put her down on the floor beside your chair. Chances are she'll join you by climbing either the chair or your pants leg. Cuddle her for a little while, then put her down and let her work her way up again.

Avian Adventures

Birds stretch after sleeping or resting, just like we do. They begin by extending both wings slightly. Next, they stretch one wing as far as it goes. The leg on the same side stretches simultaneously, and half the tail feathers fan out. Then the stretch is repeated on the other side.

Follow the Leader

Will Polly follow you anywhere? Waddling around is great exercise for her legs and feet, so try leading your flock of one from room to room. Assuming Polly's wings are trimmed, put her down on the floor and walk away slowly while calling her cheerfully. Walk all the way into another room, then wait for her to catch up. When she reaches you, give her a small treat (a sunflower seed works well). If Polly likes that game, try playing hide-and-seek. Go around a corner and call her. Then help her find you by peeking out at her and withdrawing your head once or twice. When she finds you, reward her with a treat.

If Polly doesn't follow you in a familiar room, try putting her down in a room she seldom sees. Most parrots don't like being alone in a strange place, so chances are she'll follow you out of there in a hurry. Now you have a chance to reward her. Do it several times and she'll learn that following you leads to fun, no matter what room you're in.

Follow the leader usually starts slow, but after several weeks some birds really get into it and run after their human with wings flapping. Always reward Polly when she catches up to you, no matter how long it takes her. Slow or fast, going for a walk is good for her.

Bird Brainers

Your reactions are every bit as important to Polly as a treat. Does your parrot like a neck rub? Does excitement in your voice tickle her, or would she rather hear soothing sounds? Whatever Polly prefers, reward her with the right reaction.

If you thought playing fetch was only for Rover, here's a surprise. Lots of pet parrots learn to fetch, and it's good exercise. Use a toy that Polly can pick up easily but won't want to chew. A molded plastic or nylon bead off an old bird toy works well, as does an empty spool from a spool of thread (if your bird is big enough to carry it). Begin by

187

rolling the toy only a foot from you. If Polly picks it up, show her a treat, talk her back to you with praise and trade the toy for the treat when she reaches you.

Over a period of weeks, increase the distance Polly retrieves to three feet or more. Reward every successful attempt and never do more than three retrieves at a time, or you'll bore Polly and she won't play anymore. What should you do when your bird ignores the toy after she knows how to retrieve? Nothing. Just withhold the treat and put Polly back in her cage. Gently. Never punish a parrot for refusing to perform. Instead, try again tomorrow.

Bird Brainers

Unshelled nuts are great fun for birds, but only parrots with really big beaks can crack the hardest ones themselves. Give your bird a break. Use the nutcracker and make a small crack in walnuts, brazil nuts, pecans, filberts and even almonds when they have especially hard shells.

Fun Foods for Fitness

Presenting some of Polly's food so she has to work to eat will give her additional exercise. In the wild, birds spend most of their waking hours finding food, and often have to hold it still to eat it (think of a mango attached to a tree). While it's impossible to duplicate all the effort of eating in the jungle or rain forest, you can simulate it enough to entertain and exercise Polly. Chapter 10 tells you how to present a variety of foods so Polly gets a workout during dinner.

The Least You Need to Know

➤ Exercise keeps birds physically fit and well behaved.

➤ One of the best exercises a bird can do is to flap her wings. Encourage flapping by giving your bird a bigger cage (if hers is so small that she can't spread her wings).

➤ Provide parrots with hanging toys, natural branches and supervised time on top of the cage or on a play gym. If your bird sits on your hand, teach her to flap on cue as you lower your arm.

➤ Climbing and playing follow the leader are also excellent exercises. Before letting your bird climb up your chair or follow you from room to room, bird-proof the area for her safety.

➤ Play music for your bird. Certain songs will arouse her. Dance along and she may mimic your motions.

➤ Don't start a lazy, overweight bird on an exercise program until she has been examined by an avian veterinarian.

Part 4
Taming and Training

Are you ready for some fun? How about a meaningful new relationship? Both are as close as the birdcage. In this section, I'll help you and your bird bond with each other. Soon you'll be able to hold her, train her and trade her bad habits (if she has any) for good ones. Even better, you'll be able to understand her—usually. Polly can't learn how to think like a person, but the next few chapters are going to help you interpret her feelings. Then you'll be able to bring out your bird's best by working with, not against, her nature.

Bonding with another species is special—almost magical—but is easily within your reach. Happy handling, and have fun.

Chapter 13

Building a Bond

In This Chapter

➤ Settling in together

➤ How to be your bird's best buddy

➤ Bonding with your budgie

➤ Getting cozy with your cockatiel

➤ Taming techniques for birds of all sizes

Have you skimmed some of the self-improvement books on bookstore shelves? All of them promise a better life, if only you get organized and follow their formula. No matter how different the formulas, most of those books have one thing in common: They emphasize the importance of setting goals. Do they have a point? They sure do. Setting goals and working toward them keeps us on track, but it does something else that's even better. It helps us recognize and celebrate our small successes.

How can you set goals for handling your bird when you've never trained one before? You can't. That's my job, so I have set some for you.

Your long-term goal is to create a bond based on mutual trust. In practical terms, that's a bird who doesn't fear you, and is happy to climb on your hand, come out of her cage and spend time with you. Are you in a hurry? No way. We're going to take our time, do it right and celebrate every small success along the way. Ready? Then head for the birdcage. Let's turn that pretty pile of feathers into a friend.

Ready? Set? Wait

Today may not be the best time to begin befriending your bird. If you just brought her home this morning, give her some time to settle in—two or three full days at least. In the meantime, settle down near your new pet, but not close enough to make her nervous. She'll tell you how much space she needs by either staying on her perch or fluttering around in fear. Read a book, write a letter, or watch television from a non-threatening distance, and take some time-outs to talk to Polly. Use her name often if she has one, or just tell her what a beautiful baby she is and how much fun the two of you are going to have. Don't worry about being original. Parrots love repetition. Do you like to whistle or sing? Give her a quiet concert and she'll think you're trying to speak her language.

There are exceptions to the waiting rule. Newly weaned hand-fed babies and previously owned birds used to lots of lovin' may feel rejected without physical contact. If Polly bows her head and fluffs her nape feathers, she's inviting you to touch her. Don't get her out of the cage for a day or two, but do reach in and gently pet the nape of her neck and possibly her cheeks. Parrots prefer being petted gently, and like it best when your finger moves against or across the growth of feathers. Don't even try to touch the skin. It isn't necessary when petting a parrot.

Bird Brainers

Once your bird settles in, try offering treats through the cage bars. A piece of raw broccoli or a celery top (well washed, of course) may entice your little bird to eat out of your hand. Big birds like those veggies too, but may come even closer for a sunflower seed or a peanut.

Bird Brainers

Baby birds, especially those of large species, often look full grown, even though they are still awkward and tire easily. Expect youngsters to lack motor skills and have exceptionally short attention spans. Enjoy every ungainly moment of their baby-hood. It only lasts a little while.

Contact Calls

Does Polly vocalize in any way when you leave the room? If she does, that's super. It means you've made contact. When separated from her flock or mate, a parrot can't keep in touch via telephone. Instead, she emits contact calls back and forth to let the family know where she is. Polly's call when you leave the room says she accepts you as part of her flock. It's a big step for your bird, so celebrate your success. But make it a quiet celebration or you could encourage Polly to become a screamer.

What should you do when you leave the room and your bird calls to you? Answer her softly from the other room as often as you want to. Just don't let Polly train you to come when she calls, and don't set a bad example by screaming to her from the other end of the house. Once your parrot accepts you, you're her role model.

Becoming Your Bird's Buddy

After Polly settles in and is comfortable with you sitting near her cage, you'll be able to start handling her. But first, here are some guidelines to help you bond with your bird:

➤ Never hit Polly. Her bones are delicate, and a blow could kill or maim her. She is also sensitive. Physical punishment would make it impossible for her to trust you.

➤ Avoid startling Polly. Say something to her before entering the room, and talk to her as you approach her cage.

➤ Until Polly knows you well, move slowly when you are near her cage and avoid gesturing with your hands.

➤ Never swoop down on your bird from above. Not even after you become close companions. Hawks and eagles swoop down on their prey, and parrots are genetically programmed to fear sudden movements overhead.

➤ Respect Polly's fears. She's timid about new objects because her species needs caution to survive. Instead of being upset with her when she steers clear of her expensive new toy, lay it near her cage for a few days. Sometimes, play with it while she watches. By the time you give it to her, it won't seem strange and scary anymore.

➤ Never play with Polly when you are exhausted, in a bad mood or under the influence of anything. Parrots sense bad moods immediately, and either react with anger or become fearful. Either way, it could stretch your bond to the breaking point.

➤ Keep your expectations simple. Don't imagine Polly riding toy bicycles or talking into a tiny telephone like the avian entertainer you saw at the bird park. Instead, visualize your pet as a trusting friend. That's the greatest goal of all.

➤ Make sure both of your parrot's wings are properly trimmed before bringing her out of the cage. Chasing Polly from curtain rod to lampshade will terrify her and set bonding back several days.

➤ Keep training sessions short and upbeat. Birds have the attention span of a two- or three-year-old child.

➤ Take your bird's age into consideration. Baby birds are clumsy and get tired faster than adults.

➤ Remember that every bird is unique. Just because Aunt Emma's budgie never tried to bite and learned to sit on her finger in one training session doesn't mean that yours will. Besides, people tend to brag about their pets' (and kids') good points and forget about the problems.

Bird Brainers

One of the most common mistakes pet owners make is letting their feathered or furry friend know when she makes a mistake, while ignoring everything she does right. Always let your bird know when she does something right. If you smile and say "Good bird," or "Atta girl" in your happiest voice, she'll soon learn what pleases you and will keep doing it.

➤ Understand that the majority of bird bites (and almost all budgie and cockatiel bites) occur because the bird is terrified and is trying to defend herself. It's the prey-predator mentality in action. Imagine how big you look to your bird. When you reach for her, she thinks she's on your dinner menu. She'll get over it when you win her trust.

➤ Try to empathize with Polly. She's living in a world that's foreign to her species and may not always react the way you think she should. Understand that she's programmed for survival in the jungle, rain forest or grassland—not your living room. Just as it would take us awhile to adjust to life in the jungle, she needs time to learn the ways of her human flock.

What's Coming Up?

Training methods for budgies and cockatiels follow, but don't skip ahead to the next chapter if you have a different species. Some training techniques for small birds are helpful with bigger birds too. If you start skimming, please don't skip the section called "The 'Up' Command," or anything that follows. The last few pages of this chapter give you the basics for bonding with parrots of all sizes.

Squawk!

If your birdcage has guillotine doors, be especially careful when getting Polly in and out. Avoid accidents by keeping plastic-coated twist ties or a metal clip near the cage so you can secure the door open before handling Polly.

Beginning with Budgies (Parakeets)

Budgies make great parents and young budgies tame easily, so very few breeders bother to hand-feed budgie chicks. If you happen to have a hand-fed baby budgie, consider her a tiny treasure. Most of you have parent-raised budgies, but the following training methods will turn your pets into treasures too.

If your budgie's head is covered with stripes all the way down to the cere (see Chapter 3 to find out where the cere is located), she's a baby. When you start with a baby and sit down near her while she's settling in, making physical contact is often easy. If not, don't despair. The alternative method isn't that much harder, and the results are the same—a tame, trusting bird. But we have to start somewhere, so let's try the easy way first.

Taming Baby Budgies

After a few days of sitting near Polly, she'll be used to having you near. Now you're going to get up close and personal. Sit down right in front of her cage, talk to her for several seconds, then open the cage door and slowly slip your hand inside. Polly will probably pitch a fit, but that's okay. Just keep talking or singing to her softly, and let your hand rest quietly inside the cage with as little movement as possible. Keep your hand there a full minute (time it, or you'll stop way too soon), then remove it, close the cage door and sit by Polly a little longer. The second day, leave your hand in the cage for two minutes, and the third day for four minutes. After that, five-minute periods are just right.

Soon your budgie won't be nearly as upset about your fingers invading her space. Once she relaxes, it won't be long before she becomes curious. One day, Polly will venture near to examine your fingers and explore the possibility of perching on them. Keep still and resist the urge to cheer. Let her walk all over your hand if she wants to. When she finishes and steps off, remove your hand from the cage, close the door and celebrate your success by singing softly to Polly.

After at least five more days of Polly standing on your hand, try moving your hand back and forth, and up and down slowly while she's on it. Give her a short, smooth ride. If she jumps off, keep your hand still and she'll probably climb back on. When a little movement no longer fazes her, it's time to take her out of the cage. (Why not? Her wings are trimmed, aren't they?) Be sure the area is parrot-proofed (windows closed, nothing cooking, toilet lids down—you know the drill from Chapter 12), and move your hand right out the cage door with Polly perched on it.

Squawk!

Be very careful when bringing your bird through the door. It only takes one mishap to break Polly's toes, or worse.

Walk away from Polly's cage, sit down in another parrot-proofed area and talk to your almost-tame pet. If she flutters to the floor (and she probably will), watch her walk around for a minute or so, then offer a perch. Put your finger just in front of Polly and about an inch off the floor. If she doesn't climb on, position your hand again and, in one smooth movement, push up slightly on her belly and say "up." If it works, that's great.

If it doesn't work, you may have to scoop Polly up by bringing your cupped hands together underneath her and then letting her settle back on your finger.

Bird Brainers

Your budgie may use her beak to help her balance as she climbs aboard your finger. Don't jerk away. It won't hurt.

After five or ten minutes (less if Polly panics), put your bird back in her cage. Ideally, she will ride back perched on your finger, and you will slip her inside the cage and put her on a perch. To accomplish the perch-putting part, deposit Polly just behind her perch and say "down" as she steps off your hand.

Bird Brainers

Before trying to tame your caged bird, remove mirrors and other favorite toys that are attached to the cage. Bird attention spans are small at best. You shouldn't have to compete with distractions. (Don't forget to give Polly's toys back to her when the taming session is over.)

In the days that follow, begin petting Polly while she's perched on your finger. Bring your other hand up behind her (not above her) and stroke her back gently with one or two fingers. She may jump off your finger the first several times, but eventually she'll let you touch her.

Some of you are going to accomplish all of this by the third or fourth time you try it. Go ahead, celebrate! But a lot of you will have to put off the party because you'll run into a dead end. The most common glitch occurs when you try to take Polly out of her cage and she jumps off your hand—not just once or twice, but time after time. If you have that problem or any other complication with the baby budgie method, or if your bird is an adult, read on. There's more than one way to befriend a budgie.

Having a Heart to Heart

Several years ago, when I lived in Manhattan, I walked to a bird store in Greenwich Village to buy food for my pets. As always, I visited all the birds before making my purchase. Two large cages were brimming with budgies. One had a $40 sign on it. The other said $25. The most beautiful budgie I ever saw was one of the $25 ones, so I asked an employee why there was a difference in price. "The $40 ones are babies," he said. "They'll tame easily and become pets. The cheaper ones are older. It's too late to touch them, but they're still nice to look at."

I had no intention of buying another bird, but I couldn't leave that turquoise and yellow one with the little gray saddle to become just a decorator piece, so I purchased Pinto. After a settling-in period, I set out to prove the employee wrong. Pinto was a frightened little fellow at first, and bit me a few times. He also screamed so long and so loud that I felt compelled to explain the noise to my neighbors. But after only three days (15 minutes a day) of heart-to-heart time, he sat on my finger. Within a week he climbed on willingly and rode around the apartment on my shoulder. Here's how I did it.

First I parrot-proofed the bathroom and put the birdcage on the floor. Then I went in, closed the door behind me, put a pillow on the floor by the birdcage and sat on it. Now I was committed. I had to get my turquoise terror out of his cage. Two things were certain: He was going to bite me, and I was going to put up with it. While the prospect wasn't pleasant, it wasn't as bad as it sounds because budgies can't bite hard enough to do any actual damage.

I opened the cage door and secured it with a twist tie, so it wouldn't swing shut on us while I was taking Pinto out or putting him in. Then I reached in and, after a short chase, grabbed my bird gently but firmly, making sure his wings were properly folded so he couldn't flap them against the cage. Pinto responded with nips and screams. He was sure I was about to bite off his head.

Still holding Pinto, I removed the last vestige of security from his sight by putting his cage in the bathtub. Now he would have to depend on me for comfort and safety. My immediate mission was to soothe him, so I placed my hysterical handful against my chest so he could feel my heart beat. The warmth and steady rhythm calmed him. Soon he stopped biting, and his screams became less strident and slowly ceased.

As Pinto gradually regained his composure, I shifted my hands and used my index finger to softly stroke his back while still cuddling him. Although the first touch made him scream and bite again, the steady stroking soon calmed him. After about five minutes of petting and sweet talk, Pinto's body felt relaxed enough for the next step—placing him on my finger.

Squawk!

Although it's tempting to wear gloves when handling a hysterical bird, don't do it. All gloves do is frighten the bird even more. Birds that were initially grabbed by gloves usually take longer to tame than birds that were always handled by hands.

As soon as I placed Pinto on my finger and opened my hand to free him, he fluttered to the floor as expected (I had his wings trimmed in the store before bringing him home, so he couldn't go anywhere). Now I just played with him within the confined space (my bathroom was small—all the better for bird-taming). I used one hand to herd him toward my other hand and stretched out my legs so he could climb on them. Soon, Pinto jumped on one hand to avoid the other. Every time he hopped on my hand, I held still. Finally, he sat on my finger without fear for several seconds. Enough for one day.

I tried to move toward his open cage smoothly enough so he'd remain on my finger for the ride, but after sitting in one position so long my movements were anything but fluid, and he fluttered off. Scooping him up in both hands, I held him to my heart for another minute before putting him through the door. The whole taming session took about 15 minutes.

The following day, I repeated the procedure and Pinto screamed and bit again, but he didn't protest nearly as long. After five minutes of heart-to-heart petting and talking, I herded him back on my finger. Then I put him down on the floor and got him back up on my finger several times. By the end of the session, he'd stay on my finger, even when it moved it back and forth. The third day, we made even more progress. I no longer had to use both hands to herd him to my finger. When I put my finger in front of his feet and touched his belly slightly, he climbed up on his own. Pinto was becoming a pet. And with this method, your budgie will too.

Giving Your Heart to Your Budgie

Here are the 10 steps to having a heart-to-heart with your budgie:

1. Make sure Polly's wings are trimmed and parrot-proof the bathroom.

2. Put Polly's cage and a pillow on the bathroom floor and close the door.

3. Open the cage door, and use a twist-tie or clip to keep it opened.

4. Reach in and bring Polly out. Hold her gently but firmly with her wings folded. Expect her to scream and bite you, and be prepared to grit your teeth and ignore the discomfort.

A heart-to-heart will calm a scared budgie. This is Pinto with my husband Tom.

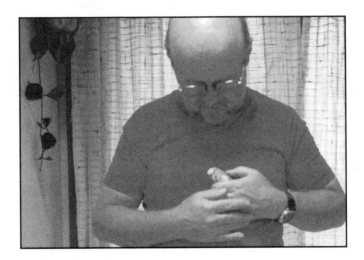

5. Cuddle Polly against your chest so she can feel your heart beat. Talk to her softly the whole time.

6. When Polly becomes a little calmer, begin stroking her back. Keep it up for five minutes while talking or singing.

7. Place Polly on your finger. When she jumps off, use one hand to slowly herd her toward your other hand. Every time she actually climbs on your finger or hand, say "up." If she is still so scared that she flutters wildly around the area and starts panting, scoop her up for another heart-to-heart.

8. After Polly sits on your finger for several seconds, the lesson is over. Talk to her softly while putting her back in her cage.

9. Repeat these steps three days in a row. Polly will probably scream and bite a little less every day, although it's not unusual to have a one- or two-day setback.

10. From the fourth day on, offer your finger after you open the cage door, instead of catching Polly. Place it just in front of and a little higher than her feet and say "up." If she doesn't move, press up gently on her tummy. If she avoids your hand, catch her and cuddle her as before.

When will Polly be a fully tamed budgie? The day she climbs on your finger as you say "up" and lets you take her out of the cage and pet her. When it happens—and it will—both of you deserve to celebrate. Polly overcame her instinctive fears, and you put up with a few little bites. Not a big price to pay for the magic of having a budgie for a buddy.

Tom's budgie buddy, Pinto.

Avian Adventures

In Chapter 3, I told you that canaries and finches don't want to be handled and are ideal pets for those who enjoy watching, rather than touching. But there are two exceptions. First, people who breed these species sometimes pick a recently hatched baby and raise it as a pet. Because the baby bird is used to people almost from birth, it has no fear of humans and enjoys riding around on shoulders and having its head and back stroked. With consistent handling, it will stay tame all its life and be a delightful companion. The second exception is people with incredible patience. It is possible, by using budgie-taming techniques, to buy an untamed canary and turn it into a friend who sits on your finger and likes to be petted. It just takes a long time and a lot of caution because canary wings should not be trimmed. Keep a net handy.

Getting Cozy with Your Cockatiel

Most cockatiels are gentle birds with sweet dispositions. If yours was a hand-fed baby, she'll always be a charmer as long as you keep her tame by handling her frequently. Let her perch on your hand while you read or watch television, and gradually introduce her to the joys of having the nape of her neck petted. You'll also want to teach her the "up" command. I'll tell you how in the next section. You can skip to it now if you want to. The rest of this section is about turning terrified cockatiels into charmers.

Squawk!

Cockatiels fly amazingly well unless every one of their flight feathers are trimmed. Before trying to tame Polly, make sure all of her flights were properly clipped and none have grown out. Crashing into the wall is not a confidence builder.

The cozier an escape-proof area you can create, the sooner you'll get close to your cautious cockatiel. Even a bathroom is too big, although a shower stall will do fine. So will any tiny corner you can construct by moving a few bookcases. The taming area should be small enough so you can touch every wall and corner while sitting on the floor (put a pillow under you and another between your back and the wall). Why such cramped quarters? Because there's not enough room for your cockatiel to run away from you. Getting up and chasing Polly would terrify her, and that's exactly the opposite of teaching her to trust you.

You'll need something to keep you occupied for half an hour or more, so put a book in your tiny taming space. (A battery-operated TV might fit, but it won't let you do as good a job. Polly should be soothed by your voice, not Seinfeld's.) Bring a twist-tie or clip for holding the cage door open and, depending on how hard your bird resists coming out of her cage, you might need a towel. Parrot-proof the area and be sure Polly's wings are properly trimmed.

Ready? Put your cockatiel's cage in the taming area, climb in and close off any avenues of escape. Sit down on your pillow, open Polly's door as wide as it goes and secure it open. Then try to coax or gently chase her out. If that doesn't work, protect your hand with the towel (or prepare yourself for a hard, but not dangerous, bite), catch your cockatiel, and bring her out of the cage carefully so she doesn't bang her wings against the bars. Then place her on the floor.

Wow! That was the hardest part and it's over. Now it's time to relax. If someone else is around, have them take the cage out of the taming area, but make sure Polly will not escape. Otherwise, just move the cage out of the way as best you can and close the cage door. Then catch up on your reading and ignore your bird. Give her time to learn that she can be really close to you without a cage to protect her, and you still won't eat her.

After 10 minutes (time it), reach out with one hand and start herding Polly (she'll move away from your hand). Keep your movements slow. Just calmly herd her a foot or two in one direction, and then a foot or two in another direction. At first, she may flap and run fearfully, but try to find just the right distance so she moves away from your hand at a walk. After a minute or two of one-handed herding, go back to reading. Then go back to herding. And so on every couple of minutes until Polly moves away from your hand without hysteria.

Now it's time to tame with both hands. Keeping your movements calm, use one hand to herd Polly toward your other hand, and then use your other hand to steer her back. Herd Polly back and forth for a minute or two, then ignore her and go back to reading—then back to two-handed herding. Eventually, something wonderful is going to happen: Polly is going to step on one of your hands to get away from the other one. When she does, hold still. Resist the urge to laugh out loud. Instead, talk to Polly quietly and tell her what a great pet she's going to be. She'll probably use your hand as a bridge and jump off the other side in a microsecond, but that's okay. Eventually, she'll get on again and you'll reward her with more sweet talk. Then one day you'll celebrate the magic moment when she sits still, cocks her head and listens to your voice.

Use one hand to herd your cockatiel toward your other hand.

Continue taming daily, and expect Polly to start out scared for several sessions. You're making progress if she calms down a little sooner just about every time (expect an occasional setback).

When Polly is perching on your finger frequently, familiarize her with the word "up" by saying it in a happy tone every time she climbs on. Try more advanced taming by raising your hand smoothly with Polly on it. Of course she'll jump off at first, but

Squawk!

Whether you bought a tame bird or tamed your own, she'll only be a companion as long as you give her companionship. Ignored birds revert to being wild birds.

she'll soon get used to it. Hold your hand about heart high, and talk or sing softly to her, and in time she'll learn to love it. When lifting your hand no longer fazes her, add side-to-side movement.

End each session by securing Polly's cage door open and gently herding her back inside. Eventually she'll ride in and out of her cage on your hand and will let you pet her (come from behind, not above, and stroke the nape of her neck and her cheeks). Soon she'll want to be cozy with you wherever you are and will no longer need close quarters. Come out of the shower stall and celebrate—listen to music or watch a TV show with your crested crony.

A fully tamed cockatiel loves to be petted.

Taming Other Small Species

Lovebirds, brotogeris (pocket or bee bee parrots), and other small species bite harder than budgies and cockatiels, so the best method for taming them depends on the bird's

Bird Brainers

If you can't make time to cuddle your lovebird, keep her happy and sane by giving her a mate of the same species.

disposition. If you have a hand-fed baby, keep her sweet by enjoying her company as often as possible. A single lovebird, for example, makes a superb pet if she gets a lot of affection, but becomes sad, and quite literally mad, if ignored.

If your small parrot isn't tame, consider her attitude before choosing a training method. The baby budgie method may work if your bird is still very young and more curious than cautious, but don't try to have a heart-to-heart with a small, scared parrot. Cuddling a little bird with a big beak before she's tame might make a bloody mess of your hands. Some small species take to the cozy cockatiel method, while others do best with the big bird-handling techniques you'll find in the next chapter.

Calling All Parrots

The following training techniques are the basics for handling parrots of all sizes. If your bird isn't ready to be handled just yet, or if she threatens to take chunks out of your finger, read Chapters 14, 16 and 17 before putting your bird through basic training.

The "Up" Command

The "up" command? Hmmm. The word *command* sounds more like training than bonding, doesn't it? Actually, it's a bit of both, but I consider it a bonding basic because once Polly knows it, you won't have to chase her around the cage every time you want to bring her out. Chasing and being chased is about as far from bonding as you can get, so let's put an end to it.

Most hand-fed baby birds have heard the word "up" often, and the budgie or cockatiel you tamed should also be familiar with it. Now we're going to give the word some meaning.

Since birds usually step up and forward when going from one perch to another, put your hand just in front of, and slightly higher than the perch Polly is on, and say "up." (Offer your index finger, but don't tuck your other fingers into a fist.) Do you have a bird on board? That's great! Tell her "Good bird," because she is one. No bland voices allowed. Tone means a lot to birds, so praise should sound upbeat and happy.

> **Squawk!**
>
> Just because you paid big bucks for a hand-fed baby doesn't mean she will stay sweet and tame while you ignore the basics of bonding. What you have is the early advantage—a trusting baby bird who wants to bond with you. Your hand-fed baby still needs to learn the "up" command and take ladder lessons.

If Polly side-stepped out of your way or simply ignored your offer, try again with a slight variation. This time put your hand just in front of her and use your index finger to apply gentle upward pressure to her belly. Say "up" as soon as your finger touches her tummy, and you should have a bird on your finger. "Good bird!"

The first few times you try this, you might have to follow Polly around the cage with your finger until you convince her to climb on. That's fine as long as she doesn't seem scared and steps on your hand after a minute or two of cajoling. But if she flutters away from you while squawking in terror, she isn't ready yet. Spend another week or two sitting near her, hand-feeding her treats and talking to her before trying to train her. When you think of how many years of fun you will have together, taking enough time to lay a firm foundation of friendship is no trouble at all.

Bird Brainers

Never stop using the "up" command—not even when your pet steps on your finger the instant it's offered. It's your ace-in-the-hole when handing a bird.

After Polly steps up on your finger almost automatically, it won't be long before she'll let you slip her out of her cage. Don't bump her head as you bring her through the door (it's easy to do if the cage door isn't very tall), and always remember to praise her.

Klutzy baby birds may be afraid to step from perch to hand, even though they want to be with you. Help your clumsy critter by lifting her off her perch, cuddling her while you arrange yourself on the carpeted floor, then placing her on your hand. Keep her low so she can't fall far if she loses her balance.

Sugar demonstrates the "up" command.

Ladder Lessons

Ladder lessons will help Polly master perching on your hand, and are one of the best exercises for reminding an unruly big bird how to behave. Begin them when Polly is calmly perched on your hand outside her cage. It doesn't matter if she came through the door on your hand, or if you had to catch her and carry her out. In fact, after Polly becomes a good ladder climber, she'll probably come out of the cage on your hand every time.

Are you sitting on the rug with Polly on your index finger? Then let ladder lessons begin. What? You don't have a bird ladder? Sure you do—it's your other hand. Your index fingers are the rungs and your goal is to get Polly to climb from one hand to the other. Assuming Polly's on your right hand (reverse this if she's on your left), put your left index finger in front of and slightly higher than her feet and say "up." If she climbs on, tell her she's wonderful. If she doesn't, apply gentle upward pressure to her tummy and praise her when she responds. Wait a few seconds and do it again. And again. Okay, that's enough for the first time. Did you praise Polly every time she stepped up? "Good trainer!"

How often should you review ladder lessons with Polly? Every time you get her out of her cage. You don't have to practice for more than a few minutes (five is more than enough), and it's best not to do it all at once, but gradually increase climbing until Polly goes up a minimum of twenty rungs a day. For example, have her climb five rungs when you get her out of the cage, ten more at intervals while watching television together, and the final five before putting her to bed.

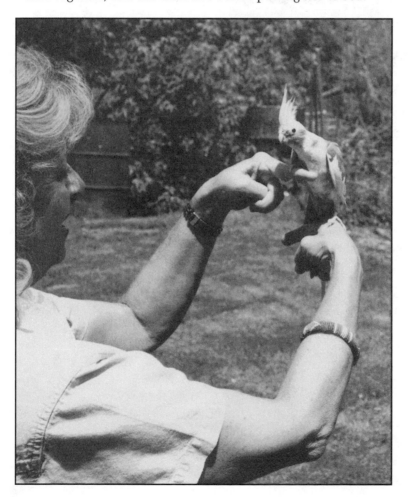

Sugar takes ladder lessons.

205

Sitting on Shoulders

Birds head for the highest perch, so once Polly starts sitting on your hand—maybe even during her first few hesitant attempts—she'll start moving upward toward your shoulder.

While having a budgie or cockatiel ride around on your shoulder is a wonderful reward for the time you spent taming, don't encourage it too soon. Insecure birds want to use your neck for a hiding place, like a shy child peering out from behind his mother's legs. Build your bird's confidence and your ability to control her with the "up" command and lots of ladder lessons first. Then put your small bird (it's a no-no with big birds) on your shoulder and enjoy.

Hands Up! (The Egyptian Grip)

Does Polly persist in heading for your shoulder or neck and fuss when you try to get her back on your hand? You can encourage her to stay on your finger by using a method that takes advantage of a bird's tendency to seek the highest perch. It's called the Egyptian grip. All it involves is making your hand higher than your arm, so Polly would have to move down rather than up to get anywhere.

Try it without Polly first. Let your arm hang down at your side. Now bend it at the elbow so your fingertips point toward the ceiling. Bend your wrist so your fingers are practically parallel to the floor, but pointing slightly upward. Lower your thumb so it's about even with your middle finger. Now imagine Polly sitting on your hand. She'd have to climb down your forearm to get to your shoulder, and that goes against her nature. Gradually get her used to feeling your thumb over her toes if she's a big bird. The gentle pressure will help steady her.

When the bird on your hand is bigger than a budgie or cockatiel, lower your elbow so your bird's head is at about the same level as your heart. I'll explain why in the next chapter.

The Egyptian grip is best for bigger birds.

The Least You Need to Know

➤ Give your bird two or three days to settle in before trying to tame her. During that time, sit near her cage to read, write or watch TV, and take the time to talk to her.

➤ Never handle your bird when you are exhausted, in a bad mood or under the influence of anything.

➤ Never hit your bird. She is sensitive and her bones are delicate.

➤ Make sure your bird's wings are properly trimmed before taking her out of the cage.

➤ Taming a bird takes lots of patience. Choose the right method for your bird and celebrate your successes one small step at a time. Every time your bird lets you get a little closer, or does something she never did before (like taking a treat from your hand), you've made progress.

➤ Always let your bird know when she does something right. Tell her what a good bird she is in your happiest tone.

➤ Hand-fed baby birds need practice to stay sweet. The "up" command and ladder lessons are just as important for them as they are for birds that had to be tamed after they were purchased.

Chapter 14

Big Babies and Secondhand Sweethearts

In This Chapter

➤ The basics of bird behavior

➤ How parrots perceive people

➤ Handling hand-raised babies

➤ Boundaries for birds

➤ Adopting previously owned birds

A parrot isn't a domestic animal like a dog. Dogs have been bred for hundreds of years to look and act a certain way, and to do useful work such as hunting and herding. But birds, those delightful descendants of the dinosaurs, have remained unchanged for millions of years. Pauly may be perched atop your book, neck fluffed and begging for petting, but he is still exactly the same animal as his wild ancestors.

Even though dogs are thoroughly domesticated, no one would think of having one in their home without training it. That's why dog obedience schools (places where people go to learn how to handle their dogs) are big business. But taming and training parrots is a relatively new idea. Getting your bird now was great timing. In the recent past, most pet parrots weren't really pets at all. They were conversation pieces or part of the decor. Today, we know better. Wild though they may be, parrots take to taming and training like kids take to candy bars. In this chapter, I'll tell you how Pauly perceives his world, and give you the basics of teaching your big bird how to be a good bird.

A Bird's-Eye View

Pretty soon, you're going to ask Pauly to learn behaviors that will make him welcome in your world. But before you begin, I want you to understand how he sees his world. Knowing how parrots react in the wild will help you handle your pet with an awareness that his sensitive nature responds to. I mentioned a few of these points earlier in the book, so one or two things may sound familiar. Please stay with me anyway. I want to put all these "parrotisms" into one package before you start taming and training your big bird.

Parrots Are Prey

No matter how big and bold Pauly looks to you, he's just a tasty tidbit to even bigger birds and many snakes. His species has feared attack from above for eons. Would you want to make friends with a masked man who climbs through your window clutching a gun? That's how Pauly feels about people who swoop down on him.

Parrots Like to Party

No, they don't stagger around with lampshades on their heads, but they are social animals. In the wild, they fly, forage, eat and sleep in large groups, and act as each other's beauticians, preening their pals' impossible-to-reach places. Pauly considers you and your family his flock, and will feel like the only teen who doesn't have a date for the prom if no one gives him any affection.

Parrots Are Cliquish

Like most teenagers, they socialize within their own circle. Pauly may respond to outsiders with fear or hostility. While that's a normal part of flock mentality, it can be modified if you introduce him to other people when he's still young. Don't skip this important step in socializing your pet.

Avian Adventures

Scientifically speaking, all dogs, from Chihuahuas to Great Danes, are the same species (*Canis familiaris*). But even birds that look somewhat similar, like the mexican red-headed amazon (*A. viridigenalis*) and the lilac-crowned amazon (*A. finschi*), are two different species. Why? Because humans have manipulated dog genetics for centuries to produce the different breeds, but bird species are still the same as nature made them.

Parrots Are Messy, Not Dirty

Pauly doesn't toss his food around to make more work for you. He's just doing what parrots have been programmed to do for thousands of years. Pauly's species sows seeds. He and other fruit- and seed-eating birds are the farmers of the rain forests and jungles. In the wild, Pauly wouldn't live near his mess. Well-groomed and glossy, he would perch high in the trees while his leftover dinner and droppings seeded and fertilized the ground below.

Parrots Are Bossy

The pecking order is important for the survival of the species. In the wild, every parrot vies for a position of leadership, even though flocks of parrots aren't led by a single bird. With so much competition for dominance, it takes a tough old bird to make it to the top, ensuring a group of strong, smart leaders.

Left to his own devices, Pauly will try to rule the roost. Trying to achieve a high position in the pecking order is part of being a parrot. But if your pet parrot succeeds (some do), he'll be nervous and lonely because he isn't genetically programmed to preside over people, and no one likes to play with a feathered tyrant. The best-adjusted pet parrots are flock members, guided by a truly benevolent person.

Parrots Are Mimics

Don't blame Pauly if he utters a bad word when Great Aunt Agnes asks him to say "Pretty bird." He had to hear it somewhere. Parrots also copy behavior. When given their own spoon, some big birds learn to use it just by watching their family eat. This copy-bird behavior can have positive or negative consequences. For example, if there's a lot of shouting at your house, your parrot will probably join in and add to the uproar.

Bird Brainers

Some parrots make good watch-birds. From his vantage point near the window, Rooster (my amazon parrot) squawks and screams to announce visitors coming down the driveway. In the wild, a similar sound would warn the flock that an intruder is near and would send them into the skies.

Parrots Adore Drama

That's why so many good talkers sometimes embarrass their owners by screaming a swear word just as the visiting preacher says grace before a meal. Pauly doesn't know a swear word from "Hello, I'm pretty Pauly," but he may say the bad words more often than the nice ones for two reasons. First, he probably heard the swear word during a moment of high drama in your household. Someone said it with great feeling when they dropped a dozen eggs on the kitchen floor or spilled cranberry juice on the carpet.

Second, every time he repeats it, it elicits more drama ("No! No, Pauly! Don't say that!"). In bird-think, a strong reaction translates into instant attention, encouraging Pauly to repeat the word again.

Avian Adventures

President Andrew Jackson's amazon parrot, Poor Poll, was the most outspoken mourner at her owner's funeral. During the ceremony, she let loose with a stream of profanity that would have shocked a sailor. The service was stopped until she was removed from the room.

Parrots Are Moody

Not as bad as a teenager who hates her hairdo on prom night, but parrots do have an attitude at times. So do many other smart and sensitive creatures—like us, for example. Just as you aren't always delighted when company drops in, there are times when Pauly won't want to be petted. That's one of the major ways parrots differ from dogs, and it is one of the hardest parrotisms for people to understand.

In the wild, Pauly would simply move away from his mate if she tried to preen him when he wasn't in the mood. If she persisted, he'd growl or squawk, and she'd get the message and give him some space. But people don't always pay attention to their bird's body language. Pressuring Pauly when he isn't in the mood to be petted could eventually force him to make his point by biting. When you pull away, Pauly will think he has finally found a way to get some time alone. Next time he wants to be alone, he'll bite sooner. But he'd rather not have to. Biting a buddy is not a natural tendency for parrots. It's a last resort. Unfortunately, people often force their parrot into biting by refusing to take his moods into consideration.

Parrots Rely on Their Eyes

In the wild, seeing a predator approach from a distance is the difference between living to greet another sunrise and becoming someone's supper. Don't be surprised if Pauly recoils or even tries to bite if you suddenly approach him looking a little different. Sunglasses, a hat or even a different hairdo are enough to momentarily put him on the defensive. Don't worry. He'll eventually get used to your styles and accessories, but it's always a good idea to talk to him before reaching for him anyway.

Eye contact is compelling when bonding with a bird. When you first get Pauly, he may be too shy to feel comfortable with eye contact, and might even appreciate it if you didn't look directly at him. But once he relaxes, looking him in the eye when you talk to him will be one of the ways into his heart.

Color also influences birds. Pauly may shriek with glee every time you wear a certain color, or may always eat the same color pellets first, even though they all taste the same.

Parrots Startle Easily

Always say something before suddenly throwing open a door and entering Pauly's area. A full-fledged scare might even make him fall off his perch. Pauly feels especially vulnerable when things go bump in the night, and would like a tiny night light near his cage so he isn't in total darkness.

Parrots Are Sensitive

They feel bad vibes faster than a husband who comes home empty-handed on his anniversary. The more relaxed you are, the calmer Pauly will be—not just during taming and training, but for wing and toenail trimming, too. Tame and train your bird during your downtime. Don't add him to the mix when you're trying to get the kids off to school or before dressing for an important presentation.

Bird Brainers

If your usually sweet bird suddenly bites when perched on your hand or arm, consider the circumstances. Did you do something that scared him, like moving so suddenly that he had to grab to keep his balance? Was he startled by a loud noise or someone suddenly entering the room? Ignore a single isolated bite, but if biting is a recurring problem, check out Chapter 17.

Parrots Become Infatuated Easily

Some of them have a thing for blondes. Others melt for a mellow voice. Some love long hair. Others get misty over mustaches. For example, one day a woman knocked on my door to ask directions. She had platinum hair and a high-pitched voice, and Rooster went to pieces. My normally feisty watchbird begged and squawked, danced and talked. The woman had no choice but to notice, and when she walked over and offered her hand, he climbed right on. Not only that, but when she started to leave and I went to take my old buddy back, he told me in no uncertain squawks that he was leaving me for his new love. Were my feelings hurt? Not at all. I know that instant infatuation is typical of parrots. Now you know it too, so don't feel bad if Pauly picks a new pal. Parrots get over puppy love faster than 13-year-olds change steadies.

Parrots Are Vocal

Screams, squawks and the shrill whistles we call noise are part of the way parrots communicate in the wild. It's natural for them to sound off at dawn and dusk, and vocalize during the day when something excites them. Sometimes seasonal changes hype up their hormones, making them call for a mate, but most of the time well-adjusted birds do not scream or squawk for hours on end.

Use contact calls (I explained those in Chapter 13) to build a bond through quiet vocalization. After Pauly responds to the "up" command (you'll also find that one in Chapter 13) and knows the boundaries of his play area (coming up later in this chapter), you can strengthen your connection through occasional louder calls.

Squawk!

When a bird owner complains about his pet, the problem is usually screaming, biting or both.

Don't worry—once your bird accepts your leadership, sporadic loud vocalization between the two of you won't teach him any bad habits. The truth is, he was born knowing how to shriek. You're just letting him know when it's okay. For example, Rooster loves to scream and dance to his favorite song. I yell. He yells. I flap my arms. He flaps his wings. The whole thing takes two or three minutes and it's a fun break (and great bonding) for both of us. Since Rooster takes his cues from me, when I quiet down, he does too.

While you should never try to put a cork on Pauly's morning and evening cacophony (it's a natural part of being a parrot), you can influence his other clamorous concertos. If your bird's screams are driving you to earplugs, there's help in Chapter 17.

Parrots Are Active and Smart

Wild parrots fly, forage for food, chew on branches, crack seeds and nuts and, in short, keep busy. A parrot with nothing to do is like a toddler without a toy. He's going to find a way to entertain himself, one way or another. Keep Pauly stimulated, physically and mentally. Give him playthings, safe branches to chew on and an exercise area other than his cage. And most important, give him your company whenever you can. He'll like that best of all.

Parrots Are Wild Animals

Now that you understand some of the ways of wild parrots, let's use those parrotisms to make sure that Pauly's a happy captive and you're a pleased parrot owner.

Beginning with Hand-Raised Babies

Is Pauly a hand-raised baby? Lucky you. He's already tame, friendly and fearless around people. In fact, he's a perfectly wonderful pet, so why bother to train him?

Even perfect baby parrots need training to stay delightful pets all their lives. That's because parrots go through stages (think about children). They have awkward ages: the terrible twos, adolescence (with its hormonal horrors) and sexual maturity, just like humans. Couple those phases with the continuous call of the wild, and you can see why Pauly needs early guidance to remain friendly and manageable as he matures.

Here are some guidelines for setting boundaries for Pauly's behavior. Follow them from day one and your pet will recognize you as the leader of the flock and happily fit in with the family:

➤ Be sure Pauly's flight feathers are properly trimmed. Chapter 18 tells you how, but I'd rather that you watched a professional do it the first time.

➤ Give Pauly a couple of days to settle in before taking him out of the cage, but sit beside him and talk to him so he senses your affection. Feed him treats by hand. Pet his head through the bars if he offers it, or reach in slowly and pet him.

➤ Baby birds need more frequent attention than older birds, just like human babies need more attention than 10-year-olds. But don't carry it to extremes. It may be hard to drag yourself away from your beautiful new baby, but force yourself for his sake. Don't let Pauly get used to rituals that you won't be able to keep up, like non-stop cuddling. While Pauly does need a certain amount of cuddling to feel secure, alternate it with talking to him, letting him perch on your hand, ladder lessons (if he isn't too clumsy), sharing toys and simply playing with him. Then put him in his cage with a couple of entertaining toys and let him amuse himself for awhile.

➤ Always use the "up" command (see Chapter 13) when getting Pauly to perch on your hand. Say "up," even when he steps on of his own accord. Soon saying it will become a habit for you, and doing it on command will become automatic for Pauly. That might not mean much now, but it will be a blessing in a few years when he's feeling his hormones.

➤ Buy or build Pauly a T-stand or similar perch that's the proper height for training purposes. When perched on it, Pauly's head should be in the vicinity of your heart. Make sure the perch is sturdy and steady with no wobble, and is the right diameter for your bird's feet (see Chapter 6).

➤ To take Pauly out of his cage, use the "up" command and bring him out on your hand. Then use the "down" command to tell him to step off your hand and onto his T-stand or

Bird Brainers

By the time parrot parents wean their babies, the youngsters are fully grown. It's hard to tell which are the adults and which are the babies, except by behavior.

Bird Brainers

While all baby parrots are ungainly, young african greys win the award for awkwardness. Pauly may want to step on your hand but be unable to keep his balance while climbing on. Help him by cupping your hands under him, lifting him off his perch and cuddling him. Then sit down on the carpet, steady him on your hand, and let him lean his head against your chest for balance.

play gym. Repeat the process when placing him back in his cage. Yes, I know all you have to do is open the cage door and Pauly will come out on his own and go back in when he's hungry. But letting your bird decide when to come and go does nothing to establish your leadership. Since birds don't attend obedience school like dogs do, they learn who's in charge in subtle ways. Determining when Pauly should be in and out of his cage is a subtle, but powerful, show of leadership. Take advantage of its simplicity.

*A T-stand is a
good training tool.*

➤ Give Pauly ladder lessons (see Chapter 13). Since baby birds of the larger species are awkward, sit on a carpeted floor so he can't fall far. If he's clumsy or scared, go real slow. One rung may be plenty until Pauly's balance improves.

Bird Brainers

A well-adjusted baby bird will not scream for constant attention. He will love being with you, but should also be capable of entertaining himself with toys.

➤ All work and no play is no life for a parrot. Make time for cuddling and fun, not just training. When you first bring Pauly out of his cage, hold him, and pet his head and neck. Then play with him a little before ladder (or any other) lessons. Play with him again at the end of each training session before putting him back in his cage.

➤ Keep training sessions short and upbeat. Pauly has a short attention span, but he'll learn to love learning if you quit while he's still interested.

➤ Encourage everyone in the family (who is old enough to handle a parrot) to play with Pauly. Supervise the child-parrot relationship closely.

Make time for cuddling if your bird enjoys it.

➤ Take Pauly to lots of parrot-proofed places in your home. It's ideal if his cage is in one room and his play area is moved from place to place (the dining room when you are eating, the family room for video viewing, and so on). Spending time in different places makes Pauly brighter and more confident, and keeps him from defending his one tiny territory (cage area) from all comers when he matures.

➤ Introduce Pauly to a varied diet, including vegetables and fruit, right away. The sooner he learns to taste new things, the less likely he is to become finicky.

➤ Sometimes, hand feed Pauly one of his favorite foods. Also, hand feed new foods.

➤ Keep in mind that parrots are mimics. It's tempting to playfully grab Pauly's nose and shake it the way you might initiate a game with a puppy. But parrots aren't puppies, and Pauly may think the game is fine, as long as he gets a turn at biting your beak. Ouch!

Hand feeding treats helps birds bond.

What If Baby Bird Bites?

Bite your tongue if your baby bird clamps down too hard on your finger. It's better than yelling "Ouch!" Remember, birds love drama. Your youngster may have innocently caught your finger to regain his balance, but if you give a yelp he'll realize he created a scene and it won't be long before he wants to repeat it. On the other hand, birds seldom repeat actions that get no reaction, so the best thing you can do is make biting seem real boring to your baby bird.

The Head-to-Heart Rule

In the previous chapter I told you to hold your bird so his head is about the same height as your heart, but I didn't tell you why. The answer deals with dominance. Jockeying for position is a perpetual part of a parrot's life. In the wild, the tough old birds who dominate the flock command from the top of the tree. It's like having the biggest corner office on the top floor in a large corporation. Meanwhile, the rest of the flock establishes its pecking order by fussing over who's perched higher than who.

Since wild parrots establish dominance by height and tame parrots are genetically the same as wild parrots, height will be important to Pauly, too. In his bird's-eye view of your living room, the tallest member of the flock rules. If that happens to be him, he'll accept the responsibility and do whatever it takes to remain in command, but the results won't be pleasant for either of you.

The good news is, you can avoid the problem altogether. When holding Pauly, use the Egyptian grip (I explained it in Chapter 13), so he won't be tempted to climb up your arm and meet you eye-to-eye from the vantage point of your shoulder. Also, make sure that his T-stand or training perch is low enough so his head is about even with your heart. If Pauly still tries to dominate, take a look at his cage. Maybe its height is empowering your parrot. Lowering the stand several inches could sweeten his disposition.

Is Pauly's play gym on top of his cage? If he willingly steps on your hand whenever you ask—except when he's on his play gym—now you know why. He's feeling bossy because he's higher than you are. Experienced parrot owners with high play gyms solve this problem by keeping a stool or small stepladder by the play gym and standing on it before taking their parrot off his power perch. Works every time.

What's Wrong with Shoulders?

Perched on your shoulder, a medium to big bird is more or less at eye level with you. That makes you equals in bird-think, so some day Pauly will probably challenge you to see who rules the roost. It may start slowly. You'll say "up" and try to take him off your shoulder, and he'll move across your back to the middle of your neck. Or he may go clear across, then hustle from one side to the other, avoiding your hands no matter which one you offer. Soon the situation becomes a bite waiting to happen. Who needs it?

Big birds do best perched on hands at heart level. If you need a shoulder ornament, stick with a budgie or cockatiel. Even if height makes them headstrong, their beaks aren't capable of doing permanent damage to your facial features.

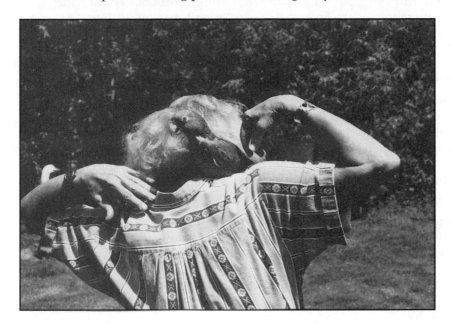

Trying to get a big bird off your shoulders is not easy.

Coconut's Story

With that said, I have a story to tell you. An umbrella cockatoo named Coconut cruises the country in a motor home, along with her human mom and dad, and a Cocker Spaniel. I met Coconut at the Manatee Hammock RV Park in Cocoa, Florida. She was perched peacefully on her owner's shoulder and they were waiting for the pay phone I was using.

When I finished, I commented on Coconut's charm and said that seeing her made me miss my birds, who were home with the house sitter. The woman reached up, Coconut stepped on her hand without hesitation, and she held the beautiful bird out to me. I said "up," and the cockatoo climbed on my hand and let me tickle her awesome crest. Her owner and I talked a bit, then I reluctantly returned the bird and the woman put her back on her shoulder.

Hours later I saw the family relaxing in lawn chairs outside their motor home. The dog was sleeping at their feet and Coconut was on such a high perch that the man had to reach way up to share his

Squawk!

Make sure your friends aren't afraid of your bird before letting them hold him. If Pauly tries to use his beak to retain his balance and they panic and fling him from their arm, the blow to his trust (and possibly his body) will be damaging.

sandwich with her. Despite shoulders to sit on and perches where she could look down on her people, this fully mature cockatoo was one of the best-behaved birds I ever met.

What's the point of this story? Nothing is written in stone. This book is just paper. It tells you what works with most birds and what usually leads to trouble. If you happen to have an exception, enjoy!

Boundaries Are Best

Pauly needs exercise outside his cage, but given free run of the house, he would chew on windowsills, piano legs, tablecloths and anything else that caught his eye. Of course the damage wouldn't go on forever. Sooner or later, he'd bite into a box or bottle containing a deadly poison (matches, mothballs, nail polish remover and suntan lotion are just a few household items that are poisonous to parrots), or burn his beak picking the plastic off an electric cord. The solution is boundary training, and it should start right away—as soon as you can bring your bird out of his cage on your hand.

A play gym with food and water dishes attached is ideal for boundary training. If you're using a T-stand, choose one with a dish at each end, and attach a couple of favorite toys to it. In either case, one of the toys should be something Pauly likes to chew. Remove ladders or any other toys that might make it easy for Pauly to climb down off the equipment and reach the floor. Put the play gym or stand in the room with you, add food and water and place Pauly on the perch. Then watch him out of the corner of your eye.

Bird Brainers

If you're a dog owner, you may say "No!" automatically, but try to retrain yourself. The words "don't try it," with their sharp T sounds, work better on birds.

When Pauly examines the toys or begins shredding his favorite chew, occasionally tell him he's a good bird. If he starts checking out escape routes, stamp your foot or clap your hands once and say "Don't try it!" in a stern voice.

If Pauly ignores your warning and tries to make like Houdini, put him back in his cage in a matter-of-fact (not angry) manner. Then close the door and let him cool his claws for five minutes. When you bring him out to try again, give him another toy you know he likes, and try to catch him doing something right so you can praise him. After several repetitions of praise for staying in place and brief banishments for being a bad bird, Pauly will learn to play on his perch.

A parrot entertains himself on his T-stand. Good bird!

How Much Praise Is Too Much?

Don't praise your Pauly just for breathing, or praise will soon become something he thinks he's entitled to just for being alive. Hold as many conversations as you want with him, but say "Good bird" only to reinforce good behavior and cooperation. If you let praise lose its meaning, you will lose one of the easiest ways to elicit avian etiquette. Eventually, you should be able to change Pauly's mood from surly to sweet just by using the cue, "Be a good bird."

Secondhand Sweethearts

Not every bird who loves being handled was purchased as a hand-fed baby. The employee at the small pet shop where I fell in love with Rooster didn't know anything about his history, except that he'd been in the store for a few weeks and didn't act like a newly weaned baby. My avian veterinarian figured he was about a year old—technically still a youngster—but had been raised by someone else.

Bird Brainers

When boundary training Pauly, make sure the play area is just as inviting as his cage, or your bright bird might train you instead of you training him. When he learns that trying to climb down motivates you to take him back to his cage, he'll use you to hitch a ride home when he gets hungry, thirsty or bored on his perch.

Bird Brainers

Help your bird learn how to play by playing with him. Get down on the floor together and let him watch you play with his toys. When he shows interest, roll the toy a few inches away from him (never toward him).

Some pet shops take birds on consignment, and birds are also offered through ads in the newspaper. While some birds lose their home because they have bad habits, many wonderful birds are sold because of divorce, a move to a place that doesn't allow pets, or their owners' allergies. Like Rooster, these secondhand sweethearts often slide right into your life like comfortable shoes. If you recently bought an amiable adolescent or an adult bird, here are some tips for reinforcing his best buddy behavior:

➤ Talk to Pauly a lot and use his name often.

➤ Trim Pauly's wings, or better yet, have a professional trim them the first time.

➤ If you bought Pauly from a private person and a cage came with him, make sure the cage is big enough so he can exercise and that the dowels are the right size for his feet (see Chapter 6).

➤ Teach Pauly what the "up" command means, and use it even if he steps on your hand as soon as you offer it. Get him used to the Egyptian grip. Practice ladder lessons. Start with just a rung or two, and work up gradually (see Chapter 13).

➤ Buy or build Pauly a play area and teach him his boundaries. Move the stand or gym to different rooms so he spends plenty of time with the family.

➤ Play "pass the parrot." Every member of the family who is old enough to safely interact with a bird should have frequent opportunities to let Pauly perch on their hand.

➤ Occasionally hand feed Pauly his favorite food.

➤ Teach Pauly flapping exercises on your hand (see Chapter 12).

Happy Endings

Whether Pauly was a hand-fed baby or a secondhand sweetie, always end his training session right after he does something right and is praised or rewarded for it. Don't take him back to his cage in frustration because he didn't respond to a new cue, and never put him away right after he bites. Why? Because if he happened to be in the mood to go home, taking him to his cage will reinforce the bad behavior. Instead, ask Pauly to do something he knows well (stepping from one hand to the other, for example), and praise him for his response before putting him in his cage.

The Least You Need to Know

➤ Parrots aren't domestic animals. They understand their world from the perspective of a wild animal who is always in danger of being eaten by a predator.

➤ Knowing how parrots act and react in the wild will help you understand your bird's behavior.

➤ Hand-raised baby birds need guidance to mature into decent adults, just as human children do. That's because parrots and people go through similar stages as they grow up. Parrots also need our help to resist the call of the wild.

➤ Use the head-to-heart rule. Have your parrot perch on your hand (not your shoulder), and keep his head at about the level of your heart.

➤ Teach your bird to stay within the boundaries of his play area when he is out of his cage.

➤ Even if you bought a secondhand sweetie who is easy to handle, don't take his good nature for granted. Instead, reinforce your bond through treats and attention, and review the "up" command often.

Talk to Me

Will Polly talk? The answer depends on several things, including her species, age and attitude. It also depends on her role model. Yes, that's you. In this chapter, I'll tell you why parrots talk and how you can encourage an attitude that leads to language. But mostly, I'll teach you to talk to Polly in ways that will make her want to parrot you.

Why Parrots Talk

The instant they emerge from the egg, parrots are vocal. They have to be. Living long enough to grow feathers depends on their ability to communicate with their parents. As helpless hatchlings, parrots compete with each other to get mommy and daddy to drop the next dollop of food down their throats. A baby bird that didn't badger its parents would soon starve to death, because her folks would ignore her in favor of the wide-open beaks of their other begging babies.

By the time a young parrot is ready for flight and independence, she knows how to communicate with the flock. She can warn other birds about intruders, tell them about a new food source, attract a mate, find the mate if they become separated in a storm, and many other skills vital to survival.

Just as young wild parrots learn the language of their feathered flock, young parrots in a human flock also try to communicate. They may mimic household sounds, meow like the family cat and try to copy speech. When Polly is very young, you may not even realize how hard she's trying. Like a human baby, it takes a parrot awhile to enunciate sounds that people recognize as words. Since parrots don't have vocal cords, they have to teach themselves to make human sounds by manipulating their trachea, and that takes a lot of practice.

Get a group of parrot owners together and sooner or later they will discuss why parrots talk. Some will say it's because they are natural-born mimics. Others say it's because of conditioning—that talking parrots were encouraged, even trained, to respond verbally to certain cues. And lately, partly because of studies done by Dr. Irene Pepperberg at the University of Arizona with an african grey named Alex, more and more parrot owners believe that birds are capable of actually understanding and responding to human speech.

Avian Adventures

Dr. Irene Pepperberg has been working with Alex the african grey since 1977, and Alex has become something of a media star. Among his many talents, he can pick out shapes and colors, request the type of food he wants to eat ("I want banana"), count the objects in front of him and announce the total and tell the good doctor when he's had enough attention and wants to go back to his cage. Dr. Pepperberg's training methods are original, and she is credited with breaking new ground in the field of human–animal communication.

What do I think? I think there is some truth to all three theories. I believe the way we interact with our pets determines how much of their speech is simple imitation, how much is learned response to a word or action, and how much is actually due to understanding. I also believe any parrot that talks, including those of the so-called "talking species," is paying her owner a great compliment. Whether she's mimicking, responding to cues or actually conversing with some understanding doesn't really matter. What matters is that Polly wants to communicate with you. In fact, she cares enough to learn a foreign language so she can fit in with her human flock.

What Type of People Have Talking Parrots?

Good verbal communicators—those who talk a lot and have expressive voices—do best when it comes to teaching birds to talk. In other words, talkative people usually own the parrots with the largest vocabularies. Does that mean Polly will never say "Pretty bird" if you're the quiet type? It could, but it doesn't have to. What it does mean is you'll have to remind yourself to talk to your pet, because parrots, being copy-birds, vocalize less in quiet places than they do in homes where conversation is constant.

Here are some tricks for making your pet want to communicate, even if talking isn't your strong suit. I know they work because I use them with my birds, and verbal communication isn't my strong suit either.

Bird Brainers

If you live alone, remind yourself to talk to Polly by putting sticky notes saying, "Talk to Polly," on your bathroom mirror, the refrigerator and other places in your home.

Tips for Teaching Parrots to Talk

➤ Start young. Even though Polly's too young to pronounce words, it's never too early to encourage an interest in speech.

➤ Don't give Polly any mirrored toys. She may bond with the beautiful bird in the mirror and talk to it in her own language, instead of learning yours.

➤ Mimic Polly's language. When she makes a neat noise you can easily copy (a clicking sound, for example), make the same sound back to her. If she responds by repeating it, praise her.

➤ Try to tantalize Polly into taking a verbal cue from you. Use her language (the click, for example) and initiate it by saying it to her first. If you can get her to copy you, congratulate yourself and praise your pet. Parroting your prompt is a big step on the road to speech.

➤ Try talking to Polly from another room. Remember contact calls? Parrots like to keep in touch by communicating with the flock when they can't see it. Many birds say their first word to an owner who is nearby, but out of sight.

➤ Sing songs. Polly doesn't care if you can carry a tune. It's your upbeat attitude that will turn her on to talking.

➤ Tell stories. Polly doesn't care what you say, as long as her name is in it often and you put lots of expression in your voice. If you'd rather not create your own stories, read nursery rhymes but change the names. For example, "Polly and Pauly went up the hill to fetch a pail of water...."

Bird Brainers

It's much easier to teach a single bird to talk than a pair. That's because the pair will bond to each other, and since they already speak the same language, they probably won't try to learn yours.

Bird Brainers

Most parrots are attracted to words and phrases with double t's in them. That's why so many birds learn to say, "Pretty bird," and "Here kitty, kitty, kitty." After your budgie learns a couple of shorter phrases, try teaching, "I'm an itty, bitty, pretty bird."

Bird Brainers

No trainer, no matter how experienced, can make a parrot talk if she doesn't want to. The best trainers make talking so attractive that their birds want to get in on the act.

➤ Repeat. Repeat. Repeat. Decide what you want Polly to say in response to certain cues, and repeat the same words every time. For example, if you want her to say, "I'm hungry," every time she hears the refrigerator door open, you say it every time. Don't alternate it with "Chow time," or "How about a carrot?"

➤ Become a good listener. Young birds need a lot of practice before their stabs at speech sound like words. For some reason, many of them practice sounds just before going to sleep. Listen when Polly mutters, and see if you hear the rhythm of the word or phrase you've been trying to teach. When you do, enunciate it back to her softly but clearly. If she repeats the rhythm, say "Good bird," and let her go back to bed.

➤ Be realistic in your expectations. Just as human babies say "mama" and "dada," before they try to talk in phrases, most parrots pick up one-, two- and three-syllable words and phrases before tackling anything tougher.

➤ Pronounce every word very clearly. After you decide on a word or short phrase, always say it clearly and with expression. Remember, parrots are drawn to drama and learn through repetition. You knew that, but it needed repeating.

➤ Keep training sessions short, sweet and upbeat.

➤ Get rid of background sounds before training. Polly will have a full plate just trying to learn a foreign language. Don't complicate it by competing with TV commercials.

➤ Create verbal cues for your daily routine. For example, you might say "hello" to Polly every time you come home, "Time to wash the dishes" as you take them from the table, and "Nighty-night" as you cover the cage. It may be a long time (a year or more) before she parrots any of it back to you, so think of it as training yourself, not her.

Rooster's First Words

When I first got Rooster, I really tried to get him to say "hello" and "pretty bird." I said "hello" every time I walked near him and often took a "pretty bird" break—letting him perch on my hand while I told him, over and over, what a pretty bird he was. Months went by and Rooster never uttered a word, although he had a hilarious laugh and used it often.

Talk clearly and happily to your bird, in a location with few distractions and no background noises.

One day I took him to a sporting goods store because my friend Julie worked there and wanted to meet him. The store wasn't busy, so I placed him on her hand. Julie looked him in the eye and said, "My, aren't you a pretty bird." Rooster puffed up, flashed his eyes and said "hello," loud and clear. "Oh wow, he talks too," Julie said, sending Rooster into gales of laughter. Rooster's one word left me momentarily speechless. When I found my tongue, I tried to get him to say it again, but he wasn't interested.

The second surprise came a week later. I was coming through the door with packages in both arms when Rooster stopped me in my tracks with, "Hello. Pretty bird." After that, he spoke more and more often.

Playing Tapes for Polly

Talking birds are usually owned by people who talk to them, but if you want to speed up the process, a tape player with auto-reverse may help. Not every bird mimics the boom box, but some of them learn to repeat recorded words while their owners are at work. There's no harm in trying.

Audiotapes and compact discs made especially for birds are available in some pet shops and through ads in avian magazines. While the older versions are monotonous enough to send Polly into a stupor, modern editions are snappier and more stimulating. Some birds respond to them and learn lots of words, but it's usually best to make your own training tapes using your voice. Here's how.

Go to an electronics store, or almost any store that sells telephone answering machines, and buy a continuous tape loop about five minutes long. Now record your voice saying a few single words and some short phrases you'd like Polly to learn. Say each one five times—slowly, clearly and with feeling—and be sure to pause between repetitions. For example, if your name is Beth you might record, "Hello Beth"…"Hello Beth"…"Hello Beth"… "Hello Beth"… "Hello Beth"… "Pretty bird"…"Pretty bird"…"Pretty bird"…"Pretty bird"…"Pretty bird" … "Here kitty, kitty" and so on. Continue for one minute, let the tape roll in silence for a minute, record a minute of a lively song Polly likes and finish with two minutes of silence. Don't skip the silence in favor of adding more words and phrases. Remember Polly's short attention span. Too much will make her tune out.

Play the tape for her during the day. Since it's on an endless loop, it will keep rewinding and replaying itself. Keep Polly from becoming bored by erasing the tape every week and making a new one. Use the same format, but use different words and a new song.

Squawk!

Don't teach Polly profanity. While a parrot who screams swear words may be a blast today, she won't be so funny after you have children or when your conservative coworker comes to dinner.

The upside of using tapes is that Polly may learn new words while you're at work or out shopping. The downside is that the phrases will be simple repetitions. While amusing and fun, they won't have the same impact as words said in conjunction with actions, such as "Did you feed the parrot?" at dinner time, and "Nighty-night" when you cover the cage.

What About Whistling?

Whistling is controversial. Some experts say it's a mistake to teach Polly to whistle if you want her to learn to talk. Whistling is easier than talking, so if your pet can communicate the easy way, she doesn't have any reason to try it the hard way. Others believe that whistling is just fine, but even they acknowledge that it's best to teach your bird to talk first.

The problem is, unless you live in a bubble, someone is bound to drop in and whistle to Polly. Why? Because whistling is the first reaction many people have when they see a parrot. And guess what Polly, who hasn't said a word after 10 months of training, will do? She'll learn to whistle by morning.

The best advice I can give you is don't encourage your young bird to whistle while you are teaching her to talk, but don't stew about it if she learns how anyway. I've never met a talking parrot who didn't whistle too.

Stimulating Speech in Slow Starters

Since talking is a way of calling attention to herself, Polly has to feel completely secure before she will attempt speech. Shy birds and pets with low self-esteem may need an attitude adjustment and a few props before sounding off in a foreign language. Try these tips:

Bird Brainers

Whistling is a wonderful way to communicate with birds who have little or no talking ability. For example, your female cockatiel may learn to whistle contact calls back and forth with you, and maybe even a tune or two, but will probably never learn to talk.

➤ Break some rules. Let Polly perch high occasionally (unless she turns into an instant tyrant). Sometimes being the tallest stimulates speech.

➤ Put Polly in places where she hears humans talk to each other. Get a T-stand so she can perch wherever the family gathers. If you live alone, put Polly by the telephone whenever you use it. Your teens can train her to talk without even trying!

➤ Use contact calls. When you're not in the same room with Polly, alternate speaking her language (copy some of her sounds) and talking to her in your language, or singing. Keep your voice mellow so you don't encourage her to scream.

➤ Set up a ritual where both of you scream, and make it dramatic. Play a special song to cue her, then dance, sing and let out an occasional whoop or yeehaw. Sometimes make a sound similar to Polly's scream. If she takes part in this craziness, it's a good sign.

➤ Using a helper and Polly's favorite food, try to get her to respond to a one-syllable word such as "hi." Show Polly the treat, and say "hi" several times in an upbeat voice. When she doesn't respond, show the treat to your helper (with Polly watching) and repeat the word "hi." When your helper answers "hi," let the helper eat the treat. Then start over with Polly. Repeat five times and then quit until tomorrow.

Squawk!

Don't make teaching Polly to talk a major project. Keep it light and fun. If Polly senses that you are disappointed in her, her self-esteem will plunge and so will her talking potential. Many birds started talking after their owners gave up on speech training.

➤ Talk or sing to Polly as often as you can. Parrots seldom copy words unless they hear them often.

➤ Sometimes another parrot is a powerful stimulus. If you have a friend with a talking parrot, ask if you can bring Polly over for a visit. Let your pet hear the other bird talk and watch it being rewarded. Then have a nice chat with your friend while the parrots interact with each other—each from the safety of her own cage.

Species with Special Speech Skills

The following species are known for their extraordinary talking ability. (To find out about other species' potential for speech, see Chapter 3.)

➤ African grey parrot

➤ Yellow-naped amazon parrot

➤ Greater hill mynah bird

And to a lesser extent:

➤ Quaker or monk parakeet

➤ Double yellow head amazon parrot

➤ Yellow-fronted amazon parrot

➤ Blue-fronted amazon parrot

➤ Blue and gold macaw

No Guaranteed Talkers

Don't take speech for granted, just because you bought one of the top talking types. Not every bird learns to talk, no matter what the species. Some parrots are serene, silent types. Others communicate through squawks and whistles. A few copy the sounds of other pets or even household appliances, but never utter even one "hello."

Does it matter if Polly talks? I hope not. Talking shouldn't have anything to do with the pleasure you get from loving your pet. It's like having a child with exceptional athletic or artistic talent. You don't love your son or daughter because of his or her superior skill. The talent is just an incredible extra. And so is speech in a pet parrot.

The Least You Need to Know

➤ Birds learn to talk because they want to communicate with their human flock.

➤ A parrot has to feel secure before she will try to talk.

➤ If you want your parrot to talk, you'll have to talk to her often. She should also hear people talk to each other.

➤ Speak clearly and use lots of expression when teaching your bird to talk.

➤ No one can make a parrot talk. Good trainers make their pets want to mimic speech.

➤ Repeat. Repeat. And keep it upbeat. Parrots learn through repetition, but only want to learn when it sounds like fun.

Chapter 16

Why Does My Bird Do That?

In This Chapter

➤ Misunderstood messages

➤ The meaning behind your bird's movements

➤ Displaced aggression

Your budgie hightails it for the far corner of his cage when you come near, your parrot bites, your canary won't sing and your once lively finches have become lethargic. What a bummer! You didn't buy a bird just so you'd have a cage to clean. You wanted a little friend, a little song, a few words or a little action. What went wrong? Maybe your bird sent you a message but you couldn't read his writing.

Both birds and people have idiosyncrasies—little habits that, when misunderstood, can affect their relationship with each other. While you and your bird probably have your share of personal peculiarities, certain actions and reactions are common to most people and their pets. This chapter will help you understand what your bird's signals mean, so you can send him meaningful messages in return.

He Said, She Squawked

Books about miscommunication between men and women have been best-sellers, even though men and women are the same species and speak the same language. That's why it's hard to imagine how many misinterpretations and mixed messages occur between species as dissimilar as people and birds. While we won't be able to read every signal our pets send us, the more we understand, the happier and better behaved our birds will be.

Here are some of the most common ways people and their pets miscommunicate. If you find yourself in any of these stories, fixing the problem will greatly improve your partnership with Pauly.

Please Pleas

When Pauly assumes a horizontal position (back flattened and wings slightly away from his body) and quivers all over while staring at something (you or your dinner, for example), please don't remove him from the room to make him feel better. He isn't cowering and trembling with fear, even though his stance may make you think so. Pauly's lowered posture says "Me, me, me!" He's begging for attention, just like kids and dogs do. It's similar to a first grader wildly waving her arm when she knows the answer and wants the teacher to call on her.

How long will an eager child try to answer questions if the teacher always ignores her? Probably several weeks. But eventually she'll give up and entertain herself with something else. Maybe she'll chatter to her neighbor or scratch her name on her desk instead of following the lesson. Your parrot will keep pleading for attention for a long time, too. But if you exclude Pauly too often, he'll quit begging, give you the cold wing and find other ways to entertain himself—like screaming and shredding stuff.

Me, me, me!

Hello Sunshine

People don't all communicate the same way. Some people tend to be undemonstrative and kind of quiet. Others are boisterous and talk with their hands. Think of birds as a clan that shouts their happiness to the skies and uses brazen body language.

Don't put Pauly in the dark by covering his cage when he shouts his version of *Oh What a Beautiful Morning*. Happy, healthy parrots always vocalize in the morning. Don't yell at him either. Pauly will think you're joining in to celebrate the new day with him. With motivation like that, he'll scream louder and longer than usual.

Wet and Wild

Please don't stop bathing your bird because you think he hates water. Lots of birds scream, raise their wings and fan their tails when sprayed with the plant mister. Their audacious attitude is not a sign of fear or anger. It's just an enthusiastic response to the excitement of showering.

Bird Brainers

Happy, healthy birds preen often. A pet that puts up with disheveled feathers and seldom grooms himself may be depressed, insecure or even sick. Sometimes birds just need to be prompted into preening. Spray your pet with plain warm water from a plant mister. If that doesn't cue him to clean up, see your avian veterinarian.

Say What?

Are you sick of hearing Pauly prattle on in parrot language when you've been trying so hard to teach him to talk? Don't let him sense your displeasure at his garbled babble. He may be practicing the very words you've been trying to teach. Most parrots practice softly, but some rehearse loud and unclear. Listen carefully. Is the rhythm of his sounds similar to the timing of the words or phrases you've been repeating for him? Then praise Pauly for practicing and ignore the noise. It would be a pity to discourage the very thing you were trying to teach.

Deserting the Perch

A boundary-trained bird will stay on his gym, cage top or T-stand (see Chapter 14 for boundary training). One of the best reasons to boundary train is that you'll be able to take Pauly from room to room. Then he can frolic outside his cage and you can enjoy his company, even when your hands aren't available for perching. If you get in the habit of carrying Pauly's perch from one room to another, he'll get in the happy habit of being with you and staying on his perch.

Naturally, you won't take him along on a quick trip to the fridge or the bathroom, and he should wait peacefully for your return. But if you take too long, he may forget his manners.

One time I forgot to cage Rooster after he spent the evening helping me write. Instead, I left him perched on his T-stand by the computer and climbed into the tub for a long soak. After about 20 minutes, his chunky green body squeezed through the slightly open bathroom door. Then he shinnied up the open shower curtain until he could see my face and greeted me with a "Hello."

When we boundary train our birds, we think we are teaching them to stay where we put them, and to a great extent we are. But I believe they learn it so easily because they want to be with us. Don't be upset with Pauly if he seeks you out when you are gone too long (don't let this happen if you also own predator pets, such as cats or dogs). Solitude isn't his strong suit. He wants to find his flock, and you're it.

I Scream, You Scream

Nothing makes a shrieking parrot happier than being screamed at. "This is a riot," he thinks. "Look at her wave her weird wings and yell. My turn. I'll give it everything I've got and maybe she'll answer me again."

Parrots need to keep in contact with their flock, so it's up to you to teach Pauly how to do it pleasantly. Otherwise, he'll go with his instincts and your home will sound like a scene from a Tarzan movie. When you're in the other room and Pauly calls, maintain contact with him through soft talk or a gentle whistle. Soon, he'll learn to copy you.

If Pauly's screaming sometimes becomes too loud or long to handle, cover the cage for ten minutes (no more). Whatever you do, don't reward the behavior with drama. For help with an incessant screamer, see Chapter 17.

Bird Brainers

Once a day, try to catch your bird doing something right and reward him for it. Walk over and talk to him or hand feed him a treat. What is something right? It's playing quietly with a toy, sitting silently on a swing or just watching you work without making demands.

Not Everybody's Buddy

You have to teach your children to stay away from strangers, but most parrots do it instinctively. If you urge a guest to reach in and bring Pauly out of the cage, and she pulls out a bloody finger instead, blame yourself. Every once in a while you'll find a parrot who is everybody's pal, but most birds trust only their family. Don't be disappointed if your performing parrot retreats to the far corner of his cage, and refuses to talk or do tricks when you have company. Most parrots entertain only their loved ones.

Why Birds Become Biters

Most bird bites are accidents, and happen because something scared Pauly. If he bites you because you approached him wearing sunglasses or a cap and he never saw you in those accessories before, the bite was a fear response. If you talked with your hands while your bird was perched on one of them, the bite probably prevented Pauly from losing his balance.

The worst thing you can do about an accidental bite is respond to it. Ignore the nip and Pauly will, too. Yell at him and you may awaken his love of drama, and make him do it again just to see if you will scream again—kind of like a puppy pouncing on a squeaky toy. If you have a bird you can't handle because he bites or threatens to bite constantly, see Chapter 17. But please don't make a big deal out of an accidental nip from a nice parrot.

Birds get moody for good reason when they *molt* (shed old feathers and grow new ones). When Pauly is molting, he may have a bunch of prickly pinfeathers in the places you usually pet. Not only are they itchy, but they may make his skin so sensitive that he squawks or nips if you touch a sore spot. Have mercy on his misery. Instead of petting him (even if he begs for it), let him know you love him by hand feeding him his favorite treats. In a few days, he'll welcome your touch again.

Wild parrots test branches with their beak before stepping on them. That's how they find out if a limb is strong enough to hold them, or will break under their weight and give them a nasty tumble. It's part of a parrot's nature to test the perch, so Pauly will probably put his beak on your finger before stepping on, no matter how many times you practice the "up" command. You'll learn to expect it and know it doesn't hurt, so it won't be any problem—for you. But what about the rest of your family?

One of the ways people teach perfectly nice parrots to bite is by pulling away when their pet tries to test their finger. When teaching your kids to handle Pauly, remind them in advance to hold their ground when Pauly leads with his beak. Pulling away makes a parrot lose faith in a fleshy perch and either avoid it or test it harder the next time.

Squawk!

Never punish your parrot by thunking him on the beak (or anywhere else, for that matter). Parrots are mimics, and aggression teaches aggression.

Bird Brainers

Sure it looks funny when your ten-inch-tall bird scares off your six-foot-tall boyfriend, but avoid the temptation to laugh. Birds love laughter, so finding the wrong thing funny reinforces bad behavior. Instead, respond by doing something your bird definitely doesn't want, like putting him back in his cage.

Quiet Canaries

Caruso won't quit singing out of spite, but his sudden silence is a message. It tells you that he either isn't feeling well or he's molting. If there are no signs of fallen feathers, check his droppings and ease of breathing, and look for hidden injuries. Also consider how much light reaches his cage. Perhaps what was a well-lighted area during spring and summer is too darn dark during the cold months.

Lethargic Finches

Finches who don't frolic and drop more food than they eat aren't becoming lazy and finicky. They are just plain sick. Don't waste time reading about behavior. Your birds need a vet, and Chapter 20 will help you make the most of the visit.

Emotion in Motion

I translated some bird body language for you in Chapter 4, but here's a quick review of what several movements mean, including a few that didn't come up earlier. Note that sometimes the same movement can mean different things, depending upon the situation:

➤ Wagging tail: I'm happy

➤ Preening: Time to tidy up. I'm so comfortable here, I'll just relax and take care of myself.

➤ Preening another bird or person: I like you a lot.

➤ Flashing or pinpointing eyes: Wow, that's interesting. I like that, or I hate that and I'm angry!

➤ Facial and neck feathers fluffed, with head bowed or scratching own head: Please scratch my head.

➤ Body low on perch, wings held slightly out to the side and quivering: Please, please, please. Me, me, me.

➤ Stretching: Gosh, I'm glad to see you.

➤ Grinding beak: It's sleepy time.

➤ Tail flared out: I'm very excited (or possibly jealous or angry).

➤ Flipping or slapping one or both wings: Get the #*%&* away from me!

➤ Wiping beak on perch: Gee that strawberry was sticky. I need the wooden napkin.

➤ Standing on one foot: Don't worry. I'm just resting. (Standing on one foot or the other is normal. Don't bother your vet about it unless your bird refuses to put one of his feet down at all or never rests on only one.)

➤ Regurgitating, when combined with head bobbing and pumping neck muscles: I love you. (No kidding! Birds regurgitate to their mates, to their young and sometimes to their favorite person. Consider it a compliment. In a mated pair, the male feeds the female in this manner while she sits on the eggs.)

➤ Pulling out healthy feathers: I'm stressed out.

➤ Fluffing all the feathers at once and giving them a quick shake: I'm about to preen. I've just finished preening. I just woke up and need to arrange my feathers.

➤ Yawning: I'm sleepy. I'm stretching my jaw muscles. (Yawning may also be a reflex, and could occur when you touch his face in just the right spot between the beak and the ear opening.)

➤ Lying flat on the back with feet waving and beak open, possibly screaming: I'm terrified, but will

Squawk!

Never hiss at your parrot. It's the sound of a snake, and some birds even use it to scare other birds away. "Shhh" is mighty close to a hiss, so don't say it either. Calm a scared or upset parrot with cooing sounds like, "You're okay," and "Pooor Polly."

fight to the death if I have to! (If your bird ever assumes this position, you have pushed him too far. Back off and let him regain his composure before handling him again. If Pauly is out of his cage and something scares him so badly that he resorts to this position, the only safe way to take him back to the security of his cage is in a towel. You'll learn how to safely "towel" a bird in Chapter 18.)

Why Parrots May Hurt the One They Love

Parrots are possessive and jealous, so they often get angry when anyone, even another family member, gets close to their favorite person. If they become enraged enough to lose their tempers and can't reach the object of their anger, they may sink their beaks into whoever is closest. Biting the nearest person when the object of their fury is out of reach is called displaced aggression. The scenario could be as simple as this:

You're watching television with Pauly on your right shoulder. Your husband comes in and gives you a peck on the left cheek. Pauly freaks out about having to share you for even an instant, and bites your nose because he can't reach your husband. If Pauly is a large parrot, he could disfigure your face (that's the best reason of all to keep a big bird off your shoulder). Had Pauly been on your hand where he belonged, the bite (if it occurred at all) would be in a less-sensitive spot.

Bird Brainers

Teach Pauly that aggression against anyone is a no-no. If he lunges at someone, or tries to bite your finger in a fit of displaced aggression while perched on your hand, wiggle your hand. He'll stop biting and try to regain his balance. If every nip makes his perch wiggle, he may learn to hold his temper.

The Least You Need to Know

➤ Misunderstandings and mixed messages are common between pets and people.

➤ Birds communicate with us through body language. The better we understand the signals our birds send us, the better adjusted our birds will be.

➤ Parrots are wary of strangers, but some do learn to talk or do tricks for people outside the family.

➤ Most parrot bites are accidents, but perfectly nice parrots can be taught to bite through mishandling.

➤ Displaced aggression occurs when a parrot can't reach the object of his rage and bites the nearest person instead. It's the best of all reasons to keep your parrot off your shoulder.

Do You Have a Feathered Fiend?

Poor you! You've been reading about petting parrots, but haven't been able to get close enough to pugnacious Polly to know what her feathers feel like.

Why does Polly act like she wants to bite your head off when you try to get near her? Or cringe in the corner when you open her cage door? Who knows? Maybe you're her second or third owner, and none of the others tried to tame her. Maybe she was captured in the wild and smuggled across the border, terrified and traumatized. Maybe she was once a sweet hand-fed baby, but reverted to wild from lack of attention. Or maybe you were inexperienced when it came to raising her and reinforced bad behavior by mistake.

You may never know what went wrong with Polly, but that's okay because it doesn't matter. What matters is teaching her to trust you, so she'll have a better life and you'll have a pleasant pet. Can it be done? Usually, but not always. This chapter will help you handle your hostile pet.

(Please note that this chapter is for people with problem parrots. If you have a new bird that just isn't relaxed enough to make friends yet, see Chapters 13 and 14.)

Think About Treats

Forget training for a moment and let's talk treats. What does Polly like best? Sunflower seeds? Corn on the cob? Peanuts? Grapes? If you've only had her a little while and don't know her favorite foods, spend a few days finding out what turns her on. Is she too scared to eat while you watch? In that case, put a variety of goodies in her dishes, leave the room and come back in five minutes to see how she did.

Bird Brainers

A taming treat should be a favorite that Polly can eat quickly, so training can continue. For example, if raw corn on the cob takes first place, give her one kernel at a time during training.

Parrots always grab their favorites first, so whatever is eaten right away should become Polly's taming treat. That means she should never find it in her food dish again. From now on, she should only see her favorite food in your hand. Offer it to her through the cage bars for a few days. Later, open the door and see if you can feed it to her with no bars between you. Feed Polly a piece of her favorite food from your hand a couple of times a day. It's good bonding.

Sometimes Polly will take a treat and throw it down. Nothing personal. Parrots in the wild do that all the time. Pick it up and offer it again or give her another one. Better yet, sometimes copy her behavior and drop a treat too. Then pick it up and give it to Polly.

Try the Quick Fix First

While adjusting the attitude of an overbearing bird often takes months, sometimes it's accomplished in just a couple of weeks. No matter what your problem with Polly, try the quick fix first. Just follow these eight easy steps:

Bird Brainers

Some parrot "problems" have solutions so simple that owners miss them. For example, if you allow your cockatiel to sit on your shoulder and she persists in playing with the attractive toys hanging from your ear lobes, she's isn't being bad—she's just being a parrot. Solution: Remove your earrings before putting Polly on your shoulder.

1. Trim Polly's wings, or have a professional do it.
2. Lower Polly's cage, T-stand, play gym and anything else she perches on (cut off the legs on the stand if you have to), so she has to look up at her human flock.
3. Make sure Polly gets plenty of exercise (see Chapter 12).
4. Spray Polly daily using warm water in a plant mister.
5. Move Polly from room to room as you and the family go from one room to another.
6. Make sure Polly sees you eat, and give her a portion of the family dinner (at room temperature).
7. Give Polly an exercise toy and a chew toy to keep in her cage (see Chapter 7).

8. At least twice a day catch Polly doing something right—like perching quietly or occupying herself with a toy. Tell her she's a good bird and hand feed her a treat.

In two weeks, you'll know if the eight steps improved Polly's personality. If they did, congratulations. Keep her on the program and have fun with your reformed friend. If they didn't make a difference, make a habit of them anyway, and read on for more help.

Befriending Belligerent Birds

You can't touch Polly and she seems to hate you—although all the growling, squawking and feigned attacks are probably her expressions of fear. Chances are you're angry at Polly by now. After all, other people's parrots perch on their hands, bow their heads for petting, beg for attention, maybe even talk, and all your bird does is snap at your fingers or cringe in the corner when you open the cage door. You wanted a pet and instead you have a problem. Poor you.

Okay, so much for sympathy. Now get over it. Polly didn't ask to be in this situation either. Parrots are social creatures, and a bird who refuses friendly advances, and consequently never gets out of her cage, is living a terrible life. Both of you need help. It's time to bite the bullet. Something has to happen to change the relationship. And that something begins with getting Polly out of her cage.

Preparing for Action

The following steps will prepare you for the process that could eventually turn your fiend into a friend:

Bird Brainers

A parrot is a wild animal. Polly doesn't know how to be a pet unless you teach her. The reason she can become such a super pet is because she's a social creature, concerned with fitting into her flock. When we encourage good behavior and don't inadvertently reinforce bad behavior, Polly responds by being a good bird.

➤ Set aside at least an hour. If you're in a hurry, your parrot will sense it and won't respond well.

➤ Eliminate the possibility of interruptions. Turn on your answering machine and let it get the phone.

➤ Don't wear anything Polly may be afraid of, like a hat, sunglasses or jewelry that jangles.

➤ Parrot-proof a small room to work in. A bathroom is ideal. Put a comfortable chair and a pillow in it.

➤ Make sure Polly's flight feathers haven't grown out.

➤ Put two 12- to 14-inch dowels in the parrot-proofed room, in case you need them. They should be the same thickness as one of Polly's perches. (Dowels are inexpensive and easily obtained at the hardware store.)

➤ Have a few of Polly's favorite treats in your pocket.

➤ Be determined. Tell yourself you are going to succeed for Polly's sake, and yours.

Ready? Me too. Good things are going to happen, so let's get started.

Extracting Your Vehement Vampire

Are you feeling brave? Then today's the day. Take Polly's cage off its stand and set it on the floor of the parrot-proofed room (it can be the room she's always in, if you have no other options). If Polly's cage is a floor model that doesn't have legs or a stand, remove the cage paper, all the dishes and any swings or toys that may hurt her. Then have someone help you take the cage to your parrot-proofed room and lay it on its side gently, with the door facing the ceiling. Now close the door to the room. From here on, it's just you and Polly.

Put a chair next to the cage. Open the cage door as wide as it goes (clip it in place if it could swing and pinch Polly's toes). Then sit down with a good book and wait. It's Polly's move.

Almost all parrots will leave a low cage and climb to its top sooner or later. When Polly does, gently close and secure the cage door so she can't return. Then sit down beside the cage and read for another five minutes. Don't guess. Time it.

After five minutes, stand up and move your hands behind Polly slowly (but don't try to touch her). She'll squawk and move away. Good. That's exactly what you want. No matter how fiercely Polly protests, keep moving your hands slowly and calmly—but relentlessly—until you have herded her down the cage and she's standing on the floor (do it with dowels if Polly's attitude makes you fear for your fingers). Now place your pillow on the floor between Polly and her cage and sit on it. Talk to your pet, using lots of soothing "ooo" sounds.

Bird Brainers

Wild parrots seldom use their beaks to bite anything but food. Biting is a learned behavior and it becomes a habit when the bird is rewarded for it. New owners just don't realize that attention (even the negative kind) and drama are big bonuses to a parrot.

Parrots like to perch in high places, so after Polly waddles around in confusion for a few minutes, make a fist and offer your forearm as a perch. Slide it in low and from the front, and stop when your arm is just in front of your parrot's feet and an inch or so higher than them. Polly will probably squawk and move away, but then again, she might accept your invitation. If she does, stay steady. Remember, Polly might lead with her beak to see if the perch is safe. Don't wimp out and jerk away. Any indecisive moves will put training back to square one. Are you sitting on the floor with your previously un-touchable parrot on your arm? Say "Good bird," and savor the magic moment. I'll get back to you soon. Meanwhile, keep your elbow low so she'll move toward your hand rather than your shoulder.

Might Polly bite? Yes, she might, although she probably won't because she accepted the invitation. But if she does, it will hurt, and the hardest part will be controlling your urge to yelp and fling her off your arm (don't do it—instead say "No!" sharply and firmly). If that big beak intimidates you and you don't want to test her temper with your forearm, using a dowel is a good alternative. After all, your Polly doesn't have a history of being a Pollyanna.

When in Doubt, Use a Dowel

What will happen if you decide against offering your arm? Well, Polly might get off the floor anyway by climbing up your shoe, or your leg. If she does, let her walk on your legs and perch atop your bent knee if she wants to, but don't let her climb your body all the way to your shoulder. Even trained parrots can be troublesome on shoulders, and Polly isn't even tame yet (although she just took a giant step in that direction). While it's great that she trusted you enough to step on your body, the real goal is getting her on your hand. That's where your dowel comes in handy.

If Polly perches on your leg, talk to her softly and give her time to become accustomed to the idea of touching you. After two or three minutes (less if she tries to climb your upper body), encourage her to perch on the dowel. Hold one end of it firmly in your hand, and offer it by bringing it toward Polly, parallel to her feet and a little above and in front of them. Then follow through by gently pushing it upward against her belly. Is Polly on board? "Good bird."

What if Polly doesn't perch on your forearm or climb up your leg? Instead, she shakes with fear or transforms into the beak-slasher-massacre-bird of B movies and dares you to befriend her? Use your dowel with her on the floor. Polly will probably back into a corner, shaking and/or screaming all the way, but eventually she'll have to climb on the dowel because you will calmly persist and won't give her anywhere else to go. Whew! "Good bird."

Squawk!

Physical punishment never works on parrots. Why? Because they can't understand that they brought on your violence by behaving a certain way. To a parrot, physical punishment is the same as being attacked, and she'll react by trying to defend herself.

Squawk!

Extremely frightened or aggressive birds, and birds with beak-shy owners, are best handled with a dowel until mutual trust develops.

Keep It Short, Sweet and Safe

By now you either have a bird on your forearm or on a dowel, and you don't need me to tell you that's major progress. Just don't be too sure of Polly yet. It's never a good idea to let a large parrot perch near your face, but it's particularly important to keep an untamed bird, who might be scared or angry, at a safe distance. Remember the head-to-heart rule (see Chapter 14). If Polly sidesteps across the dowel and winds up on your hand, lower your elbow (check out the Egyptian grip in Chapter 13). It's great that she's made contact, but maybe it's too soon for you. If so, put the dowel in your free hand, and offer it to Polly.

While Polly perches, tell her what a fine friend she's going to be and offer her a treat. She may or may not be relaxed enough to take it, let alone eat it, but someday she will be. Five minutes or less after she perches, time's up. That's more than enough stress for both of you. Carry Polly back to the cage on her dowel (or your arm), open the door and place her on a perch inside. If she opts for the cage top instead, gently herd her back through the door and close it behind her. When she settles, give her a treat through the cage bars. (If Polly's cage was on its side on the floor, set it upright before putting Polly in it.)

Possible Problems

What if something goes wrong and Polly doesn't come out of her cage? Try again another day. What if she comes out, but lies on her back in terror when you approach her with the dowel? Wait until she's calmed down, then open the door to her cage and herd her back in. Try again tomorrow. And tomorrow. Becoming friends with a frightened or furious parrot is often a slow process, but the rewards are extraordinary. Hang in there.

Another Option

Don't give up if Polly doesn't come out of her cage on her own after two weeks of trying. You'll just have to go in after her—with a dowel.

Talk softly to Polly as you open the cage door. Offer the dowel as a perch, as I've already described, being sure to put gentle upward follow-through pressure on her belly. It may not be easy. If Polly refuses to cooperate, you might have to follow her around the cage with the dowel until you get her cornered, and she has no choice but to step on it. (She'll complain loudly, but you'll ignore it.) Under those circumstances, she may quickly step up and over the dowel and climb away again. Even that's a beginning. Shut the cage door, tell her what a good bird she is, see if she'll take her favorite food from your hand and try again tomorrow.

Bird Brainers

Don't get playing mixed up with biting. If Polly pinches your arm while trying to unstring your beaded bracelet, she isn't biting. She just needs something to do. Put your bracelet away and give her a grasping toy to destroy.

The next day, get her to step on the dowel two times before quitting. The third day, three times. Then stick with three step-ups for the next several days. Within two weeks, you should see progress. One day Polly will step up on the dowel and stay longer than a heartbeat. Be sure to hold the perch steady and tell her what a good bird she is.

Once Polly steps up on the dowel and remains on it without complaining, try to bring her out of the cage on it. This may take many tries over a period of several days. Pay attention to what you are doing so you don't bump her head.

A Bird on the Hand—Hooray!

Polly may be dowel-trained, but you're still longing to feel those feet on your fingers. Here's how to make the transition from dowel to hand:

After Polly readily climbs on your 12- to 14-inch dowel, begin holding it so that less length is available to her and she has to stand closer to your hand. Proceed gradually by moving your hand up one inch every couple of days. For example, if you start with a 12-inch long dowel, in 12 days your hand will be less than six inches from Polly's feet. One special day there will be so little dowel left that Polly's feet will overlap onto your hand. That's your signal to discard the dowel and offer your hand. Congratulations! You did it. Pugnacious Polly has finally become a pet.

Once Polly perches on your forearm or hand, she's no longer a barbaric bird. But she's still an uneducated one. Use the techniques in Chapters 13 and 14 to complete her education.

Bird Brainers

Don't forget to reward Polly with "Good bird" and a treat whenever she does something right.

A T-stand is a "best buy" when it comes to taming a bird. Start using it to teach the "up" command (see Chapter 13) as soon as Polly steps on a dowel—even before she's hand-trained. Take her from the dowel to the T-stand and back again, giving the appropriate "up" or "down" command each time.

When These Methods Don't Work

If you were patient and tried everything and your parrot is still as angry, wild or terrified as ever, professional help may be the answer. Bird behaviorists can help you correct most parrot problems, and have successfully turned many demons into darlings. Ask your avian veterinarian for a recommendation.

Squawks and Screams

While some parrots (female cockatiels, for example) are rather quiet, every species makes a certain amount of noise. Periodic happy calls during the day are a pleasant sound to confirmed parrot lovers. But birds who squawk and shriek endlessly frazzle even their best human friends. If Polly's screaming is driving one of you out of your happy home, here's help.

Polly Sez

Reinforcing a behavior is the same as rewarding it because it makes your bird want to do it again. For example, if Polly's screams make you yell, "Shut the *&)%$# up!" from the other room, you've just reinforced her and she'll scream even louder. Why? Because in her parrot brain, you're communicating.

Why Some Parrots Develop Screaming Problems

Your parrot can't tell you what's wrong, any more than a human baby can, so she resorts to screaming and hopes you'll solve her problem. Of course, you know what the problem is—it's that darned screaming. Before we discuss ways to quiet your pet, let's see if Polly has a legitimate complaint. Here's what her screams might mean:

1. I'm hungry
2. I'm thirsty
3. I'm lonely
4. I'm scared
5. I'm full of energy and need an outlet
6. I'm bored
7. I'm horny

Hungry and Thirsty

Wild parrots are noisy at feeding time, and Polly will be too if her dishes are empty when her tummy is. Empty or missing food and water dishes make birds insecure. In fact, all four of my feathered friends fret and complain when their dishes are in the dishwasher, even though I don't remove the dishes until after they have eaten, and the washing cycle takes less than an hour.

Squawk!

The two punishments most often used on a noisy parrot are yelling at her and isolating her in another room. Both of these methods are guaranteed to make the bird scream even more. Not only that, but separating a parrot from her people is cruel and inhumane.

Lonely

Because parrots are social animals, they suffer when separated from their flock (that's you). In the wild, they squawk or scream to broadcast their location, and members of the flock answer. In your home, Polly can learn to maintain contact with quieter calls (see Chapter 13), provided you set a good example.

A cage on wheels or a T-stand may also go a long way in quieting a lonesome bird. Once Polly is hand- or dowel-tame, it only takes a second to get her out of her cage and put her on a perch. Take her along when you spend time in a room where she can't see or hear you.

Scared

You'll have to play detective to find out if fear is making Polly scream. First of all, did she always scream, or did the behavior start suddenly? If it started suddenly, fear is a possibility. Next, you'll have to figure out what change in her surroundings started it. Did a relative she never met move in with you? Did you put her cage in a new place—maybe near a window where she can see predators? Did you give her a new toy she may be terrified of? Did you get a new pet?

How you handle Polly's fear will depend on what she's afraid of. For example, her cage can be moved to a nonthreatening location and a scary toy can be removed. If a new person or pet is the problem, give the situation some time. Polly will get used to new faces, provided they don't threaten or tease her.

Avian Adventures

One of the best examples I ever saw of a bird screaming in fear took place in an RV park in Alabama. A fellow with a sulphur-crested cockatoo on the handlebars of his bike just passed me when the bird suddenly started shrieking. The man stopped the bike and let the bird perch on his hand, but it continued screaming non-stop. People ran out of their motor homes to see who was being slaughtered. I followed the hysterical bird's eyes and saw the reason for the ruckus. A hawk was circling overhead, and the cockatoo's instincts made him warn everyone about the predator.

Bursting with Energy

What if you were well fed, well rested and feeling fit, but were stuck in a tiny cell 24 hours a day? You might feel like screaming too. Birds have a high energy level and need plenty of exercise—especially flapping and climbing. Chapter 12 will help you start Polly on a fitness program. A little avian aerobics, followed by a gentle shower with a plant mister, may let you savor the sounds of silence.

Bored

Polly's too bright to perch around doing nothing. She needs stimulating toys (see Chapter 7). A variety of foods, creatively displayed (see "Foraging

Squawk!

The first trick a parrot teaches her owner is to take her out of the cage when she screams. Don't let Polly train you. Take her out of the cage when she's behaving and isn't expecting attention, not when she demands it.

for Fun" in Chapter 10) will also give Polly something to do with her mouth besides complain. If being alone too many hours is part of her protest, leave a radio or television set on for her. Many parrots enjoy watching TV.

Parrots who never learned how to entertain themselves may scream constantly for attention. This problem is best prevented by encouraging your young parrot to play independently and by not responding to her every peep. If you overindulged Polly when she was a baby, you'll have to put up with some noise to change her attitude. Ignore her when she screams, and give her treats and lovin' when she's quiet, and Polly will probably come around. Be patient. Depending on how badly you spoiled her, reconditioning may take several months.

Horny

Six out of seven isn't bad. Sorry, but I don't have a formula for quieting a bird who's screaming for a mate. On the bright side, it only happens during the couple of weeks that would be breeding season for the species. Your best bet? Distract your pet with a new toy or a favorite food. If that doesn't work, try calming her down by covering the cage for 10 minutes (at the most).

No matter what you do, the best you can hope for is a temporary respite. Birds make more noise than usual during mating season. Period. If you think Polly's problem is raging hormones, mark your calendar and see if she gets noisy at exactly the same time next year. With some birds, it occurs for a few days in the spring and the fall.

Demolition Demons

While destructiveness is a frequent complaint of parrot owners, the problem is theirs, not their pet's. Playing with the objects around them and chewing everything they can sink their beaks into isn't a problem for parrots. They're just doing what comes naturally. Be careful where you place Polly (see "Boundaries Are Best" in Chapter 14), and always make sure her busy beak has something safe to chew on.

Bad Biters

Since biting a buddy isn't part of being a parrot, something went wrong if your bird becomes a vicious biter. The following are the most common ways owners teach their birds to bite by mistake. If you are guilty, stop now. With luck and good handling methods, Polly may stop later.

Owners condition their birds to bite by:

➤ Being wishy-washy. (Offering your hand and then pulling it back time and again will seem like a game to Polly, and she'll try to grab your elusive hand.)

➤ Being mean. (If you use physical punishment on your parrot, she'll be terrified and will fight for her life.)

➤ Being scary. (A new look, jerky movements, the effects of alcohol or drugs and interacting with a parrot while in a hurry or a bad mood can all frighten her enough to make her bite.)

➤ Allowing the bird to be dominant. (Remember the head-to-heart rule in Chapter 14, and keep Polly perched low.)

➤ Laughing when your little bird attacks a big human. (Reinforcing aggression, no matter who it is aimed at, practically guarantees that someday it will be aimed at you.)

➤ Forcing affection on their pet. (Read Polly's body language, and respect her feelings when she isn't in a touchy-feely mood.)

➤ Over-reacting to a baby bird's nip. (Young hand-fed parrots associate hands with food and may nip fingers by mistake. The worst thing you can do is to get upset and reinforce the action with drama. Instead, ignore it and your bird will too. Next time, have a chew toy or treat handy to distract Polly when she gets too interested in your fingers.)

➤ Playing puppy-like with the bird's beak. (Look out for your fingers, toes and nose; parrots are mimics.)

➤ Housing the bird in only one place. (Parrots who stay in the same place all the time become defensive of their tiny territory. Even if you can't handle Polly yet, move her cage from one place to another often.)

➤ Becoming the bird's one and only. (Bonding with your bird is great, but too much of a good thing leads to trouble. Make sure your bird interacts with other people right from the beginning. Otherwise, Polly will become so possessive of you that displaced aggression will surely follow.)

Offering Your Hand to a Biting Bird

If Polly thinks you are unafraid of her bite, she will stop trying to bite you. Offer the back of your hand to your aggressive parrot by making a fist and bending your wrist downward. That stretches the skin on your hand so tight that your bird can't even pinch you. Now face Polly and slowly offer your safe skin. Just be sure to keep the back of your hand lined up with her beak so she can't reach around and pinch your palm. This technique will get Polly used to your hand, and should help you learn to hold your own near her beak.

Socializing Over-Bonded Birds

If Polly hates everyone but you, here are some techniques to make her more sociable:

➤ Ask family and friends to hand feed her treats.

➤ Sometimes leave the room without Polly, and have your spouse or friend "rescue" her from the T-stand and bring her to you (it's okay if they use a dowel, but teach them the correct technique).

➤ Put your bird on your partner's hand when you leave the room.

➤ Have your partner sit on the floor and read a book. Then bring Polly into the room, put her down on the floor a few feet from the person, leave the room and close the door behind you. If your parrot wants company bad enough, she'll initiate some sort of interaction with the other person, even if it's just pulling on his or her shoelaces.

Setting the Mood

Think of the times you started the day in a bad mood, but a friend or spouse changed your attitude by saying something nice just when you needed it. Like people, parrots sometimes get into bad moods for no real reason, and can be cued into a better mood with kind words. When initiating physical contact with Polly, say "Good bird" before reaching for her. That's often all it takes to turn a sour parrot into a sweetie.

Bird Brainers

Parrots never see themselves as less important than people because they can't understand the concept. Your parrot will never live to please you, but she can become your friend. Just respect her for what she is, notice good behavior and let her know she did something right.

Keeping It Up

Transforming a vehement vampire into a good bird isn't easy. Give yourself and Polly a pat on the back (okay, the nape for her). Now that you have a pet parrot, don't let her backslide into a bitch. Use the "up" command often, give her ladder lessons every day, teach her the Egyptian grip (see Chapter 13) and make the eight easy steps at the beginning of this chapter part of your daily routine. That should keep Polly in a positive mood.

The Least You Need to Know

➤ Polly's favorite food makes the best taming and training treat.

➤ Eight easy steps may be all it takes to adjust Polly's attitude.

➤ You have to get Polly out of her cage in order to tame her.

➤ If Polly has a history of biting, use a dowel as a perch instead of your hand.

➤ Parrots who won't stop screaming have a problem. If you can solve it, Polly will gradually quiet down.

➤ Wild parrots do not use their beaks as weapons unless their life is in danger. Biting is a learned behavior. We teach it to our birds by mistake.

➤ All parrots have busy beaks. Distract your pet with a chew toy when she starts checking out your fingers. If she can't leave your jewelry alone, remove it before playing with her.

➤ Don't rush your parrot into a neck rub. Help her mood by telling her "Good bird" before bringing her out of the cage.

➤ After you've corrected Polly's problem, keep her pleasant by practicing the "up" command, ladder lessons and the Egyptian grip. Make the eight easy steps a habit.

Part 5

Keeping Your Bird Healthy and Beautiful

You've picked out a healthy bird and moved him into your home and heart. Now you want to keep him in his finest form. That's what this part of the book is all about.

Healthy birds are hardier than they look, so avian health care is primarily preventive. This section begins with the regular routines that keep the vet bills at bay. But bad things can happen to even the best-kept birds, so I'll also cover emergency first aid and tell you how to recognize some dastardly diseases. You'll learn the subtle signs of a sick bird, and how you can help your veterinarian diagnose and cure your pet.

The last chapter in this section discusses the cycle of life and covers aging pets. In it, I'll try to ease you through the dreaded day when your bird dies by suggesting some simple rituals you can use to help yourself and your family recover.

Chapter 18

Grooming for Good Health

In This Chapter

➤ How to hold a bird when grooming

➤ Trimming wings, nails and beaks

➤ When feathers fly

➤ Bathing birds

Now that you know how to bring out the best in Pauly's personality, here's how you can keep him healthy and safe through good grooming. In this chapter, I'll tell you the most reliable techniques for catching and holding him, and for trimming his wings and nails. You'll also learn how to help him through his bad feathers days, otherwise known as the molt.

Toweling

Before you learn how to groom Pauly, you'll have to be able to hold him still so you can work on him. Finches, canaries and other birds whose beaks don't pinch can be held gently in your bare hands (see "Catching Canaries and Finches" in this chapter). However, hookbills, from budgies on up, can hurt unprotected hands.

Most experts recommend toweling hookbills rather than wearing heavy gloves. A bird restrained in a towel blames the terry-cloth monster for trapping him, while a bird restrained in gloves may associate his predicament with hands. Besides, you can

Bird Brainers

Birds stand still when a room suddenly turns dark, so some bird owners turn off the lights just before toweling their bird. If you try this method, note where your bird is before flipping off the switch, and be sure you can still see well enough to avoid being bitten.

control your bird's whole body with a towel, including keeping his wings still.

In addition to immobilizing your bird for grooming, toweling is also the method of choice for applying first aid (see Chapter 19). The ideal way to learn this method is to watch an expert. But whether you have that opportunity or not, please practice the technique before you need it. Here's how:

Choose a nice soft washcloth as your catcher's mitt if you have a little bird, a hand towel for a medium sized bird and a bath towel for a big bird. Beaks and toenails may snag or tear the towel, so use an old one—but not one that is worn thin. The thicker the terry cloth, the safer your fingers.

Getting Into Position

The easiest way to position Pauly for toweling will depend on whether or not he is finger-trained and has trimmed wings.

If Pauly is tame and has trimmed wings:

1. Bring him out of his cage on your hand.
2. Take him to the bathroom or to another small, noncarpeted area, and shut the door behind you.
3. Place him on the floor in a corner.

If Pauly isn't tame and/or can fly:

1. Close the doors and windows.
2. Remove the toys, dishes and perches from his cage.
3. Secure the cage door as wide open as it goes.

Bird Brainers

In all these instructions, I've assumed that you're right-handed. If you're left-handed, just switch.

Catch and Hold

When you're ready, cover your right hand or both hands with the towel (depending on the size of your bird). Moving quickly and smoothly, bring your towel-covered hand behind Pauly and grasp him from behind his head with your thumb on one side of his jawbone and your index finger on the other side. After you catch him, you have the option of leaving your thumb in position but placing your third finger where your index finger was, and moving your index finger to the top of his head for a three-point hold. Either hold works just fine, so use whichever one makes you most comfortable.

While your right hand secures Pauly's head, use your left hand to drape the towel around his body, immobilizing his wings. Then keep your left hand low and hold him near the legs and base of the tail. Make sure there's no pressure on his chest or abdomen, or he won't be able to breathe. Now you can take Pauly out of his cage (if necessary) or pick him up off the floor.

What if you missed his head on the first try? Keep trying until you succeed. A towel around your bird's body won't do any good unless you have control of his head.

When Pauly is secure in your firm but gentle grip, adjust the towel (it's best if you have a helper) and make sure his face is uncovered. Expect him to chomp into the terry cloth. It's good therapy. After all, he's taking his frustrations out on it, not you, and it gives him something to do.

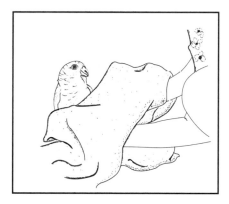

(1) Back the bird into a corner.

(2) Position your hands so the right hand is ready to control the bird's head.

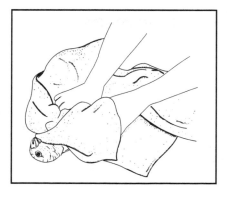

(3) Control the head while your left hand gains control of the body.

(4) That wasn't so bad, was it?

What If?

In a worst-case scenario, Pauly might assume the panic position and lie on his back while you're trying to towel him. Then you'll need more protection. Double the towel if it's large enough, or exchange it for a bigger one and fold it down the middle. Use both towel-covered hands to hold Pauly's head on the floor, then move your right hand into position as explained previously. When your bird's head is secure, put him in an upright position and arrange the towel around the rest of his body. If you're alone, pressing your bird against your chest may make arranging the towel around his body a little easier. Whatever you do, don't quit. That will only make Pauly fight harder the next time.

Toweling Tips

➤ Just do it. Tentative tries will either terrify or anger your bird. Plan your moves and make them quickly.

➤ Concentrate on Pauly's head. Catch and restrain it before grasping his body. When you finish, release his body first and his head last.

➤ Birds are breakable. Use enough pressure to do the job, but no more. With most birds, you'll need a tighter grip on the head than on the body.

➤ Organize in advance. If you're going to trim Pauly's toenails or medicate him, lay out everything you need before toweling him.

➤ Enlist a helper, if possible. He or she can gently unwrap Pauly's toes from the cage wires (if necessary), and quiet his flapping wings by making sure they are properly folded under the towel.

➤ Never hold your bird by the chest or abdomen. Too much pressure in that area interferes with breathing.

Bird Brainers

Make sure all the windows and doors are closed, and have a net handy when restraining a bird with untrimmed wings. That way, you'll be able to catch him if he escapes.

Catching Canaries and Finches

Since your canary or finch can't hurt you with his beak, it's best to catch him in your bare hands. Remove perches and other cage accessories first, then reach in with one hand (use the other hand to block the exit), corner your bird and catch him. Hold him gently in one hand with his wings properly folded against his body. Your fingers will be around his tiny neck, so be careful not to squeeze.

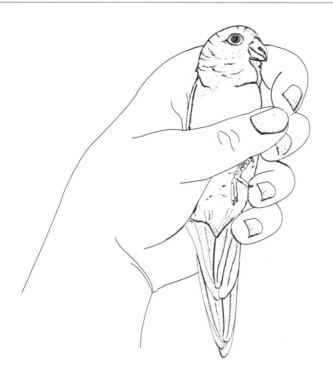

Bare hands are best for holding small birds.

Trimming Wings, Nails and Beaks

Wing, nail and beak trimming all help keep your pet safe and healthy. While almost every pet parrot should have his wings and nails trimmed periodically, only a few will ever need beak care.

Wing Trimming

The best way to learn how to trim your bird's wings is to watch an expert do it the first time. How hard will it be when you go it alone? That depends on your bird's attitude. Rooster, my amazon parrot, stands still and doesn't fuss, so it takes less than a minute to trim both sides. On the other hand, our budgie Bluebelle struggles, screams and bites, so trimming her takes two people and a small towel. In truth, that's closer to the norm. Most birds have to be restrained for wing trimming, and it's always best to use a helper.

After your bird is restrained, extend one wing out to the side and work from the top, cutting from the tip of the wing first and working inward. Using sharp, barber-quality scissors, cut the first several (five to eight) primary flight feathers just a little below the line created by the bottom of the feathers above (the dorsal major primary coverts—see the drawing on the next page). Bigger, heavy-bodied birds (think amazon parrots or cockatoos) can often get by with only five feathers trimmed on each side. But longer, leaner types (like cockatiels) need to have eight flight feathers trimmed to keep them from flying.

*A wing before and
after trimming.*

Polly Sez

Pin feathers or *blood feathers* are immature, growing feathers, protected by a sheath of keratin. Each one contains an artery and a vein. Be careful not to trim one of them, or your bird will bleed.

After you trim your bird's wings on both sides, carry him to your bed so he can get the feel of his new feather-do in a safe place. If he's learned to flap on your finger, have him do it over the bed. I also drop my birds onto the bed gently from about two feet to help them gauge their flying and gliding abilities.

There's no timetable for wing trimming, as every bird's feathers renew themselves at different times. Not only that, but the same bird may stay trimmed for four months one time and be able to fly in two months the next time. The best bet is to check your bird's wings every eight weeks and trim the two or three feathers that might have grown in—provided they are mature. *Never* cut a blood feather. You'll know which ones they are, because they still have their keratin sheath.

Nail Trimming

A bird's toenails grow continuously, just like ours do. In the wild, normal activity keeps them the right length, but a tame bird's toenails often become overgrown. How can you tell when Pauly needs a pedicure? Two ways. His nails may be so sharp that holding him on your finger hurts, or so long that they push his feet up off the ground when he walks on the floor. Ideally, nails will be blunt enough to be comfortable when he perches on you and short enough so the fleshy part of his toes touches the floor when he walks. It's best to watch a professional trim toenails before trying it yourself. Here's how it's done:

The best toenail clipper for small birds is a human fingernail clipper, while the dog toenail clipper known as the "guillotine" works best on big birds. Another must-have is styptic powder, available at most pet shops. It takes two people to tangle with toenails—one for restraint and one for trimming. Budgie-size birds can be held still in bare hands, but toweling is the best choice for bigger birds.

Bird Brainers

While some bird owners prefer trimming only one wing, it's much safer to trim both. That way, the bird is still balanced, and can glide down smoothly if he jumps or falls from his perch.

A bird's toenails curve downward. Inside the nail is the quick, containing blood and nerves. That means it hurts and bleeds if you cut it. You can see the quick if your bird has light colored nails. It's the pink tube that runs about three-fourths of the way down the nail. The rest of the nail has no feeling and won't bleed. If you can see the quick, make your cut a little beyond it and Pauly won't feel a thing. Is the nail still too long? Forget it for now, but trim it again in 10 days. Frequent trimming makes the quick recede and become a little shorter, so eventually you'll be able to cut Pauly's nails to the ideal length without spilling a drop of blood.

What if your bird has dark nails and you can't see the quick? Remove tiny amounts at a time until the nail is the proper length, or until you see the first sign of bleeding. If bleeding occurs, pack the nail with styptic power right away (cornstarch, flour or baking power are emergency substitutes).

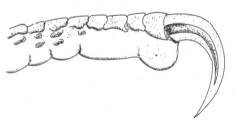

Before trimming, this nail is sharp enough to hurt when your bird perches on your arm and long enough to keep him from walking properly.

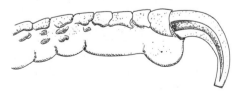

If some of Pauly's nails are too sharp, but not too long, your job will be easier. Trim only a tiny smidgen off the tip of each nail that needs it—just enough to blunt them.

Bird Brainers

An average budgie's beak grows three inches a year.

Beak Trimming

Most birds wear their beaks down as fast as they grow out, so they never need a trim. The exceptions are birds whose upper and lower beaks aren't perfectly aligned. If Pauly has a crooked bite, the upper and possibly the lower beak may become overgrown and will need to be trimmed periodically so he can eat properly. This isn't a do-it-yourself project. There are nerves and a blood supply in your bird's beak, so a mistake could injure him and make eating impossible. Beak trimming, if necessary, should be done by your avian veterinarian.

Managing the Molt

One of these days you'll find feathers floating though the air. Don't worry. You won't have to change Pauly's name to Yul Brynner. He's just shedding his old feathers and growing new ones. It's a normal process called molting and, depending on your bird, it may occur two or three times a year or almost continuously. If Pauly loses only a few feathers at a time on a regular basis, he won't need any special treatment to get through it. But if he loses a lot in a short time, it's good to give him some extra care.

During an actual molting season, Pauly will lose several feathers a day over a period of about six weeks. As worn feathers fall out, pinfeathers emerge in their place and eventually mature into a shiny new suit. Growing so many new feathers is stressful and takes a lot of energy, so Pauly needs an especially nutritious diet during the molt. If his feather loss is quite heavy, raise the temperature in his room two or three degrees to make up for the thinner layer of downy insulation.

Squawk!

After your bird molts, he'll have full-grown flight feathers and will be able to take off and fly. Trim them as they mature, but don't clip any blood feathers.

Expect Pauly to be moody during the molt. This isn't the time to teach him a new trick. Petting his pinfeathers might hurt him, so if his body language says "keep away," respect his privacy. Let him know you love him by talking to him and feeding him treats by hand, but don't pet him for a few days. Preening himself may soothe him, so encourage it by spraying him with lukewarm water from a plant mister every morning.

When feathers begin falling on your clean floor, you might get moody, too. Keep a hand-held vacuum near the birdcage until the colorful storm subsides, and you'll be able to clean up the fluffy droplets in seconds.

Avian Adventures

Many creative bird owners collect and use their pet's most striking fallen feathers. They turn the pretty plumage into earrings, dream catchers and bookmarks; or use them to decorate planters, vases and hats. Examine the beauties on the bottom of your bird's cage and see what projects they inspire.

Bird Baths and Showers

Any bird-watcher will confirm that wild birds bathe often. That's because bathing is necessary for birds. It encourages preening and is good for your pet's physical and mental health. How often should you bathe Pauly? Once a day is ideal, but three times a week will do. Always bathe him early enough in the day so he'll be completely dry before bedtime. The best bathing solution is lukewarm water, right from the tap. Never add soap or any other cleaning agents, moisturizers or perfumes.

Polly Sez

Preening is what a bird does when he uses his beak to clean, lubricate and align his feathers.

Most birds love bathing, so if Pauly doesn't, it's probably because you haven't found his favorite method yet. Here are some possibilities:

➤ Lukewarm water in a plant mister. Aim it upward so it falls down on your bird like gentle rain.

➤ A shallow bowl of warm water placed on the bottom of his cage.

➤ Let him play under the water faucet (check every several seconds to make sure the temperature doesn't change).

➤ Take your big bird into the shower with you (but keep the soap off of him).

➤ Put wet leaves (freshly washed lettuce, spinach or celery tops) on the bottom of the cage for your little bird.

➤ Buy a birdbath that fits the size of your bird and cage. They are available at many pet shops.

Birds love to bathe, and almost always preen afterwards.

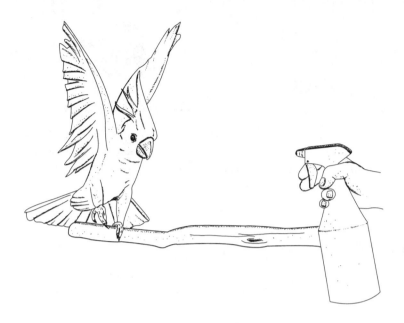

The Least You Need to Know

➤ Toweling is the best way to catch and restrain a parrot for grooming or first aid. Canaries and finches are best held in your bare hand.

➤ Most pet birds should have their wings and nails trimmed periodically. Try to watch an expert do it the first time.

➤ Be careful not to cut a blood feather when trimming wings, or the quick when trimming nails. If your bird's beak becomes overgrown, see your avian veterinarian.

➤ When birds molt, they lose worn feathers and grow new ones. The process takes lots of energy. Your bird may become moody when he's molting, and his resistance, especially to cold, may be lower than usual. Give him a variety of nutritious foods, but don't force physical affection on him.

➤ Bathing is important to your bird's physical and mental health. Some birds like baths, while others prefer showers. Use lukewarm water right from the tap, without any additives.

Chapter 19

Could It Be Serious?

In This Chapter

➤ Signs of sickness

➤ How to handle an emergency

➤ Avoiding lice, mites and parasites

The sooner you seek help for a sick bird, the better her chance of recovery. Problem is, Polly will try to hide her illness until she becomes so weak she can no longer fake it. Why? Because pretending to be healthy, no matter what, is an instinctive trait. In the wild, a weak bird quickly drops to the bottom of the pecking order, and a sick bird is driven out of the flock so she won't attract predators.

If prevention is the best kind of health care, being savvy and prepared run a close second. This chapter will help you see the signs of sickness, even if Polly's act deserves an Oscar. It will also tell you how to handle simple, but sometimes scary, situations, and what to do for a sick or injured pet until professional help is available. With luck, there's more information in this chapter than you'll ever need. Some of it is about pests and illnesses your pet may never encounter and injuries that may never occur. I hope you won't have to use it, but it's here for you, just in case.

Signs of Sickness

Many signs of sickness or stress are subtle at first—something you may sense rather than actually see—the way you instinctively know when something is troubling your spouse, child or best friend. If something seems wrong, but you can't figure out what it is, don't chalk it up to an overactive imagination. It's probably an early warning—

the very best kind, because quick treatment, before your bird weakens, has the greatest chance of success.

But what will your veterinarian think if you bring Polly in just because you sense something might be bothering her? The vet will think you're an enlightened bird owner. A lot fewer birds would die every year if their owners sought help for subtle, rather than serious, symptoms.

The better you know Polly, the sooner you'll be able to sense when something is wrong. Here are some signs of sickness that may appear insignificant to a casual observer.

Changes in Eating and Drinking Habits

Every year, hundreds of pet birds that might have been saved are too weak to recover by the time they arrive at the veterinarian's office. Why? Because of a misunderstanding on their owner's part. Many owners think their bird must be okay as long as she's still eating. But sick birds don't lose their appetites like dogs, cats and kids do. Their energy requirements are so high and their instincts to appear healthy so strong, that most sick birds eat a little (or at least appear to eat), until a few hours before their death.

Bird Brainers

Some birds, particularly cockatiels, suffer night frights and beat themselves up by thrashing around in their cages. A small night-light often stops these episodes. If it doesn't help, or if your bird hurts herself badly, see your veterinarian.

How can you tell if Polly's off her feed when she still buries her beak in her food dish? The best method is to weigh her on a gram scale (or have your veterinarian do it) when she is full grown and healthy. Then you'll have a record of her correct weight. Later, if you sense Polly may be eating less, you'll be able to weigh her and know for certain. If she has lost weight, visit your veterinarian.

Another way to find out if your bird is eating normally is to keep track of her food and water intake (any radical change in water consumption, less or more, may signal sickness). Make sure she is actually swallowing her food, not just cracking nuts and hulling seeds without consuming the kernels or moving her pellets and veggies around in her dish like an anorexic at a dinner party.

Changes in Droppings

You've been changing Polly's cage papers daily, so you know what to expect. While droppings vary in color and texture, depending upon the food your bird eats, any prolonged surprises are suspect. A change in the amount, texture or color of her droppings could signal sickness, while a buildup of droppings in only one or two sections of the cage might indicate a dip in activity level. Energetic birds usually get around more than that, and so do their droppings.

Changes in Attitude

If perky Polly loses her desire to play, sing, talk, preen or scream, and starts taking more naps, it isn't because she's growing up. A healthy bird maintains her normal activity level most of her life, so if your pet loses her zest or stops grooming her feathers, chances are, she's not feeling well. Also, suspect a physical cause when a sweet bird suddenly turns aggressive, or vice versa.

Changes in Posture and Appearance

Fluffed-up feathers, a sleepy aspect, drooping wings, frequent head flicking, swelling anywhere on the body and ragged or missing feathers are also signs that something is wrong. So is staying on the bottom of the cage for long periods of time without returning to a perch.

Fluffed-up and exhausted looking with eyes closed, this bird is obviously ill. Chances are he faked being well for several days before he was too far gone to hide it.

Obvious Signs of Trouble

Here are the most obvious signs of a bird in need of immediate help. You'll have to handle a couple of these situations yourself (don't worry, I'll tell you how later in this chapter), but an avian veterinarian is the answer for most of them.

➤ Noisy breathing, including sneezing, continuous panting and clicking sounds.

➤ Difficulty breathing, including tail-bobbing with each breath, breathing through the mouth, heavy breathing and shortness of breath.

➤ Frequently holding a cage bar in the beak while perching horizontally with neck extended (this position eases difficult breathing).

Bird Brainers

Too much dry food, poppy seed, or old, spoiled seed can cause constipation in finches and canaries. A constipated bird may strain, dance back and forth nervously on her perch, or just puff up her feathers and stay put. A variety of vegetables and fruits may solve the problem. If there is no improvement in a few hours, call your veterinarian.

271

Squawk!

Nonstick cookware and birds don't mix. If you scorch the cookware by mistake, it emits fumes fatal to birds. Best bet? Give your nonstick stuff to a birdless friend.

Squawk!

While birds get respiratory diseases, not colds like people do, don't ask for trouble by breathing on your bird when you have a cold or the flu. There's no telling how your bird's body will handle strange germs.

➤ Loss of voice, similar to a person with laryngitis.

➤ Frequent sneezing, plugged or runny nose, stained or sticky feathers around the nose or eyes.

➤ Any excessive discharge from the eyes, including tearing. Eyes partially or completely closed most of the day. Eyelids either swollen or "glued" shut by secretions. Frequent blinking, squinting or rubbing the eyes or side of the face against the perch or cage bars.

➤ Vomiting (regurgitation), other than feeding young or performing a courtship ritual.

➤ Loose droppings, and droppings containing undigested food, blood or mucus.

➤ Constipation (straining during elimination).

➤ Vent stained, wet or sticky, or feathers around the vent stuck to each other.

➤ Falling off the perch.

➤ Bleeding anywhere on the body.

➤ Ragged feathers, including broken, twisted and deformed ones. Also, bare skin showing.

➤ Constantly chewing or picking at her own feathers.

➤ A molt that seems like it will never end.

➤ White, crusty flakes around the beak and eyelids, and sometimes the legs and vent.

➤ Muscle spasms, twitching, shaking, loss of balance, flopping around on the bottom of the cage and seizures.

➤ Lumps or bumps anywhere on the body.

➤ Sore, inflamed or swollen feet.

Don't Avian Illnesses Have Names?

Avian illnesses sure do have names—like psittacosis (a.k.a. chlamydiosis, or parrot fever) and aspergillosis (a fungal disease that causes difficulty breathing). I didn't list individual diseases and their symptoms because the signs of a sick bird are so similar, no matter what the disease, that it takes a veterinarian to make the correct diagnosis. If you want to learn more about specific avian diseases, Appendix A lists books on the subject.

A healthy bird breathes through its nose. Continuous mouth breathing is one sign of a respiratory problem.

Help!—Handling an Emergency

While most sick or injured birds need the services of an avian veterinarian, it's important to handle Polly properly until she's in the hands of a pro. Keeping calm is the hardest part. If a wave of panic doesn't rush over you when you first see your sick or injured pet, you're stronger than I am. But panic won't help Polly, so take a deep breath and resolve to stay calm and think straight. Then get to work. Here's how.

Handling Sick or Injured Birds

➤ Call your veterinarian, explain your bird's problem and follow his or her instructions.

➤ Hands off, if possible. The less you handle your sick or injured bird, the better. Covering the cage may help calm her.

➤ Provide warmth. Between 80 and 90 degrees is ideal. Heat only one side of the cage, so Polly can find the place where she's most comfortable. An infrared 250-watt heat lamp (not a regular bulb) aimed at one corner of the cage from a distance of about three to four feet should do the job on a large cage, while a heating pad works well under one corner of a small cage. Keep all wires out of your bird's reach.

➤ Make eating easy. Put food and water wherever Polly is, even if she's on the bottom of the cage. Sprinkle food around her if she doesn't reach for her dishes.

➤ Don't clean the cage. Not even if Polly is eating off the floor. Something in the cage may help the veterinarian diagnose her illness. Also, changing the cage papers disturbs Polly, and she needs to be kept calm.

➤ Tempt Polly with treats. This isn't the time to worry about a balanced diet. Hand-feeding her favorite foods may help.

➤ Provide peace and quiet. Polly's room should be dimly lit, noise should be kept to a minimum and other pets should be kept out.

➤ Be prepared. Practice catching and restraining (toweling) your bird when she's healthy (see Chapter 18). Then the procedure will be familiar to both of you if the need arises.

➤ Keep first-aid supplies on hand. The items listed in the table that follows should all be kept in one place (possibly in the pet carrier), so you'll always know where they are.

Checklist for Your Bird's First-Aid Kit

✓ Avian veterinarian's office number

✓ Avian veterinarian's after hours, weekend, holiday and emergency number(s)

✓ Pad and pencil for taking instructions by phone from the veterinarian

✓ Infrared lamp and bulb, or heating pad

✓ Powdered Gatorade or Pedialyte to provide quick energy and electrolytes

✓ Honey or Karo syrup to provide carbohydrates and energy

✓ Plastic eye droppers for giving liquids

✓ Pepto Bismol or Kaopectate in case of poisoning

✓ Towel for restraint

✓ Blood stopper (styptic powder or pencil)

✓ Needle-nose pliers or sturdy tweezers in case you have to pull a blood feather

✓ Cotton balls and cotton swabs for cleaning wounds and applying pressure

✓ Nail clipper

✓ Scissors

✓ Roll of gauze for bandaging

✓ Gauze squares for bandaging and applying pressure

✓ Hydrogen peroxide for cleaning wounds

✓ Flashlight

✓ 100 percent pure aloe vera gel for burns (not moisturizer with aloe, or medication containing aloe and other things)

✓ Masking tape or surgical tape for bandaging

✓ Antibiotic powder to fight infection

✓ Pet carrier with soft towel on the bottom if your bird's cage is too large for transporting or caring for a sick bird

What Is an Avian Emergency?

Any life-threatening injury or illness is an emergency. The table that follows lists some of the most common ones. In every case, follow the guidelines given earlier in this chapter, in addition to the treatments listed here, and *get your bird to the veterinarian ASAP:*

Squawk!

Never put anything greasy or oily on your bird—not even to treat burns.

Avian Emergencies and What to Do

Emergency	Action
Injured by an animal	Apply pressure with a gauze pad to stop any bleeding.
Poisoned by ingesting something	When you call the veterinarian, identify the plant or substance. Your vet may suggest giving Pepto Bismol or Kaopectate with an eye dropper before bringing your bird in. The usual dose is about five drops for a canary or budgie-sized bird; 25 drops for a cockatiel-sized bird, and 60 to 120 drops for birds ranging in size from amazon parrots to macaws.
Poisoned by inhaling insecticide or toxic fumes	Take your bird out of the toxic air and into an area with fresh air. If that's impossible (you live in a studio apartment or it's freezing outside), ventilate the room by opening windows. Speed it up by placing a fan in the window, but

continues

Avian Emergencies and What to Do   (continued)

Emergency	Action
	keep your pet out of the draft.
Burns	Spray the burned area with cool water to lessen the pain.
Broken bones	Suspect a fracture if your bird has problems perching, holds one leg up, can't control one leg at all, or has a drooping wing. Don't move the bird unless you have to (for example, if she's out of her cage). Confine her and take her to the vet in her cage or carrier, with the perches removed and soft towels on the floor.
Shock	Suspect shock if your bird is badly hurt, suffered a severe fright or is seriously ill. Follow the guidelines for handling sick or injured birds in this chapter. The sooner your bird receives professional treatment, the better her chances of survival.

Problems You'll Have to Handle Yourself

You'll have to treat these emergencies yourself if they ever occur. Without immediate help, your pet may not live long enough to get to the veterinarian.

Broken Blood Feather

1. Restrain your bird (it's best if someone holds her while you work on her).

2. Find the injured feather.

3. Using a tweezers or needle-nosed pliers, grasp the feather as close to the skin as possible, and pull it out with smooth, firm pressure. While pulling the feather, support the body part it's attached to. For example, if it's a wing feather, hold the wing in place while pulling out the bleeding feather.

4. If the empty follicle oozes blood after the feather is removed, put pressure on it with a cotton ball

Squawk!

If your bird is poisoned and you can't reach your veterinarian, call the National Animal Poison Control Center at (800)548-2423 or (900) 680-0000. Veterinarians that are trained to treat poisoned pets are on duty 24 hours a day. You will be billed a flat fee for the 800 number, or a per-minute fee for the 900 number.

or towel for two minutes. After the bleeding stops, stay near your pet for about an hour. Sometimes bleeding resumes and you'll have to apply pressure again.

5. Follow the guidelines I've already given you for sick or injured birds by keeping Polly warm and giving her some of her favorite foods during the one-hour observation period. If she recovers quickly and seems herself soon after her trauma, the emergency is over and she won't need any further treatment. But if she lost a lot of blood and seems weak or tired, take her to the veterinarian immediately, as she may be in shock. Call first, so the staff can prepare for an emergency.

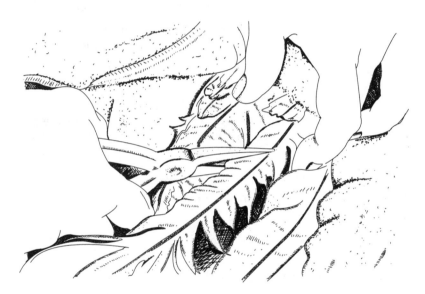

Removing a broken blood feather with needle-nosed pliers. Notice that one hand holds the wing steady, and the bird is wrapped in a towel.

(Note: Some veterinarians recommend packing an injured blood feather with styptic powder or corn starch to stop the bleeding, and calling the clinic for an immediate appointment. Since your veterinarian knows your bird well, following his or her advice is always the best bet. If bleeding isn't profuse, call before pulling the broken blood feather.)

Bleeding Wounds on the Skin

1. Restrain your bird (it's best if you have a helper).
2. Apply pressure directly to the wound with a cotton ball or a towel.
3. Using a cotton swab or cotton ball, gently wash the wound with hydrogen peroxide.
4. Apply antibiotic powder.

5. If the injury left Polly tired, weak or listless, see your veterinarian immediately. Otherwise, follow the guidelines for sick or injured birds in this chapter, while observing your bird for an hour to make sure the wound doesn't bleed again.

6. If Polly seems fine and the wound was superficial, the emergency is over. Puncture wounds or wounds with ragged edges should be seen by your veterinarian, because further repair and measures to prevent infection may be necessary.

7. Wounds caused by another animal are *always* an emergency, even if they appear superficial.

Egg Binding

If your female bird (hen) is squatting and straining on the bottom of the cage, has a swollen belly and appears weak and tired, chances are she's having trouble laying an egg.

1. Place her in a carrying cage or box (an aquarium will also do) in the bathroom.

2. Increase the temperature and humidity in the room by running the hot water (not on the bird!) to create steam.

3. Monitor the temperature in the room. Keep it around 85° by turning the water on and off as necessary.

4. Supply energy and calcium by dissolving powdered Gatorade and powdered milk in her drinking water.

5. Monitor the situation for two hours, and let your veterinarian know what's going on. If the egg doesn't emerge by then, your bird probably needs medical attention.

Heat Stroke

Signs of heat stroke include wings held away from the body, panting, weakness, inability to focus, fainting and shock (but not all of them at once). If your bird shows any of these signs and has recently been in a warm unventilated room, direct sunlight or (horrors!) inside a parked car without ventilation, act immediately. You must lower her body temperature right away to prevent permanent damage or death.

1. Get your bird out of the heat or sun.

2. Place her in a well-ventilated or air-conditioned room and mist her well with cool (not frigid) water.

3. Offer her a drink of cool water.

4. Now call your veterinarian.

Bird Stress (but They Don't Even Have a Job!)

Some problems, like a bird plucking out her own feathers, may be caused by stress. Moving the cage to another location, taking the bird from room to room with you, giving her more baths, more attention, more exercise, a larger cage and some new toys all may help. Playing the radio or TV for your pet when she's home alone is also worth a try.

Bird Brainers

Your bird doesn't have sweat glands in her skin to cool her like you do. Instead, she pants with her mouth open, and the moisture evaporating from the mucus membranes in her mouth helps cool her.

Whatever you do, don't reward Polly with attention (positive or negative) when she plucks herself. Instead, ignore her until she stops. Then catch her doing something right (such as simply sitting on her perch without picking at her feathers), and pet or praise her. Also praise her for playing with her toys and for vocalizing pleasantly—anything but plucking. If her plucking doesn't peter out after a few months, consult a bird behaviorist or your veterinarian.

What's Bugging Your Bird?

The good news about parasites, including lice and mites, is that they are most often a problem in aviaries and seldom bother one or two pet birds living in a home. But just in case, here's how you can find out if any pests are obtaining free room and board on your bird, and what you can do about it.

Banning Bugs and Other Thugs

Step one in parasite control is making sure Polly doesn't have any uninvited guests when you bring her home. That's one reason why a checkup with an avian veterinarian is a good idea, right after you get her. Step two is keeping her cage clean, and you already know all about that (if you don't, see Chapter 9). If Polly is free of internal and external pests when you get her, chances are she will never pick up any of the following felons.

Polly Sez

A *parasite* is an organism that relies on another living thing for its survival, but contributes nothing to the host organism.

Several parasitic infections have similar signs, so diagnosing and treating your bird should be left up to your veterinarian. Here's a list of the most common creepy-crawlies that may live on or in birds, and the signs most birds show when they are infected.

Red Mites

Think of these tiny bloodsuckers as vampires. They usually hide in the dark corners of your bird's cage (or in nest boxes) during the day, but drive your bird batty by crawling on her skin and biting her all night. Infected birds scratch and peck at their bodies continuously, and are up and moving most of the night. If you're not sure, cover your bird's cage with a white sheet in the evening. By morning, you'll be able to see the little red monster mites on the fabric.

To get rid of red mites, you'll have to use a special pesticide and wash or spray your bird's cage thoroughly, including perches, dishes and everything else Polly owns. Chemicals and birds are a dangerous combination, so ask your veterinarian to recommend the proper pesticide and use it carefully, according to directions.

Squawk!

Mites may be tiny, but they are mighty big when it comes to reproducing. A single female lays close to 3,000 eggs during her short, prolific life.

Feather Mites, Shaft Mites and Feather Lice

These creepy critters eat the protein parts of your pet's feather shaft, making the feathers fall out before they should and stunting the development of the replacement feathers. Treatment is the same as for red mites. Your veterinarian will take your bird's size into consideration when recommending a pesticide.

Squawk!

Several types of products advertise that they prevent mites, but I don't recommend them. Birds shouldn't be exposed to pesticides unless there is a very good reason for it. If your bird doesn't have mites or lice now, she probably won't get them and doesn't need protection. If she does have them, she needs to visit the vet.

Scaly Face

Caused by a type of mite that burrows into the top layers of a bird's skin, scaly face is most often seen in budgies. However, it should be suspected in any bird that has a white, crusty substance around the corners of her mouth and/or on her cere, beak, eyelids, vent, legs or feet. In its advanced stages, this mite infection can deform a bird's beak and legs, but it won't get that far in your pet because you know the symptoms. If you suspect scaly face, take your bird to an avian veterinarian for a simple test. If the test confirms the condition, the doc will cure it quickly and your bird's skin will soon be healthy again.

Roundworms

Roundworms (ascarids) are most often found in birds that live (or have lived) in outdoor aviaries with dirt floors. They take up residence in the intestines and can cause fatal blockages when found in large numbers. When there are symptoms, they include weight loss, pasty diarrhea, feces stuck to the vent and surrounding feathers, general weakness and depression. Catch this condition in time and your veterinarian will soon have your bird back in shape. Just don't wait too long.

Crop Worms

These parasites, also known as threadworms and capillaria, burrow into the lining of a bird's crop and esophagus, irritating and eventually thickening these organs. Symptoms include lack of appetite or thirst, weight loss, regurgitation, depression, swelling and irritation around the mouth, a droopy head and many attempts to swallow. As awful as this worm infection sounds, your veterinarian can cure it if you catch it in time.

Coccidia

This parasite inflames the intestinal tract. Infected birds often have blood in their droppings. As the parasite multiplies, symptoms include listlessness, ruffled feathers, loss of appetite and heavy consumption of grit. Your veterinarian will examine your bird's droppings (called a fecal exam) to diagnose coccidia. When caught early enough, treatment is often successful.

Bird Brainers

Your healthy bird could get mites when you bring home a new bird or rescue an injured wild bird. Just be alert to the symptoms and get professional help right away.

Squawk!

See your avian veterinarian if your bird has any symptoms of parasites. Very few birds display every sign. Most appear to have only one or two little signs, but may be very sick on the inside.

Giardia

Giardia is caused by a protozoan that spreads though contaminated water or food. Its symptoms include diarrhea, feather-picking, loss of appetite, lethargy and weight loss. Infected birds usually recover when treated in time.

Tapeworms

These flatworms live in the intestinal tract. Large infestations may cause diarrhea, weight loss, weakness and depression. Sometimes you will actually see a segment of the worm on top of your bird's droppings. It looks like a grain of rice, and may wiggle. If no worm particle is found, your vet will diagnose the problem with a fecal examination.

The Least You Need to Know

➤ Birds instinctively want to look healthy, so they try to hide their illnesses and injuries.

➤ It's important to recognize the subtle signs of a sick bird because the sooner treatment begins, the better the chance of recovery.

➤ The first thing you should do when you realize your bird is sick or hurt is call your avian veterinarian.

➤ Sick and injured birds need extra warmth, peace and quiet. Their favorite foods and fresh water should be within easy reach.

➤ Every bird owner should have a well-stocked first-aid kit.

➤ Treatment for a few emergencies has to begin at home, or your bird won't live long enough to get to the veterinarian.

➤ Few pet birds are ever bothered by mites or parasites, so mite prevention may do more harm than good.

Chapter 20

Visiting the Veterinarian

> **In This Chapter**
>
> ➤ Selecting a top-notch avian veterinarian
>
> ➤ Qualities of good clients
>
> ➤ When to take your bird to the vet
>
> ➤ How to make the most of the visit

Next to you, no one is more important to Pauly's health than his veterinarian. That makes choosing a veterinarian one of the most important decisions you will make for your pet. This chapter will help you find a veterinarian you will be able to trust with your bird's life.

But it takes two to save a sick bird—one to diagnose the illness and prescribe treatment and the other to follow up at home. Since the other is you, I'll help you become the kind of client every veterinarian wants—the one who sees the signs of sickness before they become severe, keeps calm, remembers instructions and carries them out exactly as prescribed.

Choosing an Avian Veterinarian

By now you realize how much birds differ from dogs and cats and why I told you, way back in Chapter 4, to select an avian veterinarian for Pauly. Depending on where you live, you might have several choices right in town, or you may have to drive many miles to visit the only bird specialist for five counties. Near or far, choosing a good veterinarian is a weighty decision. Someday your pet's life could depend on the bird doctor's diagnostic ability and quality of care.

Since any veterinarian can advertise that he or she treats birds, the best way to find a good avian veterinarian is by reputation. Here's how:

Bird Brainers

Write to the Association of Avian Veterinarians at P.O. Box 299, East Northport, NY 11731, or call (516) 757-6320.

➤ If you have pets other than Pauly and they have a wonderful veterinarian, ask him or her to recommend an avian practitioner.

➤ Talk to pet shop owners and employees and other bird owners. It won't be long before you find that the same few vets are recommended over and over.

➤ Call or write to the Association of Avian Veterinarians and ask for a list of members in your area. Most vets with a large feathered clientele belong to this association.

➤ A minority of avian veterinarians are board certified. That honor signifies that they passed a challenging proficiency test in avian medicine. Since the test is relatively new (it was first offered near the end of 1993), and passing it takes months of intense preparation, many excellent avian vets haven't set aside the time to take it yet. While lack of board certification doesn't mean a vet isn't qualified to treat birds, certification guarantees a vet who knows their subject inside and out.

Evaluating Your Vet

After you select a veterinarian with an awesome reputation and make an appointment for Pauly, you'll be able to decide if you're satisfied with your choice. The right veterinarian will:

Squawk!

Let your mouth, not your fingers do the walking when looking for an avian specialist. Some vets advertise that they treat birds, even though they haven't studied the fine points of avian medicine. Asking bird breeders and members of the local bird club beats looking in the Yellow Pages.

➤ Handle your bird with professional proficiency. Whether Pauly is a frightened finch or an enraged macaw, your veterinarian should handle him gently but firmly. Capture, restraint and the complete physical examination should be performed carefully but with practiced ease. Steer clean of any vet who seems frightened of your pet or becomes annoyed with him.

➤ Weigh your pet on a gram scale and take a complete history, including where you got your bird, how long you have had him, age (if known), diet, other pets (especially birds), type and size of cage, activity level, behavior and previous illnesses.

➤ Explain the examination and discuss the results with you, possibly giving you tips on how to improve Pauly's condition or keep him healthy over the long term. For example, when Rooster (my amazon parrot) had his first examination, the veterinarian said he was in fine form but the trick would be keeping him that way. He explained that it was important to give him a balanced diet, low in fat, because amazon parrots tend to cut their lives short by becoming obese.

➤ Answer your questions thoroughly in language you understand. Any veterinarian who purposely talks over your head, has an imperious attitude or acts like answering questions is a nuisance, doesn't need you (or me) for a client. Good vets answer their client's questions in plain language without talking down to them.

➤ Have a pleasant receptionist and staff and a clean waiting room.

➤ Have an organized and well-equipped facility.

➤ Be caring. If you sense coldness or indifference, Pauly's in the wrong place.

➤ Discuss fees. While most clinics expect clients to pay for regular office visits right away, you may want to ask about their policy for unexpected, expensive emergencies.

➤ Make provisions for emergency care during weekends, holidays and the middle of the night. Some veterinarians handle emergencies themselves, while others refer their clients to a service that specializes in emergencies. If your vet opts for the service, make sure an avian vet will always be available.

Bird Brainers

The first time you visit a vet, ask what kind of anesthesia he or she would use if Pauly ever needed surgery. If the answer isn't "isoflurane," politely ask why. At this time, isoflurane is the safest anesthesia available for birds.

Being the Best Kind of Client

If Pauly is ever seriously ill, it will take more than a reputable vet to pull him through. It will also take you—a conscientious and composed client. A bird does best if his veterinarian and his owner work together to cure him. Here's how you can be the type of client a veterinarian is happy to have on his or her team. A conscientious client:

➤ Calls and makes an appointment for routine visits, such as annual exams and wing and nail trims.

Bird Brainers

Remove high perches, swings and other movable toys, and empty the water dish just before driving your bird to the clinic. Covering the cage may help a nervous bird.

➤ Arrives on time.

➤ Brings their bird in his regular cage (not freshly cleaned), or in a carrier if the cage is too large for traveling. When using a carrier, bring along a sample of your pet's diet and the latest cage papers, so the veterinarian can examine the droppings.

➤ Never asks the veterinarian to diagnose their bird over the telephone. Why? Because it can't be done. Most sick birds display similar signs, no matter what their illness. It takes a hands-on examination and usually some tests to find out what's causing the trouble and decide on the proper treatment.

➤ Is understanding if the veterinarian is running late because they had to take care of an emergency.

➤ Knows their bird's normal behavior and calls the clinic right away when something doesn't seem right.

➤ Brings along a list of recent behavioral changes (loss of appetite, excessive thirst, unexplained aggression, too quiet), if there were any.

➤ Is honest. When your veterinarian asks if your bird has been on any medication, don't be ashamed to admit you tried something recommended by a pet shop employee, even though by now you feel like a fool. To make a correct diagnosis, your vet has to know exactly what your bird ingested. Besides, mixing medications can be fatal. By the same token, if your bird showed signs of illness for several days and you kept hoping he'd get better on his own, admit it. Don't say you just noticed something wrong that morning.

➤ Asks pertinent questions about bird care, but doesn't ramble. Make a list and bring it along. Vets are glad to answer questions about feeding, bathing, trimming, caging and anything else related to your pet's health, but they don't have time to hear about Aunt Carolyn's reaction when Pauly pooped on her new hair-do.

Squawk!

Never increase the dosage of a medication (not even a little) in hopes of making your bird get better faster. Medicine doesn't work that way. In fact, what cures at the proper dosage can kill when overdosed.

➤ Takes notes when the veterinarian gives instructions.

➤ Follows instructions exactly. Medications must be given at the right time and in the correct dosage or they won't work. If you don't understand how to administer a medication, ask. Your veterinarian will gladly explain or demonstrate.

➤ Stays as composed as possible, even during an emergency. The worse the injury or illness, the more your veterinarian will need you as a clear-thinking partner in your bird's treatment.

➤ Isn't argumentative or belligerent. Most veterinarians care about their clients and understand how deeply people love their animals. But they aren't magicians and can't guarantee that a sick bird will recover, no matter how skillfully they treat it. If you lose confidence in your veterinarian, the best thing to do is change clinics.

➤ Pays their bills according to clinic policy.

When Should You Visit the Veterinarian?

The best time for Pauly and his veterinarian to meet is either just before you buy your bird, or within 24 hours after. While most birds purchased from reliable pet shops and breeders are healthy, it's important not to skip the exam. Once your vet confirms that Pauly is healthy, they will have a permanent record of what's normal for your bird. Then, if he ever shows signs of sickness, tests will quickly disclose deviations. Besides, wouldn't you rather get to know your vet when Pauly is healthy, instead of trusting your pet to a total stranger during an emergency?

After the initial visit, some bird owners take their pets back to the vet (or veterinary technician) at intervals for wing and toenail trimming. Others trim at home or have it done by a professional groomer at the pet shop.

Annual examinations are a good idea because simple tests may provide an early alert that something is amiss. Birds often harbor a disease for months before showing signs of sickness, and early detection is always a bonus.

In case of emergency, take your pet to the vet ASAP. Call first and explain what happened so the staff can prepare.

Squawk!

No matter how frightening the emergency and how fast you want to get your bird to the vet, remember to secure his cage so it doesn't roll over or slide to the floor while you drive. The last thing a sick or injured bird needs is a terrifying tumble.

Making the Most of Your Initial Visit

Surely you have questions about bird care. The initial visit is the time to ask. Write your questions down as you think of them, so you don't forget anything. To get you started, here are a few questions new bird owners often ask:

➤ What do normal droppings look like?

➤ How often should my bird make droppings?

➤ What would be a good balanced diet for my bird?

➤ In what proportion should I feed seeds, pellets, fruits, vegetables and table food?

➤ Is it okay to feed my bird some fatty treats, such as peanuts and sunflower seeds? How much and how often?

Squawk!

Don't stop giving your bird his medication before you're supposed to because your bird seems better and forcing him to take medicine is a pain. The illness may reappear in a few weeks because the germs were temporarily weakened but not eliminated.

➤ What should I do if my bird breaks a blood feather?

➤ Does my bird need a vitamin supplement?

Home Again

You've had your vet visit and now you're home again, filled with new information—some of it different from what you read in this book. What should you do? Who should you believe?

Believe your veterinarian. This book is a general reference, meaning that it contains good, solid information about pet birds in general. But your bird is an individual who just had a thorough examination, and now you have personalized instructions. Follow them. They were meant especially for Pauly.

The Least You Need to Know

➤ Your bird needs an *avian* veterinarian.

➤ The best way to find a good avian veterinarian is through word of mouth. Ask other bird owners for a recommendation.

➤ Evaluate your veterinarian during your bird's first visit. The clinic should be clean, well equipped and well organized, and the veterinarian should handle your bird easily, take a complete history, give your pet a thorough examination and answer your questions in language you can understand.

➤ Follow-up care is your responsibility. Take notes so you remember what your veterinarian tells you, and follow instructions exactly.

➤ Your veterinarian should have a record of how your bird tests when he is healthy. Ideally, your bird should have his first examination right after you buy him, and a routine check-up every year.

Chapter 21

Home for the Ancient Avian

Facing the Facts of Life and Death

In This Chapter

➤ Aging avians

➤ Options for dead and dying pets

➤ Adjusting to the loss of a beloved bird

➤ Bittersweet release for you and your children

We hate seeing the signs of aging in ourselves or our pets. Yet, as the cliché goes, getting old is a whole lot better than the alternative. Besides, aging isn't all that hard on our birds. After all, they're protected from predators and their food dishes are full, so they don't need senses as sharp as their wild cousins'. In this chapter, I'll talk about the signs of aging in avians and the few simple things you can do to keep your sassy senior happy and healthy.

I'll also discuss the most painful fact of life—death. Losing a precious pet is difficult enough without having to make sudden decisions, so this chapter will cover options such as euthanasia, and different methods of caring for the body. I'll also discuss the stages of grief and healing, and tell you how to help your child cope with the loss. Then on to a happier subject—bringing a new bird into your life.

Signs of Aging

Birds age much like we do. Some senior avians get arthritis, complete with swollen joints, and wake up stiff many mornings. Others gradually develop wrinkled and pigment-splotched skin on their faces and feet, and would wear bifocals and hearing aids if they were people. Thinning feathers and crusty, sometimes crooked beaks are other characteristics of aging avians. A few oldsters seem forgetful, or just not quite as bright as they used to be. But most old birds still love life, and these venerable pets are cherished by their human families.

If you are lucky enough to share your life with an ancient avian, you can help her stay comfortable by keeping her infirmities in mind. A bird with a thinner coat of feathers needs a warmer environment, so put Polly's cage in one of the coziest corners of your home. If stiffness decreases her mobility, keep perches low, and food and water within easy reach. But don't make it too easy. Lack of exercise may speed up the loss of muscle tone that makes older birds' muscles gradually waste away—leaving them lighter and more fragile.

Bird Brainers

There's help for some of the ills of aging. For example, an injection at regular intervals (usually once a month) eases arthritis. If your bird seems stiff, discuss it with your veterinarian.

Oldsters sometimes develop digestive problems, and their organs may weaken. While special diets formulated for birds with kidney or liver problems work well, putting your bird on a new feeding plan isn't a do-it-yourself project. Consult with your avian veterinarian. After diagnosing the problem, he or she will recommend the right diet for Polly.

How Old Is Old?

How long do pet birds live? That depends on the bird. Life spans vary considerably between species, and also between individuals of the same species. For example, amazon parrots have the potential to live as long as people. Mynahs, on the other hand, are seniors at seven, and budgies are old when they reach their teens. Proper care is a deciding factor in longevity, but so is genetics. Some birds, like some people, are predisposed to illnesses that could shorten their lives.

Bird Brainers

Parrots learn all their lives. They are never too old to learn new tricks or new words, or even adjust to a new home.

The truth is, we don't know a whole lot about the life spans of many of our feathered friends. Why? Because until recent years, most parrots were caught in the wild and imported, so people didn't know how old their bird was when they got it. Today that has changed, and almost all birds offered for sale are domestically bred. In a few decades, many breeders will have birds that they raised from babies and kept until they died, so future generations will know a lot more about avian life spans than we do.

King Tut, a salmon-crested cockatoo, was the official greeter at the San Diego Zoo from 1925 to 1989. Today, a statue honoring him stands near the entrance.

What do we know about pet birds' life spans? We know that most of them don't live anywhere near what scientists believe is their potential life span, but a few become real record breakers and live exceedingly long lives. Those are the ones we hear about—the ones that make people believe all parrots have the capacity to live into their 70s. I wish!

On the bright side, only a decade ago most birds were fed seed-only diets, and today we know they need a balanced diet, similar to ours. As we learn even more about our pet's needs, their life spans will continue to increase. In the meantime, the table that follows has some rough guesstimates on the potential life spans of a few species, along with their current average life spans. Before letting these figures depress you, remember that until just a few years ago, most birds probably spent their early years on a poor diet of seeds only, simply because their owners didn't know any better.

Bird Life Spans

Species	Potential (maximum years)	Average years
Zebra finch	16	5–6
Canary	20	7–8
Budgie	18	6
Cockatiel	30	5–7
Conure	25	10
African grey	50	15
Amazon parrot	75–80	15
Macaw	50	15

When the Bond Breaks

We often know in advance when death is threatening our pet, but sometimes birds die without warning, leaving us not only saddened, but shocked. Complicating the process are the decisions we may have to make concerning euthanasia and a final resting place. Understanding these options in advance may help alleviate confusion during a time when thinking straight is difficult.

Polly Sez

Problems peculiar to aging are treated by the branch of medicine called *geriatrics*, and *gerontology* is the study of aging in people or pets.

When Is Euthanasia the Best Ending?

Relatively few bird owners have to make a choice about euthanasia because most terminally ill or severely injured birds die quickly. But if your bird is obviously suffering and there isn't any chance of recovery, euthanasia is a compassionate option to letting her linger through long days of pain. Only you can decide when the time is right, but it isn't as hard as you think. Trust your instincts. They will tell you when ending your pet's misery is the most merciful thing you can do for her.

Polly Sez

Euthanasia is the medical term for a humane, assisted death.

At your request, your veterinarian will euthanize your ailing pet. This is usually done by injecting a lethal dose of a strong anesthetic into her vein. The injection will put her to sleep instantly, and the anesthetic will stop her heart in less than five seconds. An alternative method is gas. It is also painless, but doesn't kill quite as quickly.

This healthy, 40-something macaw has lots of character lines.

Should you be with Polly when she is euthanized? Only if it makes you feel better. Some people prefer to say their good-byes in private, then deliver their pet to their trusted veterinarian. Perhaps they want to stiffen their upper lip, get in and out of the clinic quickly and mourn in private or among loved ones. Or they may want to remember their bird as vibrant and alive, instead of replaying her death in their mind's eye. Other owners want to be near their bird, maybe even hold her, during her final seconds of life. Discuss your preferences with your veterinarian, and he or she will abide by them.

Handling Your Bird's Body

Many people choose to leave their departed pet's body at the veterinary clinic. Usually the clinic notifies a service, which picks up the body and cremates it. Several birds are usually cremated at the same time, and the remains are buried in the earth. Don't hesitate to ask your veterinarian how he or she will dispose of the body. Some clinics have slightly different procedures, and others have their own facilities for cremation.

Another option is a private cremation, handled either at a pet cemetery, a private pet crematorium or your veterinary clinic. Then you can bury or scatter the remains in a place you know your pet loved. A variety of professional services may also be available, including placing the remains in an urn or interring them in a mausoleum.

Pet cemeteries also offer regular burials, and these can be as simple or as elegant as you choose (and can afford). Good pet cemeteries are neat and clean, and are nestled in lovely sections of countryside. They are also zoned for pet burials, while your home may not be.

If burying a pet in your own yard is legal, it's an excellent option. You can choose a place you know your bird would like, dig a deep hole for the body (so stray animals won't dig it up) and mark the spot by planting a flowering fruit tree or a brightly colored perennial—one that will remind you of the good times you had with your bird.

Grieving and Healing

Today we know more about grief than ever before, including the fact that when people lose a beloved companion (human or animal), they go through a series of emotional stages that gradually lead to healing. Following is a list of those stages in the order they most commonly occur, but don't take the sequence as gospel. Many people go through the stages in a different order, or suffer through several stages at about the same time.

➤ **Shock and disbelief, often accompanied by numbness.** Stunned by the news, your mind refuses, at first, to accept it.

➤ **Anger and alienation.** With understanding comes anger. Someone must be at fault. After all, that would make the pain easier to understand. If your anger turns outward, you might blame your veterinarian or your spouse. If it turns inward, you'll blame yourself.

➤ **Denial.** While grieving, you may wake up in the morning, hear a noise, and tell yourself that it's Polly playing in her cage and her death was just a bad dream. Of course this fantasy ends quickly and, after a few variations on this theme, you'll probably move out of this stage.

➤ **Guilt.** For many of us, this stage is the worst. During it, you may concoct your own guilt and flog yourself with thoughts beginning with "I should have," "could have," and "would or wouldn't have." Choosing euthanasia may cause terrible guilt, because you may irrationally blame your compassionate choice, rather than the ravages of age and disease, for your bird's death. Eventually this passes, and you'll realize that your painful choice was your final gift to Polly. It freed her from her distress and let her die with dignity.

Bird Brainers

Sometimes sadness may sweep over you at work, and your co-workers may notice. If they ask you what's wrong and you don't want to talk about it, or aren't sure how they feel about pets, just tell them you recently lost a best friend.

➤ **Depression.** While depressed, you may feel fatigued, sleep fitfully, lack appetite and have trouble concentrating. Nothing will seem to matter much or have any meaning. Although this stage is the saddest (some sufferers think they may never smile again), it usually signals the beginning of healing. In the midst of your misery, you'll finally face the reality of your pet's death and gradually learn to live with it.

➤ **Resolution.** This is the final stage of mourning. During this stage, you'll realize that although your pet is never coming back, she'll live forever in your heart. Soon you'll be able to reminisce about her fondly. One day you'll even smile while telling tales of her escapades.

When You Are at Fault

Was Polly's death preventable? Maybe you forgot to trim your cockatiel's wings and she flew into the ceiling fan. Or perhaps you noticed that your budgie wasn't quite herself, but waited a few days too many before taking her to the veterinarian. Okay, you weren't a perfect pet owner, but then, none of us are. We're just people who love our birds, but are occasionally prone to carelessness or poor judgment. Occasionally, even the best pet owner loses a bird by accident, and some mishaps result from the best of intentions. For example, Polly couldn't possibly climb into the kitchen cabinet and poison herself while your back was turned if she spent her whole life locked in a cage—but that wouldn't have been any life for a bird.

Did you cause your bird's death? Then face it, learn from it and go on. Beating yourself up endlessly won't bring Polly back. Instead, give her death meaning by resolving never to make that mistake again. Then try to forgive yourself.

Helping Yourself Through the Stages

➤ **Understand that mourning the loss of a beloved pet is natural.** Polly wasn't "just a bird." She was *your* bird. There was a strong bond between you, and broken bonds cause broken hearts.

➤ **Take time to mourn.** Don't tell yourself to "get over it," and then bury your grief so deep that it eats you up from the inside. There are no guidelines for working through the stages of grief because some of us need more time to mourn than others.

➤ **Make a few changes in your habits and decor.** Put Polly's cage and playthings out of sight. Take her treats out of the refrigerator and her pellets out of the cookie jar. If feeding her was the first thing you did every morning, create a new morning routine.

➤ **Talk about your feelings.** First, find an understanding ear—someone who also adored Polly or who loves their own pet deeply—and discuss your feelings of loss. Many cities have support groups that help people through the pain of losing a pet. Ask your veterinarian for a recommendation.

Squawk!

Never lie to your child about a dead pet. While it's easy to say, "Polly flew away and she's a wild bird now," it could come back to haunt you if Junior spends days looking at trees and calling for her. Instead, tell the truth but keep it simple and answer questions at your child's age level.

➤ **Read a book about pet loss** (see Appendix A for some suggestions).

➤ **Forgive yourself, no matter how it happened, but learn from it if you were at fault.**

➤ **If you have other pets, give them extra attention.**

➤ **Consider getting another bird.** No, not a replacement. It's impossible to replace Polly because she was an individual and there will never be another bird quite like her. But there are other birds you could love, as long as you don't expect them to be just like Polly. If you think you'll have a problem with that, buy a different species. That will help you learn to love your new bird's unique personality.

Helping Your Children (and Yourself)

Helping your children cope with the loss of their pet will probably soothe you at the same time. One of the ways adults and children come to terms with the finality of the situation (and then go on) is by combining their efforts and creating a memorial ceremony for the dead pet. This can be done, whether or not you have remains to scatter or a body to bury. In fact, it can be performed indoors if you live in an apartment and don't have a yard.

Explain the ceremony to your children as a celebration of Polly's life and all the joy she brought to your family. Then ask each one to think of why they loved Polly or something funny that she did, and tell it during the ceremony. (Young children or kids who have a problem expressing themselves might want to begin their contribution with "Thanks, Polly, for…".) Before the ceremony, the family could go out together and buy a plant (indoor or outdoor, depending on whether the memorial ceremony includes a burial) in Polly's memory.

Squawk!

Don't use Polly's death to make a point to your children. Even if you had to nag Julie when it was her turn to clean the cage, resist forever any urge to say something like, "If only you had kept Polly's cage cleaner, she might not have gotten sick." Grieving kids need compassion, not guilt.

In the days that follow Polly's death, don't be afraid to say that you miss her in front of your children. Encourage them to talk about their feelings, too. Look at pictures of Polly together, and talk about her positive traits and how pretty she was. Tell the kids (more than once) that Polly will always be part of them because the good memories they have of her are theirs forever.

If you're going to get another bird, never refer to it as a "replacement." Let your children know that Polly can't be replaced, but it's okay to learn to love another bird, too.

The Least You Need to Know

➤ Birds show signs of aging similar to people.

➤ Veterinarians can relieve some of the problems associated with aging through medication or a special diet.

➤ Some day you'll have to decide on a final resting place for your pet.

➤ When a bird is so badly hurt or so sick that there is no chance of recovery, euthanasia is a merciful option.

➤ Don't deny your feelings. It's natural to go through several stages of emotional turmoil during the period of mourning.

➤ A ceremony celebrating your bird's life may help you and your children resolve her death.

Part 6
Fun and Fancy

By now you know everything you need to know about being a good bird owner, so in this section I've thrown in the extras. I'll help you teach your pet a few easy tricks (and maybe even some hard ones), and tell you about Presidential birds and feathered superstars.

Just in case you want to go further with birds—say, breed them for fun or show—this part will also cover the basics of good breeding and tell you how to get started. Finally, we'll visit a bird show. There I'll guide you through the judging procedure and tell you how to get involved if you think the combination of competition and new friendships sounds like fun.

Tricks to Tickle Your Family and Friends

In This Chapter

➤ Getting ready for trick training

➤ Tricks your tame parrot can do today

➤ Some harder tricks

➤ Making the most of your bird's moves

Parrots of all sizes love to learn tricks. After all, during training they revel in rewards and praise, and have your full attention. There are rewards for the trainer too. Besides having fun and eventually impressing your friends, teaching Pauly a few tricks encourages closer bonding and better bird behavior.

Parrots like learning and have good memories, so you don't have to worry about following a training schedule and practicing religiously to keep Pauly performing. Missing a day or two here and there won't even matter. So how about it? Let's put Pauly on his T-stand and give him a cue or two. You've always known he was smart, and now he's going to prove it.

Is Your Bird Trusting Enough to Learn Tricks?

Although you'll be able to teach your bird a few fun behaviors even if you can't touch him (I'll tell you about them later), teaching actual tricks takes a trusting bird. If you and Pauly score 100 percent on the following test, he's ready for higher education. If not, turn to Part 4 of this book. It will help you turn Pauly into a tamer and happier pet.

Your parrot is ready to learn tricks when he:

➤ Accepts food from your hand

➤ Likes to have his head (nape and cheeks) petted

➤ Steps on your finger when you offer it and say "up"

➤ Willingly comes out of his cage on your finger

➤ Comes to you on his own (eventually) when you let him walk around on the floor

➤ Lets you touch his back, belly, feet and under his wings, even if those aren't his favorite places

Setting the Scene

Maybe you were the type of student who could study for an exam with the boom box blaring, but your parrot isn't. Pauly can only learn in a peaceful place. Kids, other pets and ringing telephones will all compete for his attention, and probably win. So select a time and a place where Pauly will have you all to himself and the background noise won't be too loud (a moderate amount is okay).

Make yourself comfortable. You'll probably want a chair, and maybe a small table or TV tray to hold treats. Pauly should be on a T-stand, close enough so you can easily touch him. If his stand is the type with dishes on each end, remove them before you begin. You can sit down or stand up while training Pauly. Your choice.

Don't worry about Pauly's head being higher than yours if you opt to sit during training. A bird who scored 100 percent on the readiness test won't change from friend to fiend that quickly.

Pushing Pauly's Buttons

Back in Part 4, when we discussed taming and training, I told you to let your pet know when he did something right by saying "Good bird." Did the words excite Pauly at first? Does he seem to ignore them now? If so, here's what probably went wrong and how you can fix it while teaching tricks.

Praising Pauly only works when your tone is sincere and maybe a little silly—okay, good and silly with some birds. Praising your pet in a drab monotone won't mean much to him, even if you mean every word of it. In fact, colorless compliments will stimulate him about as much as elevator music excites you.

How can you make the praise so powerful that Pauly wants more? By doing it with drama. Give your pet a big smile when you say "Good bird." If he's the lethargic type (some amazons are), accent the praise with a little applause when he progresses. Sometimes surprise him with a different phrase. "Way to go, Pauly!" "All Riiight! "Yeehaw!" Find the happy words that come naturally to you and use them in an excited voice every time Pauly willingly gives his trick a try. Scratch his nape. Put him on your finger for flapping (if he likes that). Read your bird's reaction. Praise should make him want to continue the lesson—not be so loud or sudden that it scares him, or so stimulating that it distracts him.

No matter what else you do, give Pauly a tiny treat that can be eaten quickly every time he tries a trick. Make it a raw kernel of corn or a sunflower seed or one bite of strawberry, watermelon, or his favorite cereal—something he craves but doesn't find in his food dish every day. Next time give him a different treat. He'll never know what the reward will be when he does something right, but he'll sure want to find out.

Bird Brainers

It's harder to give a quick training treat to a small beaked bird, like a budgie, than it is to reward a bird who can shell a sunflower seed in seconds. Try offering a flake or square of cereal and letting your little bird take one bite.

Soon you'll know which phrases tickle Pauly into trying harder. Which treat is his favorite. Whether he'd rather flap or have his neck scratched. Those are his buttons. Pauly's buttons are what turn him on and tune him in more than anything else. Pushing them makes him happy, and when he's happy he's willing to try the trick again, do it better next time, perform it on cue. And that makes you happy too.

Setting the Mood

Before beginning a training session, encourage your parrot to flap a few times. Now he's wide awake and exercised. When Pauly's perched on a bare T-stand with you sitting or standing in front of it, and with treats within easy reach, it's time to set the mood. Do it by letting your bird know he's going to get a treat every time he does something right. Start with something he knows well, preferably the "up" and "down" commands. Have him step on your hand and back down on the perch two or three times, and give him a treat and praise every time. Now he's in a cooperative mood and is ready to learn his first trick.

Turning on Cue

The first trick traditionally taught to parrots is the turn-around. Besides being easy, it sets the stage for further learning by teaching Pauly that responding to a simple signal brings rewards in the form of treats and attention. Although visual signals mean more to parrots than verbal commands, you should still choose a command for the turn-around and use the same one every time. It could be "turn," "spin," or whatever suits you.

Now put a treat in each hand and, using your right hand (I'm going to say right because that's what I use, but reverse it if you're left-handed), show Pauly the treat at about his eye level. When he reaches for it say "spin" (or whatever cue word you chose), and slowly move the treat around behind him so Pauly has to turn to follow it. When he's halfway around (facing the back), let him have the treat and tell him "Good bird."

Put another treat in your right hand, show it to him and use it as before, guiding him around to face front. But this time, reward him with the other treat—the one in your left hand. Repeat the complete circle two or three more times, rewarding and praising after each half turn.

Begin the spin by holding a treat at eye level and having your bird follow it around. This is Rooster turning for a treat.

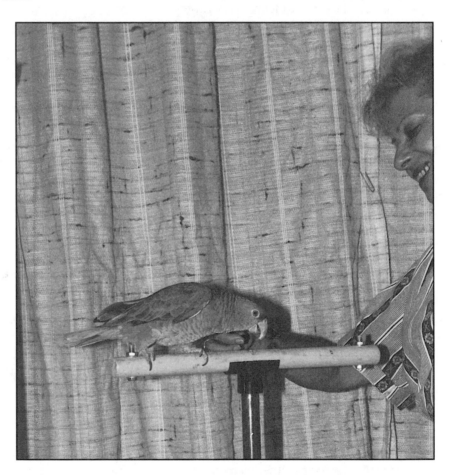

The next step is a full turn without stopping. It's done just like the half turns, except this time have Pauly follow the treat in your right hand until he completes a full circle. Then give him the treat in your left hand and lots of praise. Repeat a few times. "Good bird."

The final step is really a series of steps. Gradually raise your right hand so the treat is level with the top of Pauly's head instead of his eyes, and repeat the spin, rewarding with your left hand. Every few times you practice, raise the treat a tiny bit higher over your pet's head. Soon you won't need a treat in your right hand at all, because Pauly will turn when your empty hand circles just over his head (as long as he gets an immediate reward). The trick is perfected when Pauly does a full turn in response to your index finger painting an imaginary halo a couple of inches above his head. At that point, you can drop the verbal command if you want to.

Bird Brainers

Sometimes parrots have bad training days. They may regress—forgetting or refusing to perform behaviors they already know. Don't worry. That's natural for animals (and people). In a few days, Pauly will make progress again.

Waving Bye-Bye (or Hello)

This trick takes advantage of the fact that Pauly already knows the "up" command and lifts his foot to climb on your hand. Just a slight change of timing on your part will turn his reach for your hand into the beginning of a wave.

Start by slightly waving the fingers of your right hand at Pauly while saying "bye-bye," "hello," or whatever verbal cue you choose. Then offer him the same hand, using the movement you always use when you want him to climb on. That's where timing comes in. Just as soon as Pauly lifts his foot to step on your hand, take your hand away, tell him "Good bird," and give him the treat you were holding in your left hand. It may take several tries before he makes the connection between lifting his leg and receiving a reward. When he does, you'll know it. He'll lift the leg when you wave and you won't have to pretend to offer your hand anymore. At that point, you can also drop the verbal cue.

The next step is to get Pauly to keep his foot up longer and raise it higher. Condition him to do this gradually. Start by making him wait with his leg up just a half second more. Lengthen the wait in tiny increments, and Pauly will probably respond by lifting his leg a little higher. Reward every try when his foot is as high as you think he will raise it—if you can, give the reward just at the instant he starts lowering it. That's the beginning of the waving motion.

Some birds will just stand on one leg with the other in the air and wait patiently for their reward. If Pauly does that, lower the hand holding the treat slightly and he'll probably start lowering his foot. At that instant, reward him.

Don't overdo your training sessions. It's best to stop when your bird catches on, without trying for perfection. Over many sessions, you can gradually withhold the treat a little longer until Pauly waves like a pro. When showing off this trick, you can use any verbal cue you choose because your bird is only responding to your hand signal. A bird who knows how to wave can respond to "hello," "bye-bye," "adios," or whatever the occasion calls for.

*At first, reward even
the slightest lift of
the leg.*

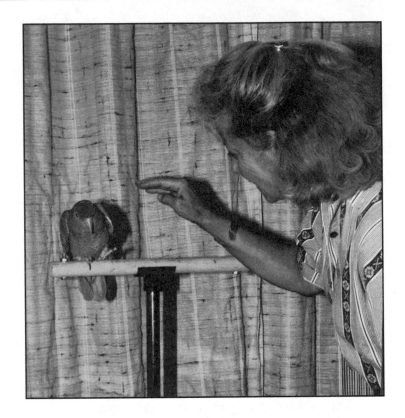

Squawk!

Don't bore your bird. Avoid repeating the same thing over and over by teaching your bird two or more tricks at the same time. Work on one for a few minutes, then go to the next. In between, alternate with behaviors your bird already knows, like "up," "down" and flapping on your finger.

Secondary School

When Pauly turns and waves on cue, he has learned how to learn. Once he knows that a correct response to your signal brings rewards and praise, the number of tricks he can learn, and their difficulty, is limited only by your time and patience. Appendix A lists books that will help you with trick training, but in the meantime, here are two more terrific tricks:

Shaking Hands

Most tricks are built from behaviors the bird already knows, and shaking hands is a good example. Don't even try it until Pauly is well started on the wave. His wave doesn't have to be anywhere near perfection, but he should be far enough along to lift his leg when you wave at him, without needing the prompt of a fake "up" signal. Most, but not all, parrots are left-footed. How can you tell? Offer your hand and give the "up" command, or watch your bird step from perch to perch. If he steps out with his left foot first, he's left-footed. Most likely, Pauly waved with his left foot, but check just to be sure, because he'll have to shake with the opposite foot to avoid confusion between the two behaviors. If he's a rarer right-handed bird, reverse these directions.

Begin the shake almost the same way you did the wave, with three exceptions. The most important exception is that you should persist until your bird lifts his right foot. Since he's used to lifting his left foot first, that could take some time. The second exception is the hand signal. For the shake, it's the same motion you would use to offer your hand to another person, toned down of course, so it won't startle your bird. The final exception is simple—change the cue words to "shake hands," or "glad to meet you," or whatever you want to say, since only the hand signal matters anyway.

Ziggy demonstrates the perfected wave.

Glad to meet you too, Rooster.

As soon as you say "shake hands" and offer your hand in greeting (toward your bird's right foot), turn your hand so it's in the same position it always is for the "up" command. Your bird will probably try to step on it with his left foot, and you'll have to maneuver your hand to prevent it. Persist gently until Pauly tries to step on your hand with his right foot. Now let him put his foot on your right hand before removing your hand. Then praise him immediately, and give him the treat you were holding in your left hand. The goal is to get his right foot on your right hand without letting him transfer his weight and climb on. As he gets the idea, gradually lengthen the time (by microseconds) that his foot touches your hand before removing your hand and giving him a reward.

When Pauly readily lifts his right foot and rests it on your hand for a second or two without transferring his weight, move your hand in a slight up and down motion before producing the treat. Little by little you can extend the time and range of motion. The final touch is just that—you will touch the top of Pauly's foot gently with your thumb while shaking hands with him.

Bird Belly Laughs

This is an advanced trick because you're going to ask Pauly for a verbal response. However, if your bird already laughs when you do, he may learn it easily. All you'll have to do is convince him to laugh on cue. That's what happened with my amazon parrot, Rooster. He already laughed when he heard people laughing, and became reliable on this trick in just a few days. If your bird doesn't laugh, see Chapter 15 for help in teaching parrots to mimic human language.

Once your bird laughs with you (or at you), cue him by touching him under the arms (wings). Tickle Pauly's pits gently, so he likes it, and laugh like crazy at the same time. You'll feel silly, until the day you start tickling and Pauly breaks into gales of laughter. Great trick!

Squawk!

There's a tendency to forget the fine line between teaching and dominating when training birds to do tricks. Please don't make that mistake. Birds learn through trust, not domination—gentle persuasion, not force.

Tickling Rooster's pits cues a long laugh.

Differences Between Dog and Bird Training

If you're an experienced dog trainer, using the same techniques on your parrot may seem like second nature. But many dog training methods won't work on birds because birds and dogs are so different. For example, dogs are genetically programmed to please people. Parrots, on the other hand, are programmed to please themselves—but if you happen to be pleased too, that's even better.

When training dogs, many successful handlers give praise and a treat until the dog knows the behavior well, then continue praising but gradually phase out the treat. Don't try that with a parrot. Although they like praise, most birds will quit performing unless they get a food reward after every trick.

Dogs learn best when training is done in small, upbeat increments. Ten or fifteen minutes, twice a day is ideal. Parrots, on the other hand, have longer attention spans. They continue trying as long as learning is still fun and they want another treat. A half hour isn't too long, provided both of you are enjoying it and you aren't trying to get Pauly to repeat the same stuff over and over. Keep every training session moving along and neither of you will become bored.

Another way that dog training differs from parrot training is that dogs understand discipline, as long as it's fair. Parrots don't. All you can do if Pauly makes a mistake or refuses to perform is skip the treat and the praise, and try again later. Birds learn only through positive reinforcement. Any type of discipline is perceived by a parrot as life-threatening, and terrified birds don't learn tricks.

Polly Sez

Positive reinforcement is training lingo for rewarding your bird for doing something right.

Finally, good dog trainers end each training session with play time, but good parrot trainers don't. Training should feel like play and be the most special part of Pauly's day. End each session when he does something right and is praised and rewarded for it, even if you have to go back to a behavior he already knows.

Name that Mannerism

Want to make your bird a performer without taking the time to teach him tricks? If you're observant, you can do it. Just watch Pauly's reaction to various stimuli, such as the family meal and certain songs on the stereo, and remember his most entertaining moves when he exercises himself. Then give that move a name and Pauly has a trick! Here are some possibilities.

Rock-a-Bye Birdie

Lots of birds like to climb around their cages and hang upside down from under the bars. If Pauly is one of them, you have the beginning of a trick. Next time he's on your finger, stand over the bed and turn your hand slowly until he's hanging upside down. If he becomes frightened, turn your hand so he's right side up again. Keep trying, and soon he'll like hanging upside down from your finger as much as from his cage.

Although an upside-down bird dangling from your hand looks like a good trick in itself, you can go further if you want to. Next time, gently put your other hand under Pauly's back. After you do this enough times (provided that Pauly likes it), he may let go of your finger and let you rock him in your hand, belly up, like a baby.

Most birds like hanging upside down.

A Silver Spoon in Your Bird's Mouth

Birds conure-size or larger may learn how to eat with a small spoon. Next time Pauly begs for some of your dinner, put his portion on a teaspoon and place the whole thing in his dish. Chances are he'll eat the food off the spoon for weeks, but one day he may surprise you by picking up the spoon and mimicking human table manners. It's worth a try.

311

Dance with Me, Pauly

Do certain songs turn Pauly on? Then make the most of your music lover. When you see him tune in, help him find the beat by dancing for him. Use your arms in ways he can copy with his wings. Turn around. Sway from side to side.

When he starts to mimic, you have three choices. You can keep rockin' and dance a duet like Rooster and I do. You can gradually slow your movements to just enough of a sway so your bird keeps going without you. Or you can put Pauly on your hand and dance with him (sometimes Rooster and I do that, too). Use the same song or album every time you want him to dance, and soon he'll recognize his special song and start without you.

Don't Stop Now

Now that you know how to make the most of Pauly's mannerisms, keep watching him. Can you predict when he will wag his tail, fluff his feathers, shake his head back and forth, bob it up and down? If so, try to get in a one-liner just as he begins the movement. "Where's your tail?" for the wag. "Are you a big bird?" before he fluffs. "Are any birds prettier than you?" as he gives a negative shake with his head. "Want a treat?" when he bobs up and down. Add a hand motion to your question (a different one for each movement), and eventually you may be able to cue Pauly rather than the other way around. In the meantime, you'll still wow your friends.

Props

When professional trainers and their performing birds do a show, lots of props are used. Parrots slam dunk miniature basketballs, ride on skates, drive toy trucks and pedal tricycles. Could your bird do that? Maybe. Some birds take to props and other don't. And since most professional trainers use several birds in their shows, the same ones don't have to excel at everything.

Squawk!

Don't let your bird play with props without supervision. Some of them aren't meant to be used as toys, and could be dangerous if chewed up and swallowed.

Props and toys for bird tricks are advertised in magazines such as *Bird Talk* (see Appendix A). Try them with caution. While Pauly may think a birdie bike is the greatest toy ever and delight friends and family by peddling around the kitchen, it doesn't always work out that way. Many birds shy away from props, at least at first, and maybe forever. If you understand that up front and won't be disappointed if Pauly refuses to try biking, skating or riding a scooter, go ahead and buy a prop. Just introduce it gradually and don't try to force props on a reluctant pet.

The Least You Need to Know

➤ Parrots have to be tame and trusting before they can learn tricks.

➤ Train your bird on a T-stand in a relatively quiet part of your home.

➤ The turn-around is a good first trick because it's easy and teaches a bird how to earn rewards for responding to cues.

➤ Give your bird a treat every time he responds to your cue, even after he knows the trick well.

➤ Parrots learn through positive reinforcement (being rewarded for doing something right). Never try to train a parrot through domination. Force scares birds, and frightened birds don't learn. Worse yet, they lose their faith in people.

Chapter 23

Bird Stars and First Birds

In This Chapter

➤ An enviable list of avian actors

➤ First birds and the roles they played in White House life

From Iago, the mean-mouthed cartoon parrot in *Aladdin* who shrieked his sarcasm from the villain Jafar's shoulder, to Paulie, the real live blue-crowned conure starring in the movie of the same name, birds have mesmerized audiences with their mischief and charisma. This chapter will tell you about some feathered superstars and where you can see them. It will also give you a bird's-eye view of the White House. Although puppies usually get the press, many of our presidents also had First Birds, and I'd like to introduce them to you.

Avian Actors

Avian actors and actresses charm thousands of people daily. They can be seen "in person" at theme parks, or you can rent a video, make some popcorn, and enjoy them in your own home. Here's how to find them.

Live on Stage

Parrots performing at theme parks thrill adults and children. Naturally, most of the parks featuring tropical birds are in sunny states, because the birds can be maintained outdoors all year. Appendix B will tell you about several of these parks. Meanwhile, I'm going to tell you about two that feature a few of my feathered favorites. Then you'll be able to look forward to seeing them the next time you plan a southern vacation.

Lolita, a yellow-naped amazon parrot with a little girl's voice, is the featured vocalist at Busch Gardens in Tampa, Florida. She answers her trainer's questions, talks to the audience and climaxes her performance with a rousing rendition of *Oh, What a Beautiful Morning*. Her co-stars include two scarlet macaws who fly free among the audience, a female eclectus who plays baseball (she's the ball), and a military macaw who swoops through hoops, then discovers an empty can and puts it in a recycling bin. Several birds of prey also appear in the show.

Parrot Jungle in Miami, Florida, showcases Pinky, a moluccan cockatoo who performed at the New York World's Fair and has been a star for 30 years. Her act includes riding a bicycle on a high wire. Other avian acrobats and orators include Megan, the macaw truck driver, and a hyacinth macaw named Henry who puts on roller skates without human help and glides off gracefully.

If a city vacation is more your style, try to see *Joseph Gabriel Magic* on Broadway at the Lamb's Theater in New York. Abra, a sulphur-crested cockatoo, is one of several bird stars in an amazing show that may be the world's largest magic act using free flying birds. Besides Broadway, Gabriel has performed in Las Vegas for a dozen years and is frequently featured on television. His credits include the *Tonight Show, The Merv Griffin Show* and *The Rosie O'Donnell Show*.

Junior, a blue-and-gold macaw owned by P. C. Musgrove, appeared in several episodes of the television series Fantasy Island *and won the role of the queen's pet in the IMAX theater production of* Behold Hawaii.

Birds on TV

Remember the TV show *Baretta,* where the hero, a detective played by Robert Blake, had a sulphur-crested cockatoo as a best friend and sounding board? If you're too young to recall the show, you can still see it in reruns. The cockatoo, one of the few animal actors to play an entire role alone (most animal actors share a role, with two or more look-alikes taking turns and performing different behaviors), won a Grand Patsy Award as the best animal actor of the year. The award included all categories of animal actors and media—feature films, television and commercials. Later, the cockatoo won the Photoplay Award as the best animal actor for the previous 10 years.

Avian Adventures

Want to buy T-shirts with colorful cartoon parrots and toucans all over them? Try Jimmy Buffet's Margaritaville Store in Key West, Florida, or wherever Caribbean Soul, the entertainer's line of clothing, is sold. Why the bird motif? Because Jimmy Buffet fans proudly call themselves Parrot Heads. Am I one of them? Well, I do have two of the T-shirts.

Fans of daytime TV probably know Flash and Lucky. The pair of blue-and-gold macaws share the role of Bird, the colorful confidant of a less-than-lovable character named Manning on *One Life to Live.* The macaws, owned by comedian Ed Richman and his wife Violet, have mated and produced a youngster who followed in their claw prints and also has an acting career. All three macaws perform in Richman's stage shows.

Birds on the Big Screen

In the spring of 1998, a full-length feature film starred a blue-crowned conure as the title character, *Paulie.* Told through the parrot's point of view, the story follows Paulie through 20 years of adventures while he searches for his first owner, the little girl who raised him. It took 14 conures to share so many stunts, but only three months to train them. A nanday, a jenday and a cherry-headed conure also steal a scene or two. It's good family entertainment.

Bird Brainers

When watching some scenes from the movie *Paulie,* you may wonder how the title character survived the filming. Never fear. None of the bird actors lost as much as a feather. When a scene was too dangerous for real birds, the directors had a robot bird stand in.

First Birds

We all read about Millie Bush, the Springer Spaniel, and the Clintons' cat, Socks, but what about our presidents' feathered friends? History remembers some of them.

He may be retired from show biz, but Junior still entertains people with his tricks.

➤ George Washington wasn't just our first president, he was the first president to share his residence with a parrot. While Washington enjoyed his horses and hounds, his wife Martha's favorite was her green parrot.

➤ Thomas Jefferson's parrot, Shadwell, had a large vocabulary and announced when he wanted a bath. Jefferson also adored mockingbirds. He often opened the cage so Dick, his favorite one, could fly around his office, perch on his shoulder and sing to him.

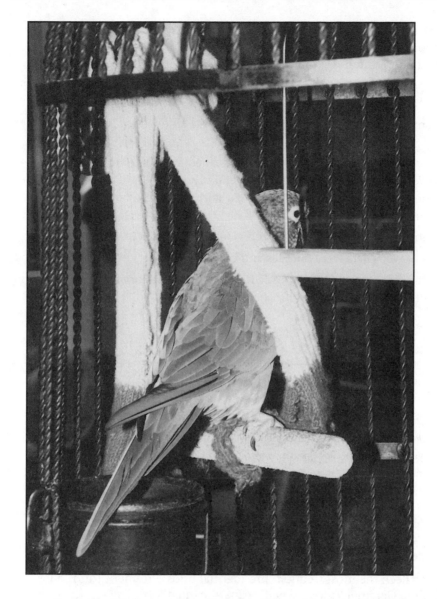

The 14 Paulies that performed in the movie Paulie *were blue-fronted conures. This blue-front, retired to his "dressing room," is named Nikki.*

➤ Dolly Madison, wife of our fourth president, James Madison, had a talented macaw named Polly. A renowned hostess, Dolly included Polly in her parties, and the parrot proved to be an accomplished entertainer.

➤ In 1827, Andrew Jackson gave his wife, Rachel, an amazon parrot named Poor Poll. Just a month before Jackson was to be inaugurated, in December of 1828, Rachel died of a heart attack. Poor Poll stayed home in Tennessee and was cared for by a custodian, but the President always asked about the parrot in his letters home. When Jackson died in 1845, Poll attended his funeral. During the service, she screamed a mouthful of profanity and had to be removed.

➤ Jesse Grant, son of President Ulysses S. Grant, kept his pet parrot in the executive mansion.

➤ A hyacinth macaw named Eli was one of many pets enjoyed by Teddy Roosevelt's family.

➤ President William McKinley's double yellow-headed amazon parrot often sang *Yankee Doodle,* and could sing or whistle several other tunes. He also flirted with women. When someone walked by wearing a skirt, the bird would scream, "Oh, look at the pretty girl!"

➤ Lady Bird Johnson's lovebirds lived in the White House.

➤ Mamie Eisenhower's pets were budgies and canaries.

➤ During her father's presidency, Caroline Kennedy had a canary named Robin and two budgies named Maybelle and Bluebell.

Avian Adventures

Many presidents and their wives owned mockingbirds, including Thomas Jefferson, Mrs. Rutherford B. Hayes, Mrs. Grover Cleveland and Mrs. Calvin Coolidge. During the Coolidge administration, a new law in the District of Colombia outlawed keeping mockingbirds in cages, so Mrs. Coolidge reluctantly parted with her pet.

Canaries in the Capitol

Canaries may have been the most frequent presidential birds. President John Tyler and his second wife, Julia Gardiner Tyler, owned a canary named Johnny Ty, who accompanied the Tylers on vacation. When their hotel caught fire, Julia ran inside the burning building and rescued her little pet.

President Rutherford B. Hayes' wife, Lucy, had four canaries. Mrs. Grover Cleveland also had several songsters, and so did Mrs. Warren G. Harding. But the Calvin Coolidges had the most birds, although they started with just Nip and Tuck, a couple of olive-green canaries. Soon a white canary named Snowflake joined the family, followed by a parrot named Do-funny. When the press told the public how much the president and his wife liked birds, gifts that peeped, squawked or sang began arriving from all over the world. Soon the second floor of the White House contained quite an aviary.

Other first canaries were owned by Mamie Eisenhower and Caroline Kennedy. When Caroline's canary Robin died, she was given a funeral ceremony and buried on the south lawn.

The Least You Need to Know

➤ Birds are terrific animal actors. If you want to see several species waddle through their routines, try one of the theme parks listed in Appendix B.

➤ If you'd rather watch birds perform without leaving your living room, look for reruns of *Baretta,* catch the daytime drama *One Life to Live* or rent the video *Paulie.*

➤ Many of our presidents and their families enjoyed pet birds.

Chapter 24

Chirp?!

Breeding Birds

In This Chapter

➤ Why be a bird breeder?

➤ Selecting superior breeding specimens

➤ Housing and management for breeding pairs

Does having one bird make you want more? Then consider breeding birds. This challenging hobby combines science, art and responsibility with a little luck, and will give you plenty to study and even more to look forward to. No, there aren't any guarantees. Sometimes things go wrong. But when they go right, you'll be privy to a special kind of joy that few people ever know. Miracles will happen in your home as eggs metamorphose into helpless hatchlings, change into prickly chicks and finally transform into beautiful young birds.

Although bird breeding is an inspiring and fulfilling hobby, it takes more equipment, space, time and money than simply keeping a pet bird or two. This chapter will tell you what you'll need, recommend a sensible start and give you the basics of breeding birds. (If you decide to go ahead with breeding, I recommend a lot more reading before you start.)

Why Breed Birds?

Breeding birds has all the attributes of a good hobby. It's educational and exciting, and can be as easy or as absorbing as you want it to be. You can enjoy it no matter what the weather, and getting started sensibly won't flatten your wallet. Friendly, knowledgeable mentors are easy to find (try bird clubs, bird shows and the Internet) and often become friends. Also, many publications are available to guide you from your first "easy" breedings through the challenge of propagating more difficult, possibly endangered species. Please read some of them before starting (see Appendix A). Like anything worthwhile, being a bird breeder demands dedication, but with good management and good luck, you'll have results worth celebrating.

Showing Your Super Specimen

Most of the exhibitors at bird shows are breeders. After all, it's fun to meet people who share your avian interests, and it's only natural to want to showcase your successes. Bird shows are also an opportunity for breeders to learn how to improve the quality of their stock by trading knowledge with each other. In addition, breeders and exhibitors learn from the judges. Some judges spread an incredible amount of knowledge in a short time by telling the audience the criteria they used when selecting the winners. For more on showing birds, see Chapter 25.

What About Making Money?

Oh, yes. Don't forget money. Let's see… if your cockatiel cost $70 and you buy one of the opposite sex for another $70 and they have four chicks, you'll sell them and double your investment instantly. And chances are they'll raise chicks twice a year. Wow! Quick money, right?

Don't believe it. First of all, propagating birds isn't that easy. Doing what comes naturally works when birds live naturally, but successfully breeding birds in captivity takes some doing. Breed birds for your own enjoyment. Do it as a labor of love, or don't do it at all. This avocation won't make you rich quick. In fact, like most hobbies, it will probably cost you money, at least at first.

Breeding to Help Save a Species

One of the best reasons for breeding birds is that without human intervention, some species may soon become extinct. Rain forests are being demolished by bulldozers at a rate that I find incomprehensible, no matter how often I hear about it. Can you visualize the loss of 50 to 75 acres (an acre is approximately the size of a football field) per minute? Neither can I. But I know it adds up to the destruction of 50,000 square miles of trees every year. Try to imagine how many birds lived in those trees and fed in those forests and you'll understand why loss of habitat is the number one threat to several species' survival.

Ultimately, you may become skilled enough to try your hand at propagating a rare species. But don't start there. Instead, find out if bird breeding is the right hobby for you, and learn the necessary skills by starting with one of the easier species. More on that later.

The Downside of Breeding Birds

Owning any bird is a responsibility, but breeding doubles and then quadruples your commitment. Besides housing and feeding both parents properly, and doing the extra cleaning chores, you are obligated to the babies. While you're marveling at their development, they are maturing. In just a few weeks, they'll be old enough to need their own housing—in other words, ready to go to their new homes, or at least, separate cages. While parting with them will surely pluck your heartstrings, housing four or five more birds could flatten your purse strings. Also, taking care of more birds than you bargained for will turn your hobby into work, and I doubt if you need more of that.

Finding excellent homes for your baby birds is something you should consider before breeding. Don't assume that the pet store will take them on consignment (although it doesn't hurt to ask), because the manager probably deals with professional breeders. That leaves giving them to friends and relatives, selling them through word of mouth, putting "birds for sale" notices on company bulletin boards and placing classified ads in the newspaper, local shopper-type publications and national bird magazines. In the meantime, the chicks are your responsibility. Besides feeding and cleaning up after them, you should begin taming them so they will be the best possible pets.

Additional birds also make it harder to travel. While you may have had a relative or friend who was willing to bird sit back in the days when you had only one, things change once you're a breeder. Now you'll need a super sitter you can rely on. Otherwise, the closest thing you'll get to a vacation will be looking at photos from last year's trip.

What's worse than having to take care of baby birds long after you thought they'd have new homes? Not having baby birds at all. Especially when you did everything by the book and were looking forward to being a surrogate mom or dad.

Squawk!

Don't decide to surprise your best friend with a bird. First of all, no one should receive a pet by surprise. If you aren't absolutely sure someone wants a bird, don't put them on the spot. Few people take good care of something they didn't want in the first place.

Polly Sez

Canaries, finches and all parrot-like birds are *altricial*, meaning naked, helpless and blind at birth. The word comes from the Latin *altrix*, which means *nurse*. This is fitting, because altricial baby birds make their parents act as nursemaids. *Precocial* birds, on the other hand, are born fluffy with down, have wide-open eyes and can run around and find food right away. Baby chickens are like this.

Unfortunately, things don't always go right when breeding birds. The most common reasons why eggs don't hatch are infertile or immature parents. Other reasons include poor diet, poor brooding (the parents allowed the eggs to get cold) and lack of humidity. Losing the first clutch is common, and the same pair often succeed on their second try.

Avian Adventures

Pets need quiet time to acclimate to a new home, so the holiday season is the worst time to transfer birds. If someone wants to buy one of your birds as a holiday gift, urge them to give the recipient a cage with a picture of the bird in it and write "coming January 1" on the back. Doing it that way has two possible endings, and neither of them will traumatize your young bird. Either the bird moves in after most of the holiday hustle is over, or only a cage has to be returned.

Choosing Breeding Pairs

Decisions, decisions. Imagine seeing sulphur-crested cockatoos or hyacinth macaw babies mature into magnificence. Now hold that thought but don't act on it—yet. Unless you've already had experience breeding birds, it's best to begin with a handsome pair of one of the smaller, easier and less expensive species.

Species Selection

Ideal species for beginning bird breeders are budgies, cockatiels and zebra finches. They cost less than larger or rarer birds, don't need as much room, are more apt to breed in captivity, usually make good parents, and their sexes can be distinguished by color—a big bonus, as you won't have to have them sexed by your avian veterinarian. But even though they are considered "easy" breeders, these species still need reliable care to successfully reproduce in captivity. If you love every minute of providing that care, you may want to expand into bigger birds later.

Handsome and Healthy

Choose Pauly's partner carefully. The offspring will contain the genetic material of both parents, so make sure the new bird is attractive, has a good disposition (after all, you'll be producing pets) and could be a poster girl for good health (see Chapter 4).

Even so, quarantine the new bird in a separate cage for a month, keeping her as far from Pauly as your home allows. When quarantine time is up, let the pair get to know each other gradually by putting their cages side by side for a few days. Even though this is an arranged marriage, it's best to let the birds think they made the decision to mate.

If you dream of producing birds elegant enough to win shows, keep your original bird as a pet and purchase a matched pair from a breeder of fine show birds. Explain your goals and let the breeder help you choose a pair with the potential to make winning a reality.

Zebra finches, budgies and cockatiels are all available in unusual color schemes called *mutations*. Steer clear of them if you are a beginning breeder. Birds sporting conventional colors and the more common mutations are generally stronger, with fewer health or breeding problems. Someday you may become interested in producing rare mutations, but by then you'll know the basics. Don't try it without reading books on breeding (see Appendix A).

The Opposite Sex

Many would-be bird breeders caged a pair together and then wondered what went wrong when poor Polly laid eggs year after year and sat on them diligently, but they never hatched. Then one day Pauly joined her and laid an egg too. Uh oh! Two Pollys and no Pauly. No wonder all those eggs were infertile.

Making sure the birds you want to breed are the opposite sex may seem elementary, but in bird breeding, it isn't. Many female birds lay eggs when the season is right, even though there is no male bird around. Others don't. So while eggs are a sure-fire way to determine sex in your bird, lack of eggs is not.

Bird Brainers

The newest method of determining a bird's sex is through DNA testing. Your avian vet will send one drop of your bird's blood to a lab, and you'll soon find out if you own Henry or Henrietta.

Bird Brainers

Once your birds bond with each other, you'll no longer be #1 in either of their lives. Expect them to defend their nest and hatchlings, and don't force your attention on them. Later, after their young leave the nest, they'll probably become pleasant pets again—provided they were tame to begin with.

Polly Sez

Breeders call a female bird a *hen* and a male bird a *cock*.

The following table gives you the most obvious sexual characteristics of typically colored mature male and female zebra finches, budgies and cockatiels (but it doesn't hold true for immature birds or unusual mutations). In most larger species, such as amazons, greys, conures, cockatoos and macaws, the sexes are so similar that only your veterinarian knows for sure—and then only after testing.

Recognizing the Sexes

Species	Males	Females
Zebra finch	Big orange patch on the cheek	Cheek is gray with no orange at all
Budgie	Cere (area above the beak, containing the nostrils) is bright blue	Cere is light brown
Cockatiel	Underside of the tail feathers is a solid color	Underside of the tail feathers is barred (striped)

The Rites of Spring

Longer days at the beginning of spring often trigger the mating and nesting instinct (although many pairs produce young, no matter what the season, under the influence of artificial light). That makes late February or the first couple of weeks of March an ideal time to provide your pair with a nest box.

Nest boxes of various types, sized for your species, are available at your local pet store. Budgies and cockatiels need one per pair. Finches are so prolific they sometimes start a new clutch before their first clutch is totally independent, so two boxes ensure that the newly fledged chicks have a place to stay while another clutch of eggs is being laid. Finches also need nest-building material, so provide them with hay and a small amount of string or sisal cut into two-inch lengths.

Polly Sez

A *clutch* is a nest of eggs or young chicks. In other words, you might say, "My cockatiels have a clutch of four eggs," or "I just finished hand feeding a clutch of lovebirds."

Budgies will use a commercially made nest box as is (be sure to buy one with a concave hollow in the bottom), but cockatiels (and an occasional budgie) seem to prefer a bit of bedding. A couple of inches of wood chips (available at pet shops) work well.

Pinto (right) fluffs and struts for Bluebell. He's trying to get her in the mood to mate. She's still aloof, but not upset by his ardor.

Laying eggs is hard work and will take a lot out of your hen, unless you provide her with a varied diet (see Chapter 11) and plenty of calcium. Cuttlebone should be available all the time. It may disappear a lot quicker than usual when your hen is laying, so check it often and make sure plenty of the soft side is still intact. Your birds may also nibble on a mineral block (available at your pet store).

Supplements formulated to help birds through the breeding cycle are worth looking into, especially if you have a finicky hen who savors only seeds. Your avian veterinarian will recommend the best one for your bird. Give it according to directions. More is not better.

How will you know when your pair feels the urge to procreate? Finches are obvious because they build a nest inside their box, but budgies and cockatiels are a bit more subtle. The hen sits transfixed, staring at the nest box, then begins peeking inside every so often. Eventually she climbs in and checks it out. After that, she goes in and out often. By then, the cock becomes extremely active. Besides following the hen in and out of the box (sometimes), he preens her, chatters to her, shows off by bouncing around on his perches, and feeds her regurgitated food. If your hen permits these advances (instead of sending her suitor packing to another perch), she's ready to be bred and will allow the male to mount her.

Bird Brainers

If you don't want to wait around for your daily peek at the eggs, entice the parents off the nest with a spray of millet.

Soon after, she will begin laying eggs—most likely one every other day. Never disturb the nest while the parents are on it or they may abandon it, but do check daily to make sure all the eggs or baby birds are okay. Take a quick look when both adults are off the nest, eating.

Bluebell decides Pinto would be a good provider. She's checking out the housing while he watches.

The young will hatch in the same order—oldest egg first—so in a clutch of four, the first chick hatched will be eight days older than the last chick. Both parents share the chick-rearing chores and make sure each youngster, no matter what its age and development, gets the right amount of regurgitated food. Your job is to provide the best possible nutrients, and plenty of them. Use top-quality seeds and pellets, and vary the diet with fresh greens, shredded carrot, kernels of raw corn, cereal and sprouts.

Chicks are born nearly naked, blind and helpless, except for the ability to beg for food. Soon they become covered with fluffy down; then quills emerge and mature into feathers. Young finches are ready to leave the nest at three weeks old, while budgies and cockatiels usually stay in their shelter for close to six weeks.

After the fledglings leave the nest, the parents usually continue feeding them for a week or two, but it isn't long before the baby birds eat independently. When you are sure your fledglings are taking food and water on their own, move them into a separate cage.

Polly Sez

To *fledge* is to grow feathers. A baby bird *fledges* out, and a *fledgling* is a young bird that just grew enough feathers to fly.

How many eggs will your hen lay? The table below gives you the usual clutch size, and lets you know how long you'll have to wait before each one hatches.

How Many Eggs?

Species	Average number of eggs	Incubation time
Zebra finches	3–4	12–15 days
Budgies	4–6	17–19 days
Cockatiels	4–6	18–21 days

Space, Time and Supplies

Two birds can't live as cheaply or as easily as one (except for finches, which should always be housed in pairs). A pair of budgies, cockatiels or any other species, needs a larger home than a single bird would. While it doesn't have to be double the size recommended in Chapter 6, approximately one-and-a-half times as large makes for comfortable quarters.

Food and water dishes have to be washed and refilled more often than before, and a nice nest box (two for finches) is a must if you want those eggs to hatch. Later, when the fledglings eat on their own, they should have their own cage away from their parents.

Squawk!

Without enough humidity, developing embryos die inside the eggs. Provide humidity with a humidifier if your home is on the dry side, and make sure your parent birds bathe when they are outside the nest box. Their damp bodies moisturize the eggs.

Good Breeders

Although everyone has their own way of doing things, top breeders have many traits in common. Good breeders:

➤ Feed a high-quality, varied diet all year long and try to make it even better during breeding season.

➤ Clean their birdcages and equipment regularly.

➤ Observe their birds daily to catch early signs of sickness, and quarantine sick birds far away from the rest.

➤ Read books about breeding and learn the fundamentals of genetics before planning their breeding program.

➤ Read the standard (see Chapter 25) for their species and try to breed birds that come as close to it as possible.

➤ Learn how to read and understand pedigrees.

➤ Choose only the best birds they can afford for breeding.

➤ Join a bird club.

➤ House their fledglings separately as soon as they become independent.

➤ Socialize and tame their young birds.

➤ Band their baby birds.

➤ Keep accurate records of each bird, including the age, weight, sex, health history and band number. These records include breeding successes and failures, as well as the number of eggs in each clutch and the number that hatched.

➤ Have a separate record for each baby bird. It includes the date it hatched, band number of the parents, weight at frequent intervals, general observations about its development and the date it began eating independently.

➤ Hand feed babies lovebird size and larger.

Squawk!

Young finches are often eager to breed as they near the three-month mark. Although they are capable, it's better to wait until they are nearly a year old. Prevent the problem by separating finches by sex when they are two months old.

The Least You Need to Know

➤ Breeding birds is a satisfying hobby, but it takes a lot of work and won't lead to easy money.

➤ Don't breed birds unless you are willing to care for the babies until you find good homes for them.

➤ The best species for beginning breeders are finches, budgies and cockatiels.

➤ Only healthy, attractive birds with good temperaments should be bred. Pick the finest pair you can afford.

➤ Two birds need a larger cage than one, and will need to have their water and food dishes washed and refilled more often.

➤ Birds need a nest box for their eggs. Sometimes attaching a nest box to the cage in late February or early March triggers breeding behavior.

➤ Learn all you can about breeding birds before you begin. You can educate yourself through books, magazines and membership in a bird club.

Let's Go to the Bird Show

Would you like to see top-quality birds of many species under one roof? Then treat yourself to a bird show. Besides seeing typical pet birds in a myriad of mutations (colors), you'll get acquainted with rarer species that are seldom seen in pet shops.

Although bird shows are interesting whether you understand the judging procedure or not, a little knowledge will make your first visit more rewarding. In this chapter, you'll learn the basics of bird judging. Following that, I'll give you the ups and downs of showing, and tell you how to get started if your love of birds leads you toward this exciting avocation.

How Birds Are Judged

Birds are in their finest feather at the bird show, and with so many beautiful specimens to choose from, your first reaction might be to pity the poor judge. But the judge has help in the form of written guidelines called a *standard*. The standard describes an ideal specimen of the species—the perfect bird every breeder-exhibitor tries to attain.

Although you'll have a great day at the bird show whether you know your chosen species' standard or not, you'll understand the judging much better if you read it first.

Appendix C has a list of bird clubs. Find the one that pertains to your species, then write and request a copy of the standard (enclose a SASE).

The Society of Parrot Breeders and Exhibitors (SPBE) Standard for Exhibited Parrots, for example, contains five categories, and each one has a different numerical value. The judge evaluates each parrot by how closely it measures up to what the standard describes as parrot perfection, and compares each individual bird to the birds competing against it. Rare birds get no special consideration, and large species have no advantage over smaller ones.

The five categories of the SPBE Standard and their weighted values are listed in the table below. I'll explain what each category means in a moment. Meanwhile, you should know that numerical scales such as this one are simply guides to help judges emphasize the points that are considered most important in each species. Birds are actually judged by comparing them one to another, so don't expect to see score sheets.

Categories of the SPBE Standard

Conformation	40 points
Condition	30 points
Deportment	15 points
Color	10 points
Presentation	5 points
Total	100 points

Conformation

Conformation is the shape of the bird's body from the top of her head to the tip of her tail, including feet and toes. It encompasses body proportions and size, both of which should be correct for the species.

Bird Brainers

Not all birds are judged on the same attributes. In fact, canaries bred for song are judged on a 100-point song standard, with certain sounds or sequences (called *tours*) worth more points than others.

Proportion is another word for balance. It means that each of the bird's body parts should be the right size and shape for the species and flow gracefully into the next body part, resulting in an attractive outline. No single part should overwhelm the rest of the bird by being too large, or weaken it by being too small. To the trained eye of a judge, a well-balanced bird looks like all its parts fit together perfectly, while birds with poor proportions appear to be made up of spare parts.

Substance is part of conformation, and you'll probably hear judges refer to it when explaining how they arrived at their placements. It deals with correct bone size and good muscle tone, denoting strength and stamina. Although the word may make you think bigger, or even fatter, is better, plumpness is not a plus. Birds don't attain substance by overindulging in fatty foods. Like us, they attain flab that way. The potential for good substance is an inherited trait, and exhibitors make the most of it by giving their birds healthy diets and plenty of exercise.

You may also hear the judge compare some of the birds' *top lines* or *back lines*. This is the line from the back of the bird's head to the tip of its tail, and ideally, it should be straight (in most species). Judges also look for a correctly shaped head and beak, proper eye placement, good wing carriage and strong, healthy feet.

Condition

While you can't control whether or not your newly purchased young bird will mature with proper proportions and substance, you can control a large percentage of your bird's condition. A bird that's in top condition is as glorious as its genetic makeup will allow. It glows with good health, appears well taken care of and is having a good feather day.

Excellent feathers are an essential part of good condition, and you grow them through good nutrition, clean, stress-free living conditions and frequent misting. Show birds should be fully feathered (none missing), untrimmed and without visible pinfeathers. That's why a small percentage of a bird's condition will always be ruled by lady luck. If a bird begins molting on the way to the show or even breaks a feather while in transit, she won't be in top condition during the judging, no matter how lovely she looked yesterday.

Bird Brainers

An excellent bird may lose simply because her tail became ragged or wet just before the judge examined her. If you have a long-tailed species, use an automatic waterer instead of an open bowl, and a T-stand in the middle of the show cage instead of a perch attached to the side.

Deportment

Deportment is the way a bird behaves and stands while being judged. Watch the top show birds. They present themselves with elegance and style, making the most of their conformation and condition. In other words, they have showmanship. A certain amount of showmanship is inborn, but much of it is taught at home.

While a correct stance for the species is something a bird may or may not be born with, you can help your bird make the most of what heredity gave her. Sure, Polly has a confident posture at home, but if she isn't used to a show cage and being stared at by strangers, she may hunch her back in fear when the judge approaches, or get off her perch entirely and huddle in a corner of the cage.

Prevent that by buying your show cage months ahead of your first show. First, place it next to Polly's cage for a few days so she can look it over. Then practice by putting

This eclectus displays himself well. He's watching the judge as she watches him.

Polly in it for a few minutes (with food and water), and gradually increase the time until she is used to spending a couple of hours in her show cage at home.

When Polly is completely relaxed in her show cage, get your friends into the act. Play "bird show" whenever you have company. Put Polly in her show cage, give her a few minutes to acclimate, then ask a friend to walk over to the cage and look at her closely from the front and the side. Once your bird is used to being stared at by both men and women, hand a friend a pointer (it can be a chopstick or an unsharpened pencil) and ask them to touch the cage with it lightly in several places. Later, have them put the pointer through the bars gently without touching Polly (you'll see the judges do that at bird shows, usually to entice a bird to turn on the perch so they can see the other side). When your bird confidently handles the show cage, the stares and the pointer, she's mentally conditioned for competition.

Bird Brainers

Does Polly prefer the bottom of her show cage? Teach her to stay on the perch by covering the bottom of the cage with Ping-Pong balls (but remove them before the show).

Color

There is no best color for a bird. Different species are supposed to be different colors, and besides that, there are color mutations within many species. So how is color judged? By its depth and uniformity. Color should be even, so in those areas where a species is supposed to be a single color, the hue should be consistent throughout. In pied birds (those with comparatively large areas of two or more colors), symmetrical markings and color contrast are both pluses.

Presentation

Presentation is up to you, not Polly. It refers to the cage she is exhibited in. When visiting a bird show, notice what type of cage the winning exhibitors use for your species (its shape, color, perch position and dimensions), and get Polly one just like it. Sometimes vendors display show cages for sale right at the bird show, and they are often advertised in bird magazines and equipment catalogs. If in doubt, ask an exhibitor. Most will be glad to help you get started.

Bird Brainers

Some birds are so full of showmanship that they follow the judge's every move with their eyes while remaining properly perched. You may be able to help Polly develop the same winning ways by having your friends give her a treat when she's on her perch and looking right at them.

Moving Left

If you ever show your bird, you'll be hoping the judge moves your bird's cage to the left. Why? Because throughout the show, from the class level all the way through the elimination contest that eventually produces Best in Show, birds are compared to each other, with the judge moving the best one to the left of the one it defeated. After every bird has been seen and compared, the victor will be on the far left. The other placements will be in order from left to right, with the second-place bird to the right of the first-place bird, the third-place bird to the right of the second-place winner, and so on.

Subjective Judging

If you have trouble understanding how the judge selects the winners, it may be because it's your first experience with subjective judging. Most of the sports we know best are judged objectively. In other words, while watching or playing baseball, football, basketball, golf or tennis, we know the score. But it's different at bird shows. There, winning or losing depends on the judge's opinion. This can be confusing at first, especially if you see a bird take Best in Show honors under one judge and fail to win her class the next day under a different judge.

Polly Sez

The word *mutation* refers to color in birds. For example, besides the original gray, cockatiels come in four standard mutations: pied, lutino, pearl and cinnamon, and a host of rarer mutations and mutation combinations such as whiteface-cinnamon-pied.

Avian Adventures

Birds can get championship titles by earning points through winning and placing at shows. Different species have different requirements. A cockatiel, for example, needs 15 points and at least one Best in Show to become a champion. The number of points a bird is awarded for a win or placement depends upon the number of birds she defeated (which depends on the number entered and present). The most points available at any one show are 10, for top honors. In that case, the second-place bird would receive nine points, the third place eight, and so on to tenth place.

The more you learn about bird anatomy and your species' standard (what it means and why those attributes are important), the better you'll understand how each judge selects his winners. One judge may be a stickler for wing carriage. Another may be swayed by superior substance. Because each judge interprets the standard in their own way, different birds may win under different judges. And that's a good thing, because it lets many deserving birds have their day. Besides, imagine how boring it would be if the same birds won the same placements at every show. Pretty soon, no one would want to exhibit anymore.

Birds are also judged in an instant of time. It's kind of the way we judge ourselves when we meet ourselves in the mirror each morning. One day we might silently congratulate ourselves on looking younger than our age, while the next day we may appear haggard. Birds have good days and bad days too. And the judge doesn't know what any of them looked like yesterday, or even five minutes ago, and can only go by what they see when it's that bird's turn to be judged. So if the owners of today's Best in Show bird keep their winged wonder up too late while they celebrate, the bird may be too bedraggled to make a good showing tomorrow morning.

To Show or Not to Show

All hobbies have their good and bad points. Here are some of the things you'll want to consider before deciding if you want to show birds.

The Upside of Showing Birds

➤ Competing in shows is fun and exciting.

➤ Depending on your goals, it can be a casual or an absorbing hobby.

➤ You'll make friends with people who have similar interests.

➤ You'll meet the top breeders.

➤ You'll probably become a breeder (at least occasionally).

➤ It's educational. You'll learn more about birds every time you attend a show.

➤ Because of all the preparation, you'll develop a stronger bond with your bird(s).

➤ Showing involves traveling.

➤ Learning from your losses will make you a stronger contender.

➤ Winning feels wonderful.

The Downside of Showing Birds

➤ A bird with trimmed wings won't win. You'll have to make special provisions so your show bird can exercise safely at home.

➤ Showing may stress your bird.

➤ Showing birds is equipment-intensive and includes many incidental expenses.

➤ Training a bird to show well can be time-consuming.

➤ Storing show equipment takes up space.

➤ Showing involves traveling.

➤ Once you become involved, you'll probably start breeding birds (at least occasionally).

➤ Losing feels lousy, until you become knowledgeable enough to turn losses into valuable learning experiences.

Getting Started

You've weighed the pros and cons and decided to give bird showing a try. Good for you. The following tips will start you down the right road and keep you from floundering into detours or dead ends.

Join the Club

Contact the national club for your species (see Appendix C) and ask for a list of local clubs in your area. Then join the one nearest you. If it's close enough so you can attend meetings, that's great. Most clubs are made up of friendly, knowledgeable people who are happy to turn new members into novice exhibitors. Many clubs also have newsletters nice enough to make belonging worthwhile, even if you can't make the meetings. Besides containing educational articles, they list upcoming shows and other activities of interest to bird lovers.

Bird Brainers

Birds become nervous showing in a regular cage because it's too open. A show cage has walls on three sides and bars only across the front. Its background should be a solid color that makes your bird stand out, but doesn't overwhelm.

Once you make friends with a few people, try putting a notice in the club bulletin. It could read something like this: "Wanted. On-the-spot training. I'll pay half the gas and be your bird sitter and assistant at the show. Just take me along and help me learn the sport." If a breeder-exhibitor takes you up on your offer, you'll find out first-hand what showing is all about. Then you can decide if you like it before making an investment.

Buying a Show Quality Bird

Sometimes the truth is hard to face, but it's better to know the facts up front than to spend money and time on an impossible dream. As much as I hate to tell you this, your pretty Polly probably isn't show quality. Why? Because you bought her to be a companion—a pal, a pet—and that's probably what she is.

The truth is, show birds seldom come from pet shops (yes, there are exceptions, but the law of averages is against you). Instead, they come from breeders who double as bird exhibitors.

Does that mean you have to buy another bird just to participate? Only if you won't be happy unless you have a contender right away. If you just want to experience showing first-hand, make Polly as beautiful as she can be through good nutrition, exercise and frequent misting, help her learn stage presence in an exhibition cage and enter her in the Novice class (or better yet, the Pet class, if one is offered). She probably won't win, but preparing Polly physically and mentally will help you learn the fine points, so you'll do an even better job with your next bird.

Bird Brainers

When attending a bird show, be sure to watch the Novice division. It's where beginners learn the sport, so many judges educate the exhibitors by offering detailed explanations of how they arrived at their placements.

Best of all, you'll begin developing an eye for a show-quality bird and furthering your understanding of the standard. Soon you'll know which traits are most important to you and which breeders' birds display those attributes. What's next? Approaching the breeders whose birds you most admire and pricing their show-potential chicks.

Entering a Show

Bird magazines (see Appendix A) also list upcoming shows. In addition to the date and location, a contact person's name and phone number (and sometimes address) will be included. Contact the person well in advance of the event and request a show catalog. If the show is so far away that you'll have to stay overnight, ask about nearby motels or RV parks. Most shows are weekend events with different judges each day, giving you two opportunities to exhibit your bird on one trip.

When your catalog arrives, read it carefully. They aren't easy reading at first, but the more catalogs you read, the easier it gets. Underline or highlight the entry fee, the date, the location, the check-in time for your species, the judging time and the deadline for entering. Take all dates and times seriously. Late entries aren't accepted, and birds that arrive after check-in time may not be allowed in the show.

When filling out your forms, you'll have to decide what division or subdivision you want to enter (go for Pet or Novice if you are new to the sport), and what section your bird belongs in (canaries, conures, cockatiels, etc.). If in doubt, ask a member of your bird club, or call the contact person.

About a week before the show, start making a list of everything you and your bird will need, and add to the list every time you think of another item. Just before you leave, reread your list slowly. Visualize the road trip, the show and staying in a motel or RV park, if applicable. If you can't think of another thing, rest assured that any item left behind won't be vital. Now check off each item as you load your vehicle.

When traveling to the show, make the trip as safe and comfortable for you and your bird as possible. Make sure the cage won't tip when you turn, and that Polly is getting ventilation, but no drafts. Estimate traveling time by using the mileage chart in your atlas. Then add an extra hour, or even two, as a safety margin.

It's good to arrive in plenty of time to get your bird accustomed to the area. Check in at the required time, listen to as many judges' explanations as you can (no matter what the species), make some friends and always keep an eye on Polly. Make a resolution to learn something new every time you show. And good luck.

Instant education. After choosing his winners, the judge explains why he lined them up that way.

Remembering What's Important

Competitive spirit is a wonderful thing. It makes us learn things we might never have known, try things we might never have tried, go places we have never been before and strive to be even better than our best. But sometimes our competitive spirit grows so strong that it changes us. It can even make us forget what's really important, and lure us into believing our happiness depends on the outcome of the next bird show.

No matter how deeply involved in bird breeding and showing you become, always remember why you wanted a bird in the first place. Birds are for companionship. Before you became competitive, you had birds in your life simply because you loved them.

Whenever competition is involved, moments of frustration alternate with times of elation. During the down days, it may help to remember that before ribbons, trophies and championships, there was still a special relationship between pet birds and people. Preparing for competition together enhances that relationship, but frustration causes some exhibitors to tear it down—and that's a pity for those people and their birds.

Please don't become so stressed out over the outcome of a show that your sensitive bird loses her confidence in you. Trust is the greatest gift our birds can give us. And, like many valuable gifts, it's extremely delicate. Don't damage your bird's trust over a piece of colored ribbon. Carry your little companion home from the show as carefully as you brought her there. There's always another bird show, but relationships are special.

The Least You Need to Know

➤ Birds are judged on how close they come to the ideal specimen described in the standard for each species. One judge's opinion rules the day.

➤ Most judges explain to the audience how they made their choices.

➤ It takes special equipment, including a show cage, to successfully show birds.

➤ Birds need conditioning and training before they are ready to show.

➤ Most pet birds are not potential show winners. Buying a show-potential chick from a breeder-exhibitor is your best bet.

➤ If possible, join a bird club and attend meetings.

➤ Bird magazines list upcoming shows and who to contact for more information. Call and request a show catalog. It will contain entry forms and details about the event.

➤ Keep your priorities straight, no matter how deeply involved in competition you become. Birds are for loving. Winning is nice, but don't ruin any relationships over it.

Glossary of Bird Words

alopreening   mutual feather grooming

altricial   naked, helpless and blind at birth; canaries, finches and all parrot-like birds are altricial

anisodactyl   a foot with three toes in front and one in back, such as the majority of birds have

avian   pertaining to birds

aviary   a large home for birds

aviculture   the care and raising of birds

barbs   feathery branches growing out of each side of the shaft of a feather

barbicels   tiny fibers attached to each barbule

barbules   smaller branches of a feather's barbs

blood feather   see *pin feather*

bristle feathers   made up mostly of shaft, but with a few small barbs at the base, they are organs of touch

budgie   short for budgerigar, the technically correct term for the bird commonly known as the parakeet

cage-top gym   see *play gym*

carotenoids   feather pigments that produce yellow, red and orange tones

cere   the area between the facial feathers and the beak, containing the nostrils

choana   a slit in the roof of the mouth

cloaca   a common chamber where all of a bird's wastes end up

clutch   a nest of eggs or young chicks

cock   a male bird

contour feathers   feathers that cover the contours of the bird

covert feathers   contour feathers that are not used for flight

crop   an area at the base of the neck where a bird can carry and store undigested food

dimorphism   differences between the sexes

disinfectant   a cleaning substance that is deadly to germs

down feathers   soft feathers that grow beneath the contour feathers and provide insulation

euthanasia   a humane, assisted death

extruded foods   sometimes called nuggets, these foods are bound under temperatures high enough to pasteurize them

fanciers   people who selectively breed and raise birds in an effort to produce exceptionally fine specimens for exhibition

fancy   the community of breeders, exhibitors, judges and those who frequently attend bird shows

filoplumes   lean, wispy feathers that grow at the base of each contour feather

fledge   to grow feathers

fledgling   a young bird that has just grown enough feathers to fly

flight cage   a cage large enough so a bird can fly in it

flight feathers   the large, strong contour feathers on the wings and tail that are used for flying

geriatrics   the branch of medicine that deals with problems peculiar to aging

gerontology   the study of aging in people or pets

germ   any microscopic organism, especially one that can cause disease; it is usually used for the toxic three: bacteria, fungi and viruses

gizzard   the muscular part of a bird's stomach

grit   a mixture of sand, tiny pieces of gravel and possibly some oyster shell; because birds have no teeth to grind their food before they swallow it, a little grit helps some species grind the shells off their seeds

hamuli   a little hook at the end of each barbicel; they interlock, keeping the million parts of the feather neatly in place

hand-raised (also **hand-fed**)   terms used interchangeably to refer to a bird that was taken away from its parents soon after birth and raised by a person

health certificate   a form signed by a veterinarian, certifying that your pet is healthy and doesn't carry any communicable diseases

hen   a female bird

hookbill   any member of the parrot family

keratin   the substance that feathers are composed of; it's a protein molecule manufactured by skin cells

melanins   feather pigments that produce brown, black or gray

molting   the normal process of periodically shedding feathers so new ones can grow in

mutation   in birds, the word is used to refer to color differences

nares   nostrils

nictitating membrane   a transparent third eyelid that moves across the eye from the inner to the outer corner and back again

parasite   an organism that relies on another living thing for its survival, but contributes nothing to the host organism

passerines   a scientific classification that is made up of perching birds, and includes canaries, finches and backyard songbirds

pellets   dry bird food formulas that are bound by compression under moderate temperatures

pin feather   (or **blood feather**)   a developing feather that has its own vein and artery

play gym   an uncaged exercise area for parrots

plumage   feathers

pneumatic bones   bones that contain air sacs and are part of the respiratory system

positive reinforcement   training lingo for rewarding your bird for doing something right

powder down   fragile down feathers found on the lower thigh, expecially on cockatoos and cockatiels

precocial   birds born with fluffy down, open eyes, and the ability to run and forage for food; chickens are precocial

preen   what a bird does when he uses his beak to clean, lubricate and align his feathers

primary feathers   the longest flight feathers; they grow closest to the end of the wing, providing most of the thrust

proventriculus the section of the stomach that adds digestive juices to food

psittacines a scientific classification that includes all the parrots

quill the hollow base of a feather that is attached to the bird's skin

raptors birds of prey, such as hawks and eagles

secondary feathers flight feathers that provide lift and help sustain the bird during flight

shaft the central part of the feather, to which the vanes are attached

softbills a family of birds that includes lories, mynah birds and toucans; the name refers to their diet and has nothing to do with their beak, which is quite hard

standard written guidelines that describe the ideal bird; standards are used to judge birds at bird shows

syrinx a membrane in the neck whose vibrations generate sound

tour a song sequence, used to judge canaries at bird shows

T-stand a bird perch shaped like a capital T

turacoverdin feather pigment that produces various shades of green

vanes the soft sides of the feather

wattle an area of featherless skin

zygodactyl a foot with two toes in front and two in back, as in parrots

Read All About It

Bird Books

Bonnie Munro Doane, *The Parrot in Health and Illness: An Owner's Guide*, Howell Book House, 1991.

Bonnie Munro Doane, *The Pleasure of Their Company: An Owner's Guide to Parrot Training*, Howell Book House, 1998.

Bonnie Munro Doane and Tom Qualkinbush, *My Parrot, My Friend: An Owner's Guide to Parrot Behavior*, Howell Book House, 1994.

Arthur Freud, *The Complete Parrot*, Howell Book House, 1995.

Arthur Freud, *The Parrot: An Owner's Guide to a Happy, Healthy Pet*, Howell Book House, 1996.

Gary A. Gallerstein, D.V.M., *The Complete Bird Owner's Handbook*, Howell Book House, 1997.

Diane Grindol, *The Complete Book of Cockatiels*, Howell Book House, 1998.

Liz Palika, *The Consumer's Guide to Feeding Birds*, Howell Book House, 1997.

Julie Rach, *The Budgie: An Owner's Guide to a Happy, Healthy Pet*, Howell Book House, 1997.

Wallace Sife, Ph.D., *The Loss of a Pet*, Howell Book House, 1998.

Dr. Matthew Vriends, *The Zebra Finch: An Owner's Guide to a Happy, Healthy Pet*, Howell Book House, 1997.

Magazines

Bird Talk, P.O. Box 6050, Mission Viejo, CA 92690

Birds U.S.A. (annual), P.O. Box 6050, Mission Viejo, CA 92690

Birds, 7-L Dundas Circle, Greensboro, NC 27407

A Directory of Bird Parks

Arizona

Phoenix: Wildlife World Zoo

Includes a large walk-through aviary and an opportunity to feed lories.

Arkansas

Hot Springs: Educated Animal Zoo; I.Q. Zoo

Both zoos present trained animal shows, including performing parrots.

California

Escondido: San Diego Wild Animal Park

Includes a walk-through aviary and bird shows.

San Diego: San Diego Zoo

Walk-through aviaries and an impressive collection of rare species, including masked shining parrots, Cuban amazon parrots and thick-billed parrots.

Florida

Winter Haven: Cypress Gardens

Offers an opportunity to feed lories in a walk-through aviary.

Miami: Parrot Jungle

Has several shows featuring avian performers. Many species on display, and several of the birds on display will eat out of your hand and talk to you.

St. Petersburg: Sunken Gardens

Walk-through aviary; trained parrot show; many parrots, especially macaws, on display.

Orlando: Walk Disney World's Discovery Island

View several species while walking a jungle path. Trainers often talk with visitors; parrots perform tricks.

Sarasota: Sarasota Jungle Gardens

Parrots and other species on display and a bird show.

Tampa: Busch Gardens

Bird shows and a large bird display, including several rare species.

Hawaii

Honolulu, Oahu: Paradise Park

This Hawaiian forest has bird shows and several displays, grouping birds according to their native lands.

Kentucky

Horse Cave: Kentucky Down Under

An Australian theme park with many birds, including a walk-through aviary where lories will eat from your hand.

Michigan

Leamington: Colasanti's Tropical Gardens

Several species, including hyacinth macaws and a colony of monk parakeets.

New York

New York: The Bronx Zoo

Several walk-through tropical aviaries with species from all over the world.

North Carolina

Asheboro: North Carolina Zoological Park

Reynolds Aviary houses many species, including mynahs.

Pennsylvania

Pittsburgh: City of Pittsburgh Conservatory-Aviary

Large, glass-domed building houses hundreds of species, including finches and softbills.

Utah

Salt Lake City: Tracy Aviary, Liberty Park

Exotic species include some rare parrots, and there is a bird show during the summer.

National Bird Clubs

Write for information on the species you are interested in, and also to find out about clubs and shows in your area.

African Lovebird Society, P.O. Box 142, San Marcos, CA 92069

African Parrot Society, P.O. Box 204-CB, Clarinda, IA 51632-2731

Amazon Society, P.O. Box 73547, Puyallup, WA 98373

American Budgerigar Society (Budgies), 1704 Kangaroo, Killeen, TX 76541

American Canary Fanciers Association, 2020 Kew Dr., Los Angeles, CA 90046, or fax (213) 656-1233

American Cockatiel Society Inc., P.O. Box 609, Fruitland Park, FL 34731

American Federation of Aviculture, P.O. Box 56218, Phoenix, AZ 85079

Aviculture Society of America, P.O. Box 5516, Riverside, CA 92517

Bird Clubs of America, P.O Box 2005, Yorktown, VA 23692

Cockatoo Society, 26961 N. Broadway, Escondido, CA 92026

Confederation of All Type Canaries, 2801 Mayfield Dr., Park Ridge, IL 60068

Macaw Society of America, P.O. Box 90037, Burton, MI 48509

Mynah News, 641 Invader, Sulphur, LA 70663

National Cage-Bird Show Club, Inc., 4910 Anthony Lane, Pasadena, TX 77504

National Cockatiel Society, 286 Broad St., Suite 140, Manchester, CT 06040

National Finch and Softbill Society, P.O. Box 3232, Ballwin, MO 63022

National Parrot Association, 8 N. Hoffman Lane, Hauppage, NY 11788

Pionus Breeders Association, P.O. Box 540, Johnson City, TX 78636

Society of Parrot Breeders and Exhibitors, P.O. Box 369, Groton, MA 01450

Index

E

F

G